PUBLICATION NO. 40: PATTERSON SMITH REPRINT SERIES IN CRIMINOLOGY, LAW ENFORCEMENT, AND SOCIAL PROBLEMS

THE EVOLUTION OF PROHIBITION IN THE UNITED STATES OF AMERICA

A CHRONOLOGICAL HISTORY
OF THE LIQUOR PROBLEM AND THE TEMPERANCE
REFORM IN THE UNITED STATES FROM THE
EARLIEST SETTLEMENTS TO THE CONSUMMATION
OF NATIONAL PROHIBITION

BY

ERNEST H. CHERRINGTON

EDITOR OF THE AMERICAN ISSUE
GENERAL SECRETARY OF THE WORLD LEAGUE
AGAINST ALCOHOLISM

Montclair, New Jersey

PATTERSON SMITH

1969

Originally published 1920
Reprinted 1969 by
Patterson Smith Publishing Corporation
Montclair, New Jersey

SBN 87585-040-5

Library of Congress Catalog Card Number: 69-14916

PREFACE

THE OBJECT of the author of this history of the Prohibition movement in the United States of America has been to assemble the facts which have to do with the liquor problem and the temperance reform and to present the same in brief chronological form, emphasizing the major note of the movement towards Prohibition in each of the several periods with which the history deals.

Each of the ten chapters into which this book has been subdivided deals with a distinct period of the temperance reform and a brief general survey of the movement in each period as the work of that period is related to the entire record of more than 300 years of temperance activity.

The facts thus presented distinctly show that the Prohibition movement in the United States has been an evolution rather than a revolution, each period plainly revealing a more advanced temperance sentiment and a more aggressive attitude of opposition to the beverage liquor traffic than that shown in the preceding period.

The volume thus presented represents research work extending over several years. Data has been gathered from practically all available sources, including colonial legislative records, histories of the early American settlements, public documents of the several states and the federal government, minutes or proceedings of the conventions of the several temperance organizations, church histories, encyclopedias, year books, compilations of important dates, temperance records, pamphlets, tracts, magazine articles and newspaper reports dealing with the temperance movement. In short, there has been used in the preparation of this work data from almost every source which has been available in public libraries and the archives of historical societies.

Among the books and documents consulted in the preparation of this volume the following deserve mention as having been particularly helpful: Temperance in All Lands, by J. N. Stearns; The Centennial Temperance Volume; One Hundred Years of Temperance, by the National Temperance Society; Secrets of the Great Whisky Ring, by General John McDonald; The Prohibitionist's Text Book, by the National Temperance Society; New Encyclopedia of Social Reform, by W. D. P. Bliss; The Life of Frances E. Willard, by Anna A. Gordon; Fifty Years' History of the Temperance Crusade, by J. E. Stebbins; A Century of Drink Reform, by August F. Fehlandt; The Temperance Reform, by W. H. Daniels; the Lincoln Legion, by Louis Albert Banks; Women and Temperance, by Frances E. Willard; The Liquor Problem in All Ages, by Daniel Dorchester; History of the Woman's Crusade, by Annie Wittenmeyer; Intoxicating Drinks and Drugs in All Lands and Times, by Wilbur F. Crafts; The Temperance Movement, by Henry W. Blair; Temperance Progress, by John G. Woolley and William E. Johnson; Great Temperance Reforms, by James Shaw; Temperance Recollections, by John Marsh; Glimpses of Fifty Years, by Frances E. Willard; History of Temperance in Massachusetts, by

George F. Clark; The Federal Government and the Liquor Traffic, by William E. Johnson; Life of John B. Finch, by Frances E. Finch and Frank J. Sibley; Memories of the Crusade, by Mother Stewart; Autobiography and Personal Recollections, by John B. Gough; History of the Independent Order of Good Templars, by T. F. Parker; Forty Years' Fight with the Drink Demon, by Charles Jewett; Cyclopedia of Temperance and Prohibition, by Funk and Wagnalls; Battling with the Demon, by J. A. Dacus; minutes or reports of the proceedings of the national conventions of the Woman's Christian Temperance Union, the Independent Order of Good Templars, the Sons of Temperance, the Anti-Saloon League of America and other temperance organizations; also files of the New Voice, the National Advocate, the Union Signal, The American Issue, the Scientific Temperance Journal, and other temperance periodicals.

This volume is presented to the public in the hope that it may prove to be of service to the temperance reform at this particular time, when the victory which has been secured for Prohibition in the United States must be made permanent through the proper enforcement of the law and the education of all the people as to the reasons for and the benefits from such a governmental policy.   E. H. C.

September 1, 1920.

CONTENTS

CHAPTER I

CHAPTER II

CHAPTER III

CHAPTER IV

CHAPTER V

CHAPTER VI

CHAPTER VII

CHAPTER VIII

CHAPTER IX

CHAPTER X

THE EVOLUTION OF PROHIBITION
IN THE UNITED STATES OF AMERICA

CHAPTER I

THE PIONEER PERIOD OF TEMPERANCE ACTIVITY IN THE UNITED STATES OF AMERICA—1607-1775

THE American liquor problem is as old as the white man's knowledge of the American continent, and it may be said that primitive phases of the question antedate the discovery of America by Christopher Columbus in 1492, since the traditions of practically all American Indian tribes include references to ancient customs and rites having to do with the indulgence of the aborigines in native intoxicants.

The age-old liquor habits and customs of Europe were introduced on this continent at a very early date. In fact, they came with the first explorers. The earliest settlers appear to have given particular attention to the kind and quantity of intoxicating liquors which accompanied them on their voyages across the Atlantic to their new homes amid the forests of the Western world.

English, Dutch, Spanish and French pioneers each made a distinct contribution to the beginnings of American civilization, but each also bears responsibility in the matter of the introduction of liquor-drinking customs different from any which the Indian had known and which promptly became the deadly enemy of the American savage, the cause of many of the internal difficulties of the colonists, and the principal factor in the numerous early mis-understandings between the whites and the Red Men.

At the earliest formal meeting between the French and the Indians, in 1535, on the island of Orleans in the St. Lawrence river, Jacques Cartier is reported to have celebrated the occasion by spreading a feast of bread and wine for the great chief Donnaconna and his Indian warriors.

The introduction between Henry Hudson and the Delawares in 1609 was in the form of a ceremony which consisted in presenting to the chiefs of the tribe a large drinking vessel filled with liquor, from which Hudson himself first drank.

The seed of drinking customs thus early planted in the New World yielded a prolific harvest. The use of intoxicating liquors as beverages, begun at those early dates, increased by leaps and bounds. There was no condemnation of intoxicating liquors as such. There was no attitude of hostility to in-toxicants even on the part of the moral and relig-ious forces. The only phase of the question which served to arouse any opposition was that which presented itself in the form of drunkenness. There was indeed in those days no scientific knowledge of the evil physiological effects of alcohol on the human system. The only sin therefore which in any sense came under the ban of social condemna-tion was that of excess which expressed itself in speech and manner.

This general condition characterized the entire colonial period. All that could be designated as temperance reform work in the 168 years from the founding of Jamestown in 1607 to the outbreak of the Revolutionary War in 1775 was the activity which contented itself in agitation and legislation against the evil of drunkenness. Liquors in themselves were considered wholesome and necessary. When used in the kind of moderation which stopped short of drunkenness they were considered helpful and stimulating. Only when used to excess were they condemned.

The efforts of the colonists to reduce and finally to prohibit the sale or gift of intoxicating liquors to the Indians were due to the fact that the havoc which intoxicants quickly wrought among the Indians indicated clearly and emphatically their possibilities for evil, since it quickly became apparent that it was all but impossible for the Red Man to drink in what the white man considered moderation.

The temperance reform movement of the colonial period, if indeed it can properly be considered as approaching the dignity of a reform, readily subdivides itself into three phases: first, the effort to prevent the excessive consumption of intoxicating liquors by the Indians on account of the fact that such abuse caused serious trouble with the savages and thus menaced the safety of the whites; second, regulations to prevent the excessive use by servants and apprentices, which tended to promote idleness and loitering among them thus interfering with the efficiency of those whose time and labor were supposed to belong to others; and third, the attempt to discourage drunkenness among those who had become so addicted to the habit of liquor consumption that their drunken condition interfered with the peace and good order of the communities in which they lived.

One of the first important commodities to be used by the early settlers in trade with the Indians was intoxicating liquors. The Indian was unable to drink in moderation, and in fact he did not desire to drink in moderation, for the sensation of drunkenness was to him the most attractive feature of the white man's liquor, which was readily able to turn the most peaceful Red Man into a savage of the most ferocious type. Many a chief, seeing the destruction wrought among his people by the white man's liquor, exerted every effort against it, both in trying to influence the members of his own race, and in appealing to the Colonial governments to discontinue the sale of ardent spirits to his people. The fact is well established that the war known as the Pequod War in 1638 was largely caused by the depredations of Indians who had become intoxicated on liquor secured from the whites, and it is also well established that King Phillip's War of 1676 was caused in the same way.

Early efforts in the Massachusetts Colony to prevent the sale of intoxicating liquors to servants and apprentices were due to economic rather than to humanitarian motives. While this may be considered the primitive stage of the movement against intoxicating liquors in the interest of labor efficiency, it was evidently not championed by the early colonists for any other reason than that which grew out of class distinction, which was strongly marked in the early days of American history. The time and services of servants and apprentices were supposed to belong absolutely to their masters and principals. Consequently any time spent in loitering, drunkenness, or even in idling around public inns, was so much lost time; hence the early regulations against the sale to servants and apprentices were purely conservation measures from the viewpoint of the master and employer.

Laws intended to assist in the suppression of drunkenness during colonial days were for the most part drawn to regulate the conduct of the individual consumer rather than to curb the activities of the seller. Yet there were numerous instances in which regulation as that term is used by the advocates of liquor even in this day, was brought to bear on innkeepers of the seventeenth century in the interest of making the sale of intoxicating liquors entirely "respectable." Among the provisions thus enacted by the several Colonial governments were included the prohibition of the sale to persons under certain ages, the limiting of the amount of liquor sold to one person at a given time, the regulation of beermaking so as to insure a wholesome product, and provisions for closing all public houses at stated hours.

Taxation of the liquor traffic for revenue purposes began in the colonies as early as 1650. During that year the Colony of Connecticut passed a law imposing a duty on imported liquors and an excise tax on liquors manufactured in the United States. From that time forward for two hundred and seventy years, one of the principal arguments of the liquor traffic in its own defense has been that it has served the public by providing revenue for the government.

The Church of colonial days did not recognize the liquor traffic as a great evil. On the other hand, even the immoderate use of liquors was common at church functions and especially at weddings, church councils and funerals. This condition existed until about the middle of the eighteenth century, when the colonies one by one either by law or by action of the church bodies themselves began to insist upon the elimination of liquor consumption in connection with funeral ceremonies. The first recorded action of this character was taken by the General Court of Massachusetts in 1742, the decree of the court forbidding the use of wine and rum at funeral services.

The relationship between the liquor traffic and the African slave trade began in the early part of the eighteenth century. It is not too much to say that the slave traffic and a large part of the slavery problem which presented itself in later years were properly chargeable to the desire of some of the early colonists to secure a foreign market for American intoxicating liquor products. Something of the extent to which this traffic had gone in the early part of the eighteenth century is shown by the fact that in the year 1734 there were sent from the colony of Rhode Island to the coast of Africa eighteen vessels of rum which were exchanged for a cargo of African slaves.

The most outstanding movement against the sale

and use of intoxicating liquors during the colonial period was the so-called Oglethorpe Experiment in the colony of Georgia. Upon the arrival of Governor Oglethorpe in Georgia in 1733 he declared the importation of ardent spirits illegal. The following year the Councilors of Georgia acted upon the advice of Oglethorpe and prohibited the importation of rum. In 1735, the English Parliament, at the request of Oglethorpe, enacted a law prohibiting the importation of ardent spirits into the colony of Georgia. At first this provision was rigidly enforced but through the influence of Europeans who later came to the colony and those who visited Georgia from other colonies, the enforcement became lax and the law finally drifted into disrepute.

The following chronology for the period shows something of the gradual growth of the liquor traffic during colonial days as well as the slow but decidedly progressive tendency throughout the period toward emphasizing the evils of the traffic as they appeared and insisting upon remedial provisions.

CHRONOLOGY OF THE TEMPERANCE REFORM FOR THE COLONIAL PERIOD—1607-1775

1609

Henry Hudson, the British navigator, sails into New York Bay, lands in the midst of some Delaware Indians on the island who are fishing, and makes friends with them by giving them their first introduction to intoxicating liquor. One of the chiefs drinks the cup of liquor offered by Hudson, be-

comes dead drunk so that his comrades think he has
expired.   When he is finally aroused and confesses
to having been pleased with the sensation, all the
Indians follow his example.

(There is a tradition that the Indians thereafter referred to this island as "Manahachta-nienk," which
in the Delaware language means "The island where
we all became intoxicated," and that this name given
to the island by the Delawares was afterward cor-
rupted by the white man into "Manhattan.")

1619

The Colony of Virginia enacts a law against playing dice, cards, drunkenness, idleness and excess in
apparel.   This law also requires that drunkards shall
be publicly reproved by ministers.

1620

Massasoit visits the settlement at Plymouth and
is treated by the Governor to a military salute with
music and "a pot of strong water."

1623

The Dutch Reformed Church is established on the
Island of Manhattan and takes strong grounds
against "the excessive use of intoxicating drinks."

1629

The office of the Massachusetts Colony in London
directs Governor Endicott as follows:

"We pray you endeavor, though there be much
strong water for sale, yet so to order it that the savage may not, for our lucre sake, be induced to the
excessive use or rather abuse of it; and at any time
take care our people give no ill example; and if any
shall exceed in the inordinate kind of drinking as to

become drunk, we hope you will take care his punishment be made exemplary for all others."

The ship "Arabella" bringing Governor Winthrop to Massachusetts Bay has among its supplies the following: "42 tuns of beer, 14 tuns of water, 1 hogshead of vinegar, 2 hogsheads of cider and 4 pumps for water and beer."

The Virginia Colonial Assembly enacts a law providing that "ministers shall not give themselves to excess in drinkinge, or riott, or spending their tyme idellye by day or night."

1630

Governor Winthrop of Massachusetts discontinues the practice of drinking healths one to another and "wishes others to do the like."

1632

Massachusetts Bay Company gives to John Winthrop Governor's Island on condition that he shall plant an orchard upon it.

Virginia enacts the provisions of the law of England against drunkenness.

1633

Massachusetts Bay Colony stipulates that the Governor's permit is necessary to sell liquor, and it is declared that already many are "distempering themselves with drinke."

Robert Cole of Massachusetts Colony having been frequently punished for drunkenness is ordered to wear a red D about his neck for a year.

Plymouth Colony passes a law against permitting drunkenness in one's house. Innkeepers are to sell "not over twopence worth to any one but strangers just arrived."

John Holmes of Plymouth Colony is censured for drunkenness and ordered "to sitt in the stocks, and amerced in twenty shillings fine."

1635

Plymouth Colony heavily fines an unlicensed liquor dealer.

Massachusetts enacts a law providing that licenses shall be issued by the court; heavy penalties are added.

1636

Thomas Savery of Plymouth Colony is found guilty of drunkenness and ordered whipped.

1637

Wm. Reynolds of Plymouth Colony is found guilty of being drunk.

The first brewery in America is built by Captain Sedgwick in Massachusetts Colony.

Massachusetts, in order to discourage drunkenness, orders that no person shall remain in any inn or victualing house "longer than necessary occations, upon payne of 20 shillings for every offense."

The general court of Massachusetts applies in part the principle of Prohibition to the traffic in strong drink, prohibiting the selling of "sack or strong water" to Indians.

1638

New York sells liquors only at company stores.

The Dutch on Staten Island first distil brandy.

One person in each of eleven named Massachusetts towns is authorized to sell "sack or strong water."

The Pequod War with the Indians is caused largely by troubles growing out of the liquor traffic with the Indians. Connecticut orders among the supplies for troops one hogshead of "beare, three or four gallons of strong water, and two gallons of sacke."

Massachusetts Colony prohibits the drinking of healths.

A tippling housekeeper is publicly whipped in Massachusetts.

1639

Massachusetts orders retailers of wine not to allow it to be drunk in their houses.

1640

Major La Frediere, commandant of the garrison stationed at Montreal, turns his quarters into a dramshop for selling liquor to Indians, and systematically swindles them.

1641

The cultivation of hops is introduced into Massachusetts Colony.

John Appleton is said to be the first maltster in the Colony of Massachusetts.

1642

Maryland adopts a law providing against drunkenness under penalty of a fine consisting of 100 pounds of tobacco. If the offender is a servant and unable to pay, he is to be set in the bilboes and compelled to fast for 24 hours, or be imprisoned.

It is declared in New York that "many accidents

are caused by quarrels, fighting, and the multitude of low groggeries badly conducted" compel stricter measures.

1643

Connecticut enacts a law prohibiting anyone from selling wine or strong water without a license.

1644

Virginia Assembly prohibits the illegal sale of wine or strong liquor; strong beer only is permitted, and no liquor debts are "pleadable or recoverable" by law.

Liquor revenue pure and simple appears in Massachusetts laws.

The court of Pennsylvania issues the following order: "The court, apprehending that it is not fit to deprive the Indians of any lawful comforts which God alloweth to all men by the use of wine, orders that it shall be lawful for all who are licensed to retail wines, to sell also to Indians."

James, Duke of York and Albany, issues an ordinance against the manufacture and use of malt liquors on Long Island.

New York Colony levies an excise tax on beer, wine and brandy.

There is a temporary letting down in Massachusetts of the law prohibiting the sale of liquors to Indians.

1645

It is determined in Massachusetts that "more than half of a pint at one time" is excess, and tippling "above ye space of half an hour" is forbidden.

New Plymouth, Massachusetts, disfranchises citizens for drunkenness.

Connecticut prohibits the selling of intoxicating liquors to Indians under penalty of 40 shillings to 5 pounds.

The Massachusetts Colony law of 1639 relative to drinking of healths is repealed.

The Massachusetts Colony provides for fining innkeepers 5 shillings for suffering drunkenness or excessive drinking in their houses.

West India rum is introduced into the American colonies.

1647

Rhode Island prohibits drunkenness under penalty of 5 shillings or 6 hours in the stocks if unable to pay. Selling liquor to Indians is also forbidden under penalty of 5 pounds.

Connecticut prohibits tipling in "ordinaries."

Massachusetts gives county courts the right to grant licenses.

1648

It is ordered that only one person in Boston shall be allowed to sell wine to the Indians.

Probably the first distinctive temperance meeting on American soil is held at Sillery (Canada) under the auspices of Father Jerome Lalemant. The meeting is addressed by an Algonquin chief, who in his own name and the name of the other chiefs proclaims the Governor's edict against drunkenness, and exhorts the Indians to total abstinence, declaring that all drunken Indians will be handed over to the French for punishment.

1649

Virginia boasts of six public brew houses.

The Massachusetts Colony orders that "every victualler, ordinary keeper or taverner should always keep provided with good and wholesome beer for the entertainment of strangers who, for want thereof, are necessitated to much needless expenses in wine."

The Colony of Rhode Island enacts a license law for Roger Williams, permitting him to sell wine or "strong water" to sick Indians.

1650

Connecticut lays a heavy duty on all imported liquors and an excise tax on all manufactured at home.

Connecticut passes a law providing that no licensed dealer is to suffer any one to be drunk or to drink excessively (viz., above half a pint at a time) or to tipple above the space of half an hour, or at unreasonable times. The penalties are as follows: For drunkenness appearing in speech or gesture only, 10 shillings; for excessive drinking, 3 shillings 4 pence; for tippling over half an hour, 2 shillings 6 pence; for tippling at unreasonable hours or after 9 o'clock, 5 shillings. The penalty is doubled in case of second offenses.

1651

The people of East Hampton, Long Island, at a town meeting pass an ordinance providing "That no man shall sell any liquor but such as are deputed thereto by the town, and such men shall not let youths, and such as are under other men's management, remain drinking at unreasonable hours, and such persons shall not have above half a pint at a time among four men."

Three grades of malt beer are fixed by Massachusetts laws.

1654

The preamble of a liquor law in Massachusetts says, in part: "Notwithstanding the great care this court hath had and the laws made to suppress that swinish sin of drunkenness, yet persons addicted to the vice find out ways to deceive the law."

The Colony of Massachusetts prohibits licensed persons from allowing excessive drinking, under fine of 20 shillings.

1655

The Colony of New Haven passes a liquor regulation law.

The sale of liquors to Indians is forbidden in Pennsylvania.

Virginia grants to the commissioners of each county the power to license ordinaries.

The townspeople of East Hampton, Long Island, pass an ordinance "for the prevention of drunkenness among the Indians," also against "selling to them or sending any to them or employing any one to sell for them," also against selling them liquor "in the town for the present drinking above two draws at one time; and to sell to no Indian but such as are sent by the Sachem and shall bring a written ticket from him, which shall be given him by the town, and he shall not have above a quart at a time."

1656

Rhode Island grants to constables and ordinary-keepers the right under warrant to search any man's house to see what quantity of liquor he may have.

Connecticut fixes the rates at which liquor is to be sold.

1657

Selling liquor to Indians in Massachusetts is prohibited under penalty of 40 shillings, the original law of 1639 being invoked.

John Barnes of Plymouth Colony is fined 5 pounds for abusing himself with drunkenness after admonition.

1658

Plymouth Colony passes a law disfranchising drunkards.

Maryland prohibits drunkenness under penalty of confinement in the stocks for 6 hours or a fine of 100 pounds of tobacco (half to the informer); for a second offense the law provides public whipping or a fine of 300 pounds of tobacco; for a third offense the offender is adjudged infamous, and disfranchised three years.

Virginia enacts a law which provides that one convicted of drunkenness three times is accounted a common drunkard. Those convicted of drunkenness are incapable of being witnesses or holding office.

The Virginia Assembly requires bonds for the sale of liquor and taverns are limited to one or two in a county.

1659

Connecticut prohibits the distillation of corn or malt into liquor, and fixes a fine of 20 shillings on any person found drunk in a private house. A fine of 10 shillings is also fixed for the owner of the house.

1660

"The greatest chief of the Mingoes" complains of D'Hinoyossa, the director of the Dutch Colony of New York, and states that the outrageous conduct of the Indians arises from his not restricting the sale of liquor.

New Plymouth, Massachusetts, laws forbid liquor sales on Sundays; also forbid sales to children, servants or tipplers, who are all forbidden to visit inns.

1661

The Massachusetts General Court decrees that "No person shall practice this craft of stilling strong water nor shall sell or retail any by lesser quantity than a quarter caske."

The Massachusetts Bay Colony enacts a law to regulate the sale of liquors.

1662

D'Hinoyossa, director of the Dutch Colony in America, prohibits the sale of liquors to Indians, under penalty of 300 guilder and authorizes the savages to rob those who bring them strong drink.

Plymouth Colony enacts a law providing that "All persons that doe or shall still any strong waters, shall give account of their disposal of them both of the quantity and the persons to whom sold."

Thomas Lucas of Plymouth Colony, found guilty of drunkenness for the third time, is publicly whipped.

1663

D'Hinoyossa, upon his arrival at Altona, prohibits distilling and brewing even for domestic use.

1664

An ordinance against the manufacture and sale of malt liquors in New York is published by "His Royal Highness James, Duke of York and Albany," at Hamsted, on Long Island.

The Virginia Assembly enacts a law providing that "Ministers shall not give themselves to excess in drinking or riot, spending their time idly by day or night, in playing at dice, cards, and other unlawful games."

1665

New York prohibits the sale of liquors to Indians, fixes a maximum retail price of two pence a quart for beer and 12 shillings a gallon for any liquor, under penalty of 20 shillings a gallon, so sold.

1667

Prior to this date a law is enacted in Massachusetts Colony providing that "beer should be made with 5 bushels of good barley malt at least to a hogshead without any mixture of molasses, cane, sugar, or other materials instead of malt, and that it should not be sold above 2 pence a quart."

1668

The Indians appeal to the New York authorities asking that no liquors be sold to the Indians at any place along the river.

New Jersey passes a law prohibiting persons drinking after 9 o'clock, and fines drunkenness 1 shilling, 2 shillings, and 2 shillings 6 pence for first, second and third offenses.

A Virginia law fixes a fine of 2,000 pounds of tobacco for unlicensed innkeepers and provides that only two ordinaries are to be licensed in each county.

1669

New Plymouth, Massachusetts, laws forbid laborers to be paid in drink and provide that liquor debts are not collectible by law, and that dealers trusting customers shall be fined for each offense.

1670

Massachusetts requires selectment to post drunkards' names in public houses and to prohibit sales to them.

The town of Attleboro, Massachusetts, is settled by John Woodcock, who builds a fortified tavern on the "Bay Road." On July 5 he is "allowed by this court to keep an ordinary at the Ten Mile River, and likewise enjoined to keep good order, that no unruliness or ribaldry be permitted there."

1671

Deputy Governor Lovelace of New York leaves to the discretion of the military officers the selling of liquor to Indians.

1673

Rhode Island prohibits the sale of liquor on Sunday.

Rev. Increase Mather, D.D., of New England, preaches and publishes "two sermons testifying against the sin of drunkenness."

1674

Plymouth Colony Church complains that some of its members "walk disorderly, sitting long in public houses, with vain companions and drinking."

1675

All who sell drink in Plymouth Colony are forbidden to sell to Thomas Lucas, an habitual drunkard.

By a special order of the court of New York, "strong liquor is not to be sold to the Indians in quantities of less than two gallons at a time under penalty of 5 shillings sterling."

1676

The new constitution of Virginia applies in part the principle of Prohibition to the traffic in strong drink, prohibiting the manufacture and sale of ardent spirits.

The Virginia Assembly prohibits the sale of wines and ardent spirits outside of Jamestown.

King Philip's War breaks out, caused largely by a long series of outrages resulting from the sale of liquor to Indians and renegade whites at John Woodcock's tavern (Attleboro, Mass.).

Virginia law provides that justices who get drunk on court days shall be fined 500 pounds of tobacco for the first offense, 1,000 pounds for the second, and forfeiture of position for third. Ministers who become drunk are fined a half-year's salary for the first and second offenses and stripped of every right for the third offense.

1677

New Jersey forbids the sale of liquor to Indians under penalty of $100, doubling the amount for each subsequent offense. If the violator is unable to pay, he receives 20 stripes.

Virginia enacts a law providing that only two licenses may be granted in each county and that those must be granted to taverns.

1678

At the funeral of Mrs. Mary Norton, widow of John Norton, who had been minister of the first church in Boston, 51½ gallons of the best Malaga wine are consumed by the mourners.

1679

New Jersey forbids selling liquor to Indians on penalty of 20 lashes for the first, 30 for the second, and imprisonment for an indefinite period for the third offense.

1681

Delaware Indian chiefs request the Governor and Council of Pennsylvania to permit liquors to be sold to the Indians until it is prohibited in New Castle and in the government of Delaware.

The West New Jersey Assembly prohibits the sale of ardent spirits to red men, and permits criminals other than murderers to be pardoned by the person injured.

1683

The manufacture of beer is begun in Pennsylvania under the direction of William Penn.

South Carolina passes a law preventing unlicensed taverns and punch-houses.

1685

At the funeral of Rev. Thomas Cobbett, minister

of Ipswich, there are consumed by the mourners one barrel of wine and two barrels of cider.

The Yearly Meeting of Friends in Pennsylvania and New Jersey declares against the sale of ardent spirits to the Indians in the following language: "This meeting doth unanimously agree and give as their judgment, That it is not consistent with the honor of truth, for any that make profession thereof, to sell rum or any strong liquors to the Indians, because they use them not to moderation but to excess and drunkenness."

Mr. John Comb of Plymouth Colony is disfranchised for drunkenness.

1686

South Carolina prohibits the sale of intoxicating liquors by anyone who does not have a license from the Governor.

1687

Rum is imported into New York and yields a revenue to the government, according to the report of Governor Dougan to the committee of trade on the province of New York.

1688

The Treasurer of Massachusetts Colony is authorized "to rent, let or farme let the impost of wine, brandy and rhum, and the rates upon beere, cider, ale and mum."

1689

Connecticut imposes a fine of five pounds on persons selling liquor without license.

1691

"Rumm" is imported from the West Indies in return for flour exported to those islands from New York.

Governor Sloughter of New York is made drunk by Royalists, who thereby secure his signature to the death warrants of the patriots, Leister and Milborne.

1692

Massachusetts re-enacts liquor license provisions.

1694

South Carolina passes an act regulating public houses.

1695

South Carolina enacts the statutes of the common law of England for the regulation of public houses.

1697

New York forbids the frequenting of tipling houses on the Sabbath.

1700

New Hampshire prohibits innkeepers from permitting townspeople to remain in their houses drinking on Saturday night or Sunday under penalty of 5 shillings. The same fine also is provided for the drinker.

As a result of strong drink and pestilence in Carolina the Indians are reduced to a small number. Out of 1,000 warriors but a dozen weak men remain.

New Plymouth, Massachusetts, orders inspectors and gaugers for distilleries, the sales to fix the fee paid.

The cultivation of grapes is begun in New York, Virginia and the Carolinas, as well as in Canada.

The manufacture of New England rum is begun in Boston, the raw material being drippings from West India sugar-making, which are shipped to Boston for rum manufacture.

1701
Pennsylvania forbids the selling of liquor to the Indians.

New Hampshire imposes a fine of 5 shillings on drunkards.

1705
Rev. Francis Makenzie, first Presbyterian minister in America, preaches against intemperance.

1709
Sales of liquor by planters in South Carolina are limited to sales not to be drunk on the premises.

1710
New York imposes an excise tax on liquors sold at retail.

1711
The authorities of Lynn, Mass., provide half a barrel of cider for the Widow Dispaw's funeral.

1712
New York fixes a fine of five pounds for selling liquors without license.

1714
New York requires retailers of strong liquors to pay a special tax which is appropriated for the support of the colonial government.

The largest and most important distillery on the continent is set up in Boston by Henry Hill.

1715
Maryland prohibits the carrying of liquor to In-

dian towns under penalty of 5,000 pounds of tobacco and forbids the selling to an Indian of more than one gallon of liquor a day under penalty of 3,000 pounds of tobacco.

1719

New Hampshire prohibits the sale of liquor to drunkards and decrees that their names shall be posted in public houses.

New York enacts a law providing for a fine of 3 shillings on any "Christians" who are convicted of drunkenness, cursing or swearing, and a number of stripes at the discretion of the magistrate on "Negroes and Indians" guilty of those offenses.

1720

New York places a duty on imported wine and distilled liquors.

1721

Town councils in Rhode Island are given the power to post prohibitions against selling liquor to persons named as drunkards.

1726

Rev. Cotton Mather, D.D., of Massachusetts Colony, together with 22 other ministers, publishes "A serious address to those who unnecessarily frequent the tavern."

1728

The town of Salem, Mass., provides a gallon of wine and a gallon of cider for the funeral of a pauper.

1729

Salem, Mass., provides six gallons of wine for the funeral of a pauper.

1733

On the second day after his arrival in America, Governor Oglethorpe of Georgia declares that "the importation of ardent spirits is illegal."

1734

The Councilors of Georgia prohibit the importation of rum into the colony.

Rhode Island sends 18 vessels to Africa laden with rum in trade for a cargo of slaves.

1735

The English Parliament prohibits the importation of liquors into Georgia.

Rum is manufactured in increasing quantities in Massachusetts.

1738

New York enacts a law restraining tavern-keepers from selling strong liquors to servants or apprentices, and from "giving large credit to others."

1740

Delaware requires all keepers of inns or alehouses to obtain licenses of the Governor.

1741

The Indians of Pennsylvania complain to the Governor of the colony about rum being brought among them by traders.

1742

The General Court of Massachusetts forbids the use of wine and rum at funerals.

The prohibition of the importation of liquors into Georgia is rescinded by act of Parliament.

1743

The General Rules of the Methodist Church are formulated by John and Charles Wesley, among which rules is the prohibition against "drunkenness, buying or selling spirituous liquors, or drinking them, except in cases of extreme necessity."

The prohibitory laws of Georgia are first evaded and later defied, improvident English settlers contending the rum is necessary to resist the climate.

1744

The grand jury in Philadelphia, of which Benjamin Franklin is a member, reports as follows: "The grand jury do therefore still think it their duty to complain of the enormous increase of publick houses in Philadelphia, especially since it now appears by the constables' returns that there are upwards of one hundred that have licenses which, with the retailers, make the houses that sell strong drink by our computation near a tenth part of the city, a proportion that appears to us much too great."

1746

There are three rum distilleries in New York.

1748

More than 15,000 hogsheads of rum are manufactured in Massachusetts annually, and a large portion is used in trade with the Indians and with the French.

1751

Massachusetts prohibits the selling of liquors to any "Negro, Indian or mulatto slave." This law is afterwards repealed.

1753

Rev. Andrew Eliot of Massachusetts preaches against the growing liquor evil.

1754

Whisky drinking is reported to be practically universal in Huntington County, Pennsylvania.

1756

On September 26 the Colony of Pennsylvania enacted an excise law levying a tax on retailers of foreign spirits.

1757

Georgia enacts a law providing that "no liquor license shall be granted to any joiner, bricklayer, plasterer, shipwright, silversmith, goldsmith, shoemaker, smith, tailor, tanner, cabinet maker or cooper, who should be capable of getting a livelihood by honest labor and industry."

1759

Sir Geoffrey Amherst, as commander of the English in the French and Indian War, directs that "every soldier who shall be found guilty of intemperance shall receive twenty lashes per diem until he discloses the name of the person from whom he procured the liquor."

1760

The History of New Sweden, by Acrelius, just published, enumerates 48 drinks in use in North America.

Virginia and Carolina pass laws compelling ministers to abstain from excess of drinking and riot.

The Friends of Pennsylvania make an effort to abolish the use of liquor at funerals.

John Wesley strongly and urgently sets forth the evils of intemperance and the sin of distilling liquors.

The diary of John Adams, February 29, 1760, says: "At the present day, licensed houses are becoming the eternal haunt of loose, disorderly people of the same town, which renders them offensive."

1761

The first invoice of goods taken on a hand-sled to the new town of Francestown, New Hampshire, includes a five-gallon keg of rum.

Massachusetts allows justices to grant a license to a representative of a deceased licensee.

1762

The Friends of Pennsylvania abolish the use of ardent spirits so far as their societies are concerned.

Ministers in Virginia decline to officiate at funerals where ardent spirits are introduced.

1763

The rum traffic among the Indians is introduced by the English into Ohio, the French having previously prohibited it.

1765

The Stamp Act of March 27 contains provisions requiring stamps on liquor licenses.

1766

Methodism begins its career in the United States. The movement is committed to the provisions of the English discipline which declares against using, buying and selling distilled liquors.

1767

Rhode Island places the liquor license fee at five pounds.

1772

The Act of 1756 is amended by the Colony of Pennsylvania, on March 2, extending the excise to rum, brandy and domestic spirits.

1773

John Wesley declares for prohibition of distilling.

1774

Anthony Benezet, a member of the Friends Society in Pennsylvania, issues a pamphlet entitled "The Mighty Destroyer Displayed in Some Account of the Dreadful Havoc Made by the Mistaken Use, as Well as the Abuse, of Distilled Spirituous Liquors," in which the author advises against the common use of any drink "which is liable to steal away a man's senses and render him foolish, irascible, uncontrollable and dangerous."

The New England Yearly Meeting of Friends disowns a member for drunkenness.

CHAPTER II

THE FIRST serious and effective efforts against the use of distilled liquors as beverages began with the movement for American independence. Prior to that time the principal agitation along temperance lines was against drunkenness. The harmful effects of the use of intoxicants in moderation had not been generally accepted.

The necessity of facing the problem presented by the use of intoxicants among American soldiers at the outbreak of the Revolution, when all the man-power of the Colonies was needed at its best, compelled not only the Colonial Legislatures but the Continental Congress to give serious consideration to the scientific phases of the alcohol problem.

Medical science blazed the trail for the temperance reformers in this new field. The early Methodists and several other church denominations had already recognized the habitual use of distilled liquors as an evil, but the attitude of those bodies was indicated, as a rule, by declarations of a very general character and their activities were confined for the most part to resolutions affecting the individual members of the several communions.

Anthony Benezet, who belonged to the Society of Friends in Pennsylvania, had published a pamphlet in

1774 which advised against the use of intoxicants. But the publication of this pamphlet did not result in any direct and immediate effort to press for remedial measures along temperance lines, although the reading of the pamphlet must have had its effect upon men who afterwards became instrumental in presenting the same truth in a way that received more serious attention.

Doctor Benjamin Rush, a noted physician of his day, who was also a very public-spirited man and one of the principal figures in the drafting and signing of the Declaration of Independence, is generally recognized as the pioneer in the movement against the use of distilled liquors. When the war was at its height in 1777, Doctor Rush prepared a strong document against the use of ardent spirits, which document was approved and adopted by the War Board of the Continental Congress and was printed and circulated among all the troops in the United States Army. The object of this document was to urge all the soldiers to abstain from the use of distilled liquors while in the service of their country. This was the first appeal against the use of distilled liquors which was recognized in any official way by the government.

Doctor Rush frequently has been referred to by historians as the pioneer advocate of total abstinence from the use of alcoholic liquors. As a matter of fact, however, his activities and writings were limited to the fight against distilled liquors. This was quite in harmony with the general attitude toward the question in that early day, since even those who were the strongest advocates of temperance seemingly had no thought of placing under the ban such intoxicants

as beer and light wine. It is not unlikely that this attitude upon the part even of religious forces and temperance reformers may have been due in part to the
fact that the consumption of beer and wine during that
period was very small. Distilled liquors, which constituted the principal intoxicant, were consumed at the
rate of about two and one-half gallons per capita
annually. From these and other facts it is evident that
the liquor problem had not assumed anything like the
comparative proportions it did in later years when the
liquor interests and more especially the beer interests
began active propaganda to promote the use of beer
as a beverage and thus strongly appealed both to appe-
tite and greed.

In this connection it is significant to note that the
struggle for prohibition in the United States has been
largely a struggle against the consumption of fermented liquors. During the nineteenth century the per
capita consumption of distilled liquors as well as the
per capita consumption of wine gradually decreased
until at the close of the century the per capita annual
consumption of distilled liquors was slightly more than
one gallon, the annual per capita consumption of wines
was slightly less than one-half gallon, while the annual
per capita consumption of malt liquors was more than
16 gallons. It is safe to say that had it not been for
the remarkable increase in the consumption of beer in
the United States the temperance reform would not
have reached the stage which it did reach.

The suggestion that beer and wine are less harmful because they contain a smaller percentage of alcohol, is not confined to the pro-liquor arguments of the
twentieth century. This same suggestion was respon-

sible to a very great degree for the substitution of beer for so-called ardent spirits in the early days of the American Republic. The one vital factor which has not been and is not taken into account by those to whom such a suggestion appeals, is that the consumption of beer, wine and whisky, is primarily due to the demand for the alcohol contained in such liquors, and that the size of the drink has invariably been regulated according to the kind of intoxicating liquors consumed, so that the average drink of whisky, wine or beer, would contain about the same amount of alcohol.

Before the appearance of Doctor Rush's document which was circulated by the War Department, the Federal Government had already taken measures to restrict the sale and use of distilled spirits in the army. General George Washington on March 25, 1776, issued orders at Cambridge, Mass., enjoining upon all officers of the Continental Army the obligation to prevent, so far as possible, the frequenting of tippling houses by American soldiers. Prior to these orders, Maryland had already fixed the ration for Maryland troops in the Continental Army at one-half pint of rum per man daily. When the Pennsylvania Colonial Assembly, however, fixed the ration for Pennsylvania troops on April 4 of that same year the ration included one quart of small beer per man per day. Other colonies followed the example set by Pennsylvania in fixing the ration in beer instead of distilled liquors. The Continental Congress on September 20 prohibited the sale of all kinds of liquors to soldiers by sutlers, thus limiting the alcoholic drinks of the members of the American Army to the ration as prescribed by the several Colonial Legislatures and the Continental Congress.

The crusade against the use of distilled liquors especially in the army had its effect. The Continental Congress in session at Philadelphia by strong resolutions appealed to the several Colonial Legislatures immediately to pass effective laws to stop the practice of distilling. The colony of Pennsylvania took steps against the distilling of grain in 1779. This action, together with the action taken in other colonies as well as the expressed attitude of the Continental Congress, compelled the attention of the moral and religious forces throughout the colonies. While John Wesley had already in 1773 declared against the practice of distilling, the Methodist Church in America officially condemned the practice in 1780. The Brethren took the same action in 1783, while the New England Society of Friends made a similar declaration in 1784.

Doctor Rush in 1785 published his famous pamphlet entitled "An Enquiry Into the Effects of Ardent Spirits Upon the Human Body and Mind." This pamphlet proved to be the greatest and most effective arraignment of distilled liquors that had ever been presented and its effect upon the public mind was soon evident.

While Doctor Rush was the first to speak out against distilled liquors from the viewpoint of medical science, physicians and surgeons in many parts of the country promptly followed his lead in calling attention to the evil results of the use of distilled liquors. The College of Physicians of New York in 1790 presented to the United States Senate a memorial deprecating the use of ardent spirits and recommending high duties upon their importation as a measure to help discourage their use. Similar action was taken by the College of Physicians and Surgeons of the city of Philadelphia as a result of which the question engaged Congress and the agitation for restrictive legislation became more and more persistent.

Just at the time when medical associations and public-spirited men generally began to see the need of restrictive legislation in connection with the production, importation and sale of distilled liquors, Alexander Hamilton was trying to find some way to establish the financial credit of the new Federal Government and to secure necessary revenues for current expenses. Mr. Hamilton promptly hit upon the plan of raising revenue from taxes and imposts upon distilled liquors. As early as 1787 Hamilton urged Congress to place a tax upon distilled liquors. In 1789 his suggestion was repeated with emphasis through the columns of the Federalist. The following year he presented to the House of Representatives an elaborate argument in favor of taxing ardent spirits in order to provide revenue for the government. Mr. Hamilton's efforts were finally successful, the Revenue Act being adopted by Congress in 1791, which act Mr. Hamilton himself estimated would bring to the Federal Government an annual income of $826,000.

The Second Congress of the United States, in 1792, amended the original act which changed the amount of duty on distilled liquors and provided for license fees on distilleries as well as placing a special tax on liquors distilled from foreign materials. This action by the Federal Government was the immediate cause of the breaking out in western Pennsylvania of what is known as the Whisky Rebellion, the putting down of which compelled the United States Government to expend something like $1,500,000 in war preparations.

It is a significant fact in this connection that the Whisky Rebellion in western Pennsylvania was encouraged by the action of the Legislature of the state of Pennsylvania, which called into question the right of the Federal Government to place such taxes as had been placed on the production of distilled liquors. This was the first outbreak, after the formation of the Federal Government, on the question as to where the rights of the state governments on the question of taxation ended and those of the Federal Government began.

Thus the Whisky Rebellion not only presented the problems of states' rights in general, but it presented in particular the question which involved the possibility of solving the liquor problem under the American form of government. From that time on it was evident that the liquor problem in the United States could never be permanently solved except by national action and that before the problem could be put in the way of permanent solution the states' rights doctrine, which had already asserted itself both in the North and in the South, would have to be settled, as it was settled seventy-five years later.

Following the suppression by the Federal Government of the Whisky Rebellion in Western Pennsylvania, practically every Congress for the next eight years amended the Federal revenue act, increasing or decreasing the various tax provisions until the election and inauguration of Thomas Jefferson as President of the United States. President Jefferson in his first message to Congress advocated the repeal of the internal revenue law. Congress acted upon President Jefferson's suggestion, and as a result the whole internal revenue system established by Mr. Hamilton was wiped out.

This period was also marked by the action of the Federal Government in taking strong measures to suppress the sale of intoxicating liquors to the Indians and in Indian countries. President Jefferson in 1802 urged Congress to prohibit the sale of liquor among the Indians. Congress replied by authorizing the President of the United States to take such measures to prevent the sale or distribution of spirituous liquors among the Indians as might seem necessary. The President acted under the authority given by Congress and during the following years the Federal administration made every possible effort to establish the prohibition of liquor selling among Indians.

In 1805 William Henry Harrison, Governor of the Northwest Territory, representing the Federal Government, called upon the territorial Legislature to pass a law prohibiting the sale of liquor to Indians. The following year the territorial Legislature acted upon the Governor's suggestion in a degree by prohibiting the sale of intoxicants to Indians within forty miles of Vincennes.

The following chronology covers the principal items of interest in connection with the temperance reform during the period.

CHRONOLOGY OF THE TEMPERANCE REFORM FOR THE
PERIOD 1775–1810

1775

The Colonial Congress of New Hampshire in August passes a preamble and resolution deploring the great prevalence of intemperance and recommending that the treats given to soldiers on muster day be diminished.

On November 4 the Continental Congress fixed the army ration at "one quart of spruce beer or cyder" per day, and on November 28 fixed the ration for the navy at a half-pint of rum per man, with discretionary allowances when on extra duty or in time of engagement.

1776

Dr. Benjamin Rush, who later wrote the notable pamphlet entitled "The Effects of Ardent Spirits on the Human Mind and Body," is chairman of the Committee on Independence in the Continental Congress.

A general movement against intemperance is waged in practically all the colonies.

The regulations for the government of the army, adopted by Congress September 20, provide that "No sutler shall be permitted to sell any kind of liquors or victuals or keep their houses or shops open, for the entertainment of soldiers, after nine at night, or before the beating of the reveilles, or upon Sundays, during divine services, or sermon."

General George Washington issues orders at Cambridge, Mass., (March 25) enjoining upon all officers of the Continental Army to prevent, as much as possible, the soldiers from frequenting tippling houses.

The Continental hospital regulations, promulgated in July, provide a corporal's guard "to prevent persons from going in, without orders, to disturb the sick, or carry liquor to them."

The Pennsylvania Assembly on April 4 fixes the ration for Pennsylvania troops at one quart of small beer per man per day.

On February 1 the Maryland Council of Safety fixes the ration for Maryland troops at one-half pint of rum per man per day and discretionary allowances for particular occasions.

1777

Dr. Benjamin Rush prepares a paper against the use of ardent spirits which is adopted by the Board of War and printed and circulated among all the troops in the United States Army. This paper urges all to abstain from the use of liquors while in the service of their country.

Congress in session at Philadelphia passes the following resolution: "Resolved, that it be recommended to the several Legislatures in the United States immediately to pass laws the most effective for putting an immediate stop to the pernicious practice of distilling grain, by which the most extensive evils are likely to be derived if not quickly prevented."

General Stephen, one of Washington's division commanders, is dismissed because of intemperance.

1778

The annual meeting of the "Brethren" or "Dunkards" passes a resolution requiring brethren of the brotherhood to put away distilleries from among them.

Richard Allen and Absalom Jones organize the "Free African Society," which is a temperance organization, excluding men of drinking habits from its membership.

1779

Pennsylvania lays an embargo on the exportation of wheat and flour, and prohibits the distillation of all kinds of grain or meal as a conservation measure. Rye and barley are later excepted.

The Colony of Pennsylvania still further amends its excise provisions. The act proves unsatisfactory and is soon repealed.

Vermont prohibits drunkenness under a penalty of a $2 fine if noticeable in speech, gesture or behavior.

1780

The General Conference of the Methodist Church condemns the practice of distilling liquors and proposes to disown "all persons who engage in distilling."

1783

The annual meeting of the "Brethren" or "Dunkards" resolves that those who refuse to comply with the third admonition to put away distilleries from among them shall be shut out from church communion and from the kiss.

Congress recommends to the states that it is necessary for the restoration of public credit to vest Congress with power to levy certain specified duties on spirits, wines, teas, pepper and other commodities.

The Indians of western Pennsylvania, in council at Pittsburgh, March 15, resolve to take matters into their own hands and "spill all rum among them for the term of five years."

1784

The Society of Friends at the New England Yearly Meeting in the Discipline of the church recommends against the distilling, importing, trading in or handing out to others of spirituous liquors.

At an ordination of a minister in Hartford, Conn., on May 24, the account of the South Society shows that there was used for the occasion "15 boles of punch, 11 bottles of wine, 5 mugs of flip and 6 boles of toddy."

The Methodist Church declares for the prohibition of "drunkenness, buying or selling spirituous iquors or drinking them unless in cases of extreme necessity."

1785

Dr. Benjamin Rush publishes his "Enquiry into the Effects of Ardent Spirits Upon the Human Body and Mind."

Rev. Phillip William Otterbein organizes his Church, excluding from partaking of the communion all those who indulge in strong drink.

1787

The General Assembly of the Presbyterian Church endorses the Law and Order League for the enforcement of the law against criminals.

Major John F. Hamtramck, commandant of Post Vincennes, Northwest Territory, issues a proclamation dated October 3, forbidding the sale of liquor to Indians.

Alexander Hamilton in a letter to the New York Packet declares that ardent spirits, under Federal regulation, might be made to furnish a considerable revenue. He shows that the quantity imported into the United States, at a shilling a gallon, would produce two hundred thousand pounds.

1788

The Yearly Meeting of Friends of New England binds all of the members of the church against the use of ardent spirits.

Dr. Benjamin Rush, a warm personal friend of Bishops Asbury, Whatcoat and McKendree and Dr. Coke, appears before the General Conference of the Methodist Episcopal Church to beseech the conference to use its influence to stop the "use as well as the abuse of ardent spirits."

1789

The second act placed upon the statute books of the United States under the Constitution is a bill providing for the following duties upon imported liquors and malt:

Ale, porter and beer—in bottles, per dozen, 20 cents; otherwise, per gallon, 5 cents.

Spirits—Jamaica proof, per gallon, 10 cents; all other, per gallon, 8 cents.

Wines—Madeira, per gallon, 18 cents; all others (bottles or cases), 10 cents; all others (otherwise), per gallon, 10 cents.

Malt—per bushel, 10 cents.

The pamphlet "The Federalist," a series of essays dealing with the formation of the Constitution of the United States, by Alexander Hamilton and others, argues for heavy duties for Federal purposes, particularly a duty on ardent spirits.

On April 8 James Madison offers a resolution in the United States House of Representatives declaring for a duty on rum, other spirituous liquors, wines, molasses, tea, pepper, sugar, cocoa and coffee.

The General Assembly of the Presbyterian Church votes to do all in its power to make "men sober."

The Federal Herald, of Lansingburg, N. Y., on July 13 says: "Upwards of two hundred of the most respectable farmers of the county of Litchfield, Conn., have formed an association to discourage the use of spirituous liquors, and have determined not to use any kind of distilled liquors during their farming work the ensuing season."

John Wesley's rule against the use, sale and buying of distilled liquors is amended by striking out the words "unless in cases of extreme necessity," thus greatly strengthening the Methodist attitude against the liquor evil.

John Wesley urges total abstinence on the ground of Christian expediency.

1790

A memorial from the College of Physicians of New York is presented to the United States Senate, deprecating the use of ardent spirits and recommending the imposition of high duties upon their importation.

It is estimated that the consumption of distilled spirits and wine in the United States is 2½ gallons per capita.

The rule of John Wesley against the use and sale of distilled liquors is modified by the addition of the words "unless in cases of necessity" and the elimination of the words "buying and selling."

A volume of temperance sermons makes its appearance in Philadelphia; it is supposed to have been prepared by Dr. Benjamin Rush.

The second session of the First Congress of the United States increases the duty on the importation of distilled and fermented liquors.

Dr. Benjamin Rush of Philadelphia urges a special hospital for inebriates.

On December 29 Robert Morris introduces into the Senate of the United States a memorial from the College of Physicians and Surgeons of Philadelphia praying that "such heavy duties may be imposed upon all distilled spirits as shall be more effectual to restrain their intemperate use." On the following day the same memorial is introduced in the House of Representatives by George Clymer.

On March 5 Alexander Hamilton sends to the United States House of Representatives an elaborate argument in favor of an excise tax on ardent spirits.

The United States House of Representatives on April 27 passes a resolution providing for an internal tax on distilled spirits. A committee is appointed to draft the bill, which is defeated on June 14 by a vote of 26 to 13.

The Act of Congress approved April 30 provides an army ration of half a gill of rum, brandy or whisky, or the value thereof for each man.

The action of Major Hamtramck of Post Vincennes, forbidding the sale of liquor to Indians, is confirmed by Acting Governor Sargent and the Judges of the Northwest Territory, acting in a legislative capacity.

1791

The Pennsylvania Legislature, on June 22, passes resolutions strongly protesting against any action on the part of the United States "tending to the collection of revenue by means of excise" as being established on principles subversive of peace, liberty and the rights of the citizens.

Alexander Hamilton expects a revenue of $826,000 annually from the general excise law passed by Congress.

On March 3, the last day of the closing session of the First Congress of the United States, an elaborate measure is passed increasing the duty on all imported distilled liquors and placing a tax on such liquors manufactured in the United States, the duty being from 9 cents to 30 cents per gallon.

The county courts of South Carolina are given the power to grant liquor licenses.

1792

There are 2,579 distilleries in the United States; the per capita consumption of liquor is 2½ gallons.

The Second Congress of the United States passes a measure changing the amounts of duty on imported distilled liquors and providing for licensing distilleries.

In the United States liquors distilled for consumption in this country amount to 5,171,564 gallons; spirits imported amount to 4,567,160 gallons; wines imported amount to 1,267,723 gallons.

1793

The Whisky Rebellion breaks out in western Pennsylvania, occasioned by the action of the Federal Congress in placing an excise tax of 11 cents a gallon on spirits distilled from foreign materials.

William Graham, an ex-saloonkeeper from Philadelphia, is appointed as collector by the Treasury Department to collect the excise from the counties in Pennsylvania where the "Whisky Rebellion" is at its height. Many outrages are committed against collectors; seventy suits are instituted against distillers and are promptly set aside by the courts. The President of the United States calls on the Governors of the states of New Jersey, Maryland, Virginia and Pennsylvania for 15,000 men, and when the troops appear on the scene the insurgents finally agree to pay the excise taxes.

The United States Government expends about $1,500,000 in war preparations on account of the "Whisky Rebellion."

1794

Dr. Benjamin Rush issues a book entitled "Medical Enquiries into the Effect of Ardent Spirits on the Body and Mind," which creates a stir among medical men.

The President of the United States is authorized by Congress to increase the quantity of liquor to a gill for troops on the frontiers.

The Philadelphia meeting of Friends rules that those who import, make, sell or grind grain for liquors "should not be employed in any service in the church nor their contributions received," and that if not "reclaimed they must be disowned."

Congress orders that a half-pint of spirits or a quart of beer shall constitute a part of the rations of the navy.

The Act of June 5, passed by the Third Congress of the United States, contains the following proviso: "That no license shall be granted to any person to sell wines or foreign distilled spirituous liquors who is prohibited to sell the same by the laws of any state."

This act also provides for a license tax on retailers of "wines and foreign distilled spirituous liquors by retail." A license fee of $5 is required for each class of licenses.

1795

President Washington on July 10 issues a proclamation of general amnesty to all persons implicated in the "Whisky Rebellion."

A uniform ration of half a gill of liquor daily is ordered by Congress for each soldier in the army.

One James Chalmers, a citizen of Nassau, N. J., who had become such a victim to strong drink that he could not control himself, issues the following document to the saloonkeepers: "Whereas, the subscriber, through the pernicious habit of drinking, has greatly hurt himself in purse and person, and rendered himself odious to all his acquaintances and finds that there is no possibility of breaking off from the said practice but through the impossibility to find liquor, he therefore begs and prays that no person will sell him for money, or on trust, any sort of spirituous liquors, as he will not in future pay for it, but will prosecute any one for action of damage against the temporal and eternal interests of the public's humble, serious and sober servant." (Signed and witnessed.)

1796

The following statement is prepared at the suggestion of the General Conference of the Methodist Episcopal Church and received the sanction of the General Conference of 1800: "Far be it from us to wish or to endeavor to intrude upon the proper religious or civil liberty of any of our people, but the retailing of spirituous liquors, and giving drams to customers when they call at the stores, are such prevalent customs at present and are productive of so many evils, that we judge it our indispensable duty to form a regulation against them. The cause of God, which we prefer to every other consideration under Heaven, absolutely requires us to step forth with humble boldness in this respect."

The Act of May 30 leaves the spirit ration for the army unchanged, except that it takes away from the soldier the right to commute the ration for the value thereof.

The African Methodist Episcopal Zion Church declares that strong drink is "a monster of frightful mien" and requires the ministry to discountenance its use themselves and to insist upon principles of total abstinence on the part of their congregations.

1797

The chief of the Miami Indians, Mechecunnaqua, or Little Turtle, begins an agitation for relief from the whisky peddlers. He visits Philadelphia and petitions President John Adams for the abolition of the liquor traffic among the Indians.

The Fourth Congress of the United States enacts a law repealing certain duties on distilled liquors, imposing certain duties on the capacity of stills of a particular description, and providing certain penalties for distilling without a license.

Seventh-Day Baptists enforce Prohibition as affecting their places of yearly meeting.

The Quarterly Conference of the Methodist Episcopal Church of Virginia passes a resolution pledging the honor as well as the words of the members as Christians, not only to abandon the use of ardent spirits themselves, except as a medicine, but also to use their influence to induce others to do the same.

The Presbyterian Synod of Pennsylvania enjoins its ministers to preach against the evils of intemperance and its causes.

The New Jersey Legislature passes a prohibitory vendue law.

1798

Vermont places a license fee upon liquor retailers of from one to thirty dollars, according to the profits.

The Presbyterian Synod of Pennsylvania adopts a temperance platform pledging its ministers to abstain from the use of intoxicating liquors, and enjoining upon them the duty of preaching against its use by the people. The last of August is appointed a "day of humiliation, fasting and prayer" on account of intemperance.

The Fifth Congress of the United States passes an amendatory act laying duties upon stills and upon liquors distilled in the United States.

Town Councils in Rhode Island are given privilege of granting licenses to sell liquor at their discretion, the license fee being fixed at $20.

1799

The Army Organization Act of March 3 eliminates the spirit ration, except as to those soldiers who are allowed such a ration by the terms of their enlistment; and at the same time authorizes the issuance of a ration not exceeding one-half gill of spirit per day, and more in case of fatigue, service, or on "other extraordinary occasions."

The power to grant liquor licenses in South Carolina is transferred from the county courts to the Commissioners of Roads.

1800

Handsome Lake, the Seneca prophet, inaugurates a total abstinence movement among the Iroquois. He organizes temperance societies, in which lectures are given by the head men of the nation.

The art of distilling intoxicants is introduced into Hawaii by convicts from Botany Bay. King Kamehameha I. later orders all the stills destroyed and forbids the manufacture of rum.

Micajah Pendleton of Nelson County, Virginia, signs and circulates a total abstinence pledge, thus starting the first pledge signing movement in America.

The Sixth United States Congress increases the duties on wines.

The Universalist Church resolves to hold no further sessions of the council of its convention in any hall connected with a tavern or public house, and to assemble in the private dwelling of some person.

1801

The Seventh United States Congress repeals certain duties on liquors and modifies the regulations governing distilled liquors.

Congress withdraws the option of a quart of beer in the navy ration instead of a half-pint of spirits.

Little Turtle, chief of the Miami Indians, travels from Indiana to Baltimore to attend the Baltimore Yearly Meeting of Friends, which body had previously proposed to establish schools among the Indians. The committee having this matter in charge reports that the selling of liquor to Indians creates such a deplorable condition that it is doubtful if good could be accomplished. Little Turtle makes an earnest appeal to the whites to stop the selling of liquor.

The Baltimore Yearly Meeting of Friends sends an address to Congress embodying the speech of Little Turtle.

Chief Little Turtle visits President Jefferson at Washington and begs him to aid in the movement to prevent the sale of liquor to aborigines.

President Jefferson writes letters to the Ohio Legislature asking it to enact legislation prohibiting the selling of intoxicants to Indians.

William Henry Harrison, Governor of the Northwest Territory, in a report to the Secretary of War, deals with the outrages and atrocities committed in the Indian country on account of liquor selling.

Thomas Jefferson, in his first message to Congress as President of the United States, suggests that they may henceforth dispense with all internal taxes, excises, licenses, etc. Congress later acts upon this recommendation and does away with the internal revenue system established by Hamilton.

South Carolina provides for the using of revenue derived from liquor licenses in the repairing of public roads.

1802

President Jefferson, in a message to Congress (Jan. 27) relating to Indian affairs, urges that body to prohibit liquor selling among Indians.

Congress, in the Act of March 30, authorizes the President of the United States to take measures to restrain or prevent the selling or distributing of spirituous liquors among the Indian tribes.

Congress restores the spirit ration for the army and doubles the amount, making it one gill per man.

1804

Congress provides that an equivalent of malt liquors or wine may be substituted for spirits in the army at certain seasons of the year.

A Total Abstinence Society is organized in Virginia by Micajah Pendleton and a large number of people in the Shenandoah Valley sign the pledge of this society and become abstainers. ,

The "Brethren" or "Dunkards" unanimously decide, in annual meeting, that no member of the church shall be permitted to sell ardent spirits or wine.

A drunken row in St. Louis and other outrages

committed by drunken Indians are instrumental in causing the Black Hawk War.

1805

A remarkable total abstinence campaign is carried on among the Indians by the Shawnee chief "The Prophet." In a meeting of Shawnees, Wyandots and Senecas at Wapakoneta, Ohio, he announces to the Indians that he has received a revelation warning him to denounce certain evil practices among the Indians, and especially firewater. His influence on the Indians is so strong that intoxication became practically unknown among the western tribes for a number of years.

William Henry Harrison, Governor of the Northwest Territory, in his message to the first Legislature, July 29, strongly recommends the Prohibition of liquor selling to Indians.

An association to promote temperance in Philadelphia is organized by persons engaged in the manufacture of paper, most of the members being journeymen paper-makers.

Rev. Ebenezer Porter, pastor First Congregational Church, Washington, Conn., preaches a strong temperance sermon from text Isa., 5:11, declaring that the American republic has more male and female drunkards in proportion to population than any other country.

The Sober Society is founded at Allentown, N. J.

1806

An act of the Legislature of the Northwest Territory approved December 6 forbids the sale of intoxicants to Indians within 40 miles of Vincennes.

1808

Dr. Lyman Beecher preaches a strong temperance sermon at East Hampton, Long Island.

Dr. B. J. Clark (Billy Clark) founds the Union Temperance Society of Moreau and Northumberland at Saratoga, N. Y. The constitution of this society declares: "No member shall drink rum, gin, whisky, wine or any distilled spirits, or compositions of the same or any of them, except by advice of a physician or in case of actual diseases, also excepting at public dinners, under the penalty of 25 cents; provided that this article shall not infringe on any religious rite; no member shall be intoxicated under penalty of 50 cents; no member shall offer any of the above liquors to any person to drink thereof under the penalty of 25 cents for each offense."

1809

A Total Abstinence Society is organized in Greenfield, Saratoga County, N. Y.

CHAPTER III.

PRIOR to the year 1810 the temperance activities of the Christian Church were largely limited to the attitude of outstanding ministers who preached against the traffic, and resolutions of church bodies, couched in general terms of advice and restriction intended to affect the conduct of individual members.

Rev. Increase Mather of New England was one of the first of the early temperance prophets. In 1673 he preached and published two sermons against the sin of drunkenness. Rev. Francis MacKinzie, frequently referred to as the first Presbyterian minister in the United States, preached against intemperance as early as 1705. Rev. Cotton Mather with the co-operation and endorsement of twenty-two other ministers, published a "Serious Address to Those Who Unnecessarily Frequent the Tavern" in the year 1726, just one hundred years before Dr. Lyman Beecher preached his famous series of six sermons against intemperance.

John Wesley, the founder of Methodism, made his first pronouncement against the liquor traffic and the liquor habit in 1743, but since Methodist activities did not begin in the United States until 1766, the Wesley declaration and the attitude of the Wesley movement in behalf of temperance was not brought to bear on the liquor problem in America until that time. The provision of the English Methodist discipline against the sale and use of distilled liquors, was strongly approved by the Methodists when Methodism began its career on the American continent in 1766 and John Wesley's declaration against distilling, issued in 1773, became the temperance battle cry of the Methodists in America during the last quarter of the eighteenth century. Thirteen years later, in 1789, John Wesley sent forth a ringing declaration for total abstinence from all intoxicants, which declaration was the foundation for total abstinence activities among Methodists.

Rev. Andrew Elliott of Massachusetts in 1753 sounded the alarm against the growing evil of intemperance, and the Rev. Phillip William Otterbein in 1785, when he organized his first church in America, took perhaps the strongest stand that had been taken officially by any minister up to that time by excluding from partaking of the communion all those who indulged in strong drink. The Rev. Heman Humphrey, who afterwards became president of Amherst College and served in that capacity for twenty-two years, was one of the early advocates of temperance. In 1810, while a pastor of the Congregational Church at Fairfield, Conn., he preached a series of six temperance sermons which are recorded to have had a profound effect on that section of New England.

While these and many other ministers of the different church denominations repeatedly preached against the liquor traffic and strongly urged upon the church the necessity of combatting the evil of intemperance, the great pioneer of the church's activity in temperance reform in America was the Rev. Lyman

Beecher, D.D., who as pastor of the Congregational Church in East Hampton, N. Y., in 1808 spoke out boldly in the interest of temperance, and who, after moving to Litchfield, Conn., in 1810, began activities in behalf of the temperance cause which resulted in stirring the Congregational Church of New England to aggressive action, out of which developed various local organizations in New England, the Massachusetts Society for the Suppression of Intemperance, and the first organized movement of a general or national character in the interest of temperance reform.

The declarations of various church bodies prior to the year 1810 indicate a constantly growing interest in individual temperance and an increasing tendency upon the part of the several church denominations to urge upon their members the importance of divorcing themselves from any connection with the traffic in distilled liquors. The Society of Friends in Pennsylvania at the Yearly Meeting held in 1685 declared against the sale of liquors to Indians on the ground that the Indians were wont to use such liquors "not in moderation but to excess." Seventy-seven years later, in 1762, this same society declared against the use of ardent spirits among the members of that society. The general rules of the Methodist Episcopal Church formulated in England in 1743 and adopted by the Methodists in America, who became active on this continent in 1766, contained a prohibition against "drunkenness, buying or selling spirituous liquors or drinking them except in cases of extreme necessity." The Brethren or "Dunkards" at the annual meeting of that body held in 1778 by action of the body required all members of the society to refrain from engaging in distilling. Five years later this same society declared that all those who failed to obey the injunction set forth in the declaration of 1778 should be shut out from "church communion and the kiss."

The Society of Friends of New England in 1784 incorporated in the discipline of the church a provision against distilling, importing, trading or handing out to others spirituous liquors. In 1788 this society at its Yearly Meeting bound all members of the church to refrain from the use of ardent spirits.

The Methodist Episcopal Church in 1780 strongly condemned the distilling business and declared the purpose of Methodists "to disown all persons who engage in distilling." The old John Wesley rule was reaffirmed by the Methodists in America in 1784 and again in 1788 after a strong appeal had been made to the General Conference of 1788 by Doctor Benjamin Rush, who was a close personal friend of Bishop Asbury and other pioneers of Methodism in America. In 1789 the American Methodists took a stronger stand than that represented by the Wesley rule, when they cut out of the rule the words "unless in cases of extreme necessity." In 1790, however, the rule was weakened by cutting out the words "buying or selling." The second regular General Conference of the Methodist Church, however, in 1796 again set forth the historic attitude of the church in no uncertain terms.

The General Assembly of the Presbyterian Church in 1789 went on record in a strong resolution which committed the church to the policy of doing all in its power to make men sober. The Philadelphia Yearly Meeting of Friends in 1794 declared that all those who imported, made or sold distilled liquors should not be employed in any service of the church and their contributions should not be received for the support of the church. This appears to be the first record of a church refusing to receive money made in the conduct of the liquor traffic.

The Seventh Day Baptists made a pronouncement in 1797 and enforced Prohibition so far as the place of the yearly meeting of the Assembly was concerned. The Universalist Church in 1800 resolved to hold no further sessions of the council of its convention in any hall connected with a tavern or public house. The Brethren or "Dunkards" in 1804 unanimously decided against any member being permitted to sell ardent spirits or wine.

The temperance sermons which had been preached prior to 1810, and the resolutions of the several church denominations prior to that date, however, had to do almost entirely with the individual habits and privileges of the members of the several organizations. The church had repeatedly admonished and adopted restrictive rules for its members, but the church as such, prior to 1810, had not put itself into the temperance movement in such a way as to influence public opinion outside of church communions and to bring to bear the force of public sentiment in behalf of temperance reform. Perhaps the nearest exception to this general attitude of the church was the action of the Baltimore Yearly Meeting of Friends in 1801 when that body after hearing the pathetic appeal of the Indian Chief "Little Turtle" sent to Congress a copy of "Little Turtle's" address in behalf of his people.

The new policy on the part of church bodies in con-

nection with the temperance reform was inaugurated
by the General Assembly of the Presbyterian Church
in 1810 when that body, recognizing the growing evil
of intemperance and realizing that a new policy must
be adopted by the churches if the growth of the liquor
traffic and the liquor habit was to be arrested, appointed
a special committee to consider and report to the General Assembly the conditions in respect to the liquor
traffic. The following General Assembly of the Presbyterian Church in 1811 after receiving a report from
the special committee appointed the previous year,
appointed another special committee to devise ways
and means to arouse public sentiment on the liquor
question. This committee reported to the General Assembly of 1812 recommending that all ministers of the
Presbyterian Church be urged to deliver public discourses on the sin and mischief of intemperate drinking and that they further be urged "pointedly and
solemnly to warn their hearers and especially members
of the church not only against actual intemperance but
against all those habits and indulgences which have a
tendency to produce it." This report, moreover,
strongly arraigned drinking places as public nuisances
and urged action against them. The report of the
committee was adopted by the General Assembly and
the Presbyterian Church was thus committed to an
aggressive movement against every phase of the traffic
in distilled liquors. The sessions of the General
Assembly of the Presbyterian Church in the following
years took no backward step, but repeatedly empha-
sized the obligation of the church to press the movement for temperance reform and to urge coöperation

to this end upon the part of all Presbyterian ministers and members of the church.

At the General Conference of the Methodist Episcopal Church held in 1812 the Rev. James Axley, a strong advocate of temperance and one of the reform leaders of the church, presented a resolution declaring that no stationed or local preacher should retail spirituous or malt liquors without forfeiting his ministerial character. This resolution attempted to go further than the declaration of any church organization had previously gone, since it included fermented liquors in the same class with distilled spirits. The General Conference of the Methodist Church was not ready to take such an advance step and the resolution was defeated. The same General Conference, however, sent out a strong letter urging activity in the interest of temperance reform. At the following General Conference in 1816 the same resolution which had been introduced by Doctor Axley at the General Conference of 1812 was presented again by him with the elimination of the reference to malt liquors, whereupon the resolution was promptly adopted by the General Conference. From this time forward each succeeding General Conference of the Methodist Episcopal Church took advance ground on the liquor question until it reached the point eventually of declaring unequivocally for the total Prohibition of the sale and use of all kinds of intoxicating liquors as beverages.

The Eastern Conference of the United Brethren Church held in 1814 incorporated in the discipline of that church a provision insisting upon abstinence from strong drink and the use of liquors except in cases of necessity as medicine. In 1821 the United Brethren

Church took a decidedly advanced step when in its General Conference Resolutions it not only declared that preachers and lay members should not be permitted to carry on distilleries but enjoined the ministers of the church to labor against the evils of intemperance and indicated that the next General Conference would take up the subject for further consideration and action. In the General Conference of the United Brethren Church held in 1833 even a stronger resolution was adopted. From that time forward the General Conferences of the United Brethren Church aggressively continued the fight against the liquor traffic, thus being one of the first church organizations to declare for the total prohibition of the liquor traffic in all its forms.

The General Convention of the Universalist Church in 1814 by resolution requested the Universalist societies not to permit liquors at subsequent meetings of those bodies. The African Methodist Church which was organized in 1816 declared in its discipline strongly against drunkenness and drinking spirituous liquors unless ordered to do so by a physician. Similar action was taken by the Baltimore Yearly Meeting of Friends in 1821 and was urged by the Rev. William Metcalf on the Bible Christian Church in 1823. Other denominations during this period spoke out in resolutions against intemperance and distilling, but the resolutions and activities of most of the churches did not reach further.

The most important forward movements of the church along temperance lines during the entire period from 1810 to 1826 were directed by the Congregational denomination through its state associations and through the local and state organizations created and directed largely by ministers of the Congregational Church. When Doctor Lyman Beecher moved from New York to Litchfield, Connecticut, in 1810, the organized movement for temperance reform in the United States was destined to have its beginnings on New England soil, by virtue of the fact that more than any other single factor the great personality of Doctor Beecher undoubtedly had to do with committing the church to a relentless coöperative fight against the liquor traffic and fostering the spirit of general organized activity along temperance reform lines.

The General Association of the Congregational Church in Connecticut in June, 1811, appointed a committee to coöperate with the committee appointed by the General Assembly of the Presbyterian Church. Similar action was taken the same year by the General Association of Congregational Churches of Massachusetts and the General Association of Congregational Churches in New Hampshire.

Something of the general character and remarkable qualities of leadership of Doctor Lyman Beecher is indicated by the report of the Congregational Association of Connecticut, held in Litchfield in 1812. The committee on temperance, which had been appointed the previous year, reported at the Association meeting in Litchfield in 1812 deploring the evil of intemperance but indicating that probably not much could be done to remedy conditions. Doctor Beecher, amazed and disgusted at the apathy and lack of courage shown by the report of the committee, promptly moved that the committee be discharged and that a new committee be appointed. This action was taken, and the newly appointed committee with Dr. Beecher at its head promptly brought in a ringing resolution outlining a plan of action in behalf of the temperance reform, which was heartily adopted by the Association. A stronger resolution was also adopted by the Association the following year.

Second only to those of Doctor Beecher in the early days of this period were the efforts in behalf of temperance reform by the Reverend Heman Humphrey, D.D., afterwards president of Amherst College. The Rev. Justin Edwards, moreover, who began to be heard on the temperance question in 1815 and 1816, was destined to play a conspicuous part in the forward movement which had been inaugurated in the Congregational Church by Doctor Beecher. In 1822 Doctor Edwards advanced the idea that the only means of preventing sober men from becoming drunkards is by entire abstinence. During the next few years Doctor Edwards took an active part in the temperance reform agitation and published several articles and pamphlets in the interest of the movement. It is probably fair to say, however, that no other temperance declarations, comparatively speaking, have had such wide publicity throughout the American continent and the world as have the famous six temperance sermons preached by Doctor Lyman Beecher in 1826. These sermons served the purpose of what might well be described as a call to arms for the temperance forces of the nation. They had a profound effect on temperance organization work, which began on a nation-wide scale the same year these sermons were preached.

One of the most significant facts in connection with the forward movement of the church along temperance lines which began in 1810 was that it marked the dawn of a new age in church activity, since it suggested the importance of coöperative effort on the part of the churches of different denominations, and since it suggested also the necessity for social service activity on the part of the churches, which activity should of necessity reach outside the close church communion into the realm of the social life of the nation and the world. It is more than a coincidence that the period of larger church activity in coöperative effort for temperance reform began at the time when the church throughout the United States was in the midst of one of the greatest revivals of religion, comparatively speaking, which has ever swept over the American continent. It is undoubtedly true that the period of religious fervor which seemed to prevail throughout the nation at that time was responsible for greatly hastening the progress of the temperance movement which grew out of the activities of the church and for which the church was responsible both in the matter of leadership and sentiment.

The following chronology covers the principal items of interest in connection with the temperance reform during the period.

Chronology of the Temperance Reform for the Period 1810–1826

1810

Dr. Lyman Beecher moves to Litchfield, Conn., and immediately becomes active in the cause of temperance.

Rev. Heman Humphrey, D.D., pastor of a church

in Fairfield, Conn., and afterwards for 22 years president of Amherst College, preaches a series of six temperance sermons.

Jeremiah Evarts of the Congregational Church, editor of the "Panoplist," begins to write against the evils of intemperance.

During the year 25,499,382 gallons of ardent spirits are distilled in the United States, of which only 133,823 gallons are exported. In addition to this, over 8,000,000 gallons of spirits are imported into the United States.

There are 14,191 distilleries in the United States; the per capita consumption of distilled liquor is 4 4-7 gallons.

The Presbyterian General Assembly appoints a committee to consider and report on conditions in respect to the liquor traffic.

1811

Dr. Benjamin Rush appears before the General Assembly of the Presbyterian Church urging the necessity of inaugurating a plan to arouse public sentiment on the liquor question; a committee is appointed to devise ways and means.

The General Association of the Congregational Church in Connecticut held at Litchfield in June appoints a committee to co-operate in the temperance movement with the committee appointed by the General Assembly of the Presbyterian Church.

The General Association of the Congregational Church of Massachusetts appoints a committee on temperance to correspond with and act in concert with the committee of the General Assembly of the

Presbyterian Church and with the committee appointed for the same purpose by the General Association of Connecticut.

The General Association of the Congregational Churches in New Hampshire, in session at Dunbarton, September 17, appoints a temperance committee to act with the committee appointed by the General Assembly of the Presbyterian Church.

The General Convention of Vermont, the Synod of New Jersey, the Synod of New York and the Presbytery of Suffolk, Long Island, take steps against the evils of intemperance.

A temperance society is organized in Weathersfield, Conn.

On November 5 Rev. Nathaniel S. Prinne preaches a strong temperance sermon before the Presbytery of Long Island.

1812

Upon presentation of the report of a committee appointed in 1811 by the Congregational Association of Connecticut to the effect that nothing can be done to check the evil of intemperance, Dr. Lyman Beecher, Litchfield, moves that the committee be discharged and a new committee appointed. This being done, the new committee, with Dr. Beecher as chairman, promptly reports recommending entire abstinence on the part of individuals and families from all spirituous liquors and advance steps against the traffic.

The Congregational Association of Fairfield County, Conn., publishes a strong appeal to the public against the drinking usages of society. This was probably written by Rev. Heman Humphrey, afterwards president of Amherst College.

The General Assembly of the Presbyterian Church adopts the report of a committee appointed the year before, which report urges upon all the ministers of the Presbyterian Church in the United States "to deliver public discourses on the sin and mischief of intemperate drinking." This report further admonished every minister "pointedly and solemnly to warn their hearers, and especially members of the church, not only against actual intemperance but against all those habits and indulgences which may have a tendency to produce it," and arraigns drinking places as public nuisances.

The report of the Secretary of the Treasury of the United States closes with an appeal to the ministers of the gospel and others to put forth active, practical efforts for the suppression of intemperance.

Rev. Mr. Weems, the biographer of George Washington, publishes a temperance pamphlet.

The General Conference of the Methodist Episcopal Church defeats a resolution presented by Rev. James Axley declaring that "no stationed or local preacher shall retail spirituous or malt liquors without forfeiting his ministerial character among us," but sends out a circular letter to the churches regarding the liquor question.

A temperance society is organized at Portland, Maine, on April 24.

A temperance society is organized at Saco, Maine.

A temperance society is organized at Bath, Maine.

Rev. Calvin Hill and Rev. Roswell Swan of the Congregational Church advocate total abstinence.

An Indian council is held at Batavia, N. Y., on March 2, at which Chief Hauanossa makes a strong plea for total abstinence.

The Religious Magazine of Maine declares that "the selling of spirituous liquors at a place of worship should be discouraged and that a man who indulges in the use of ardent spirits is in a poor situation to either hear or preach the gospel."

A gill of rum, whisky or brandy is made a part of the regular daily ration of each soldier in the United States Army.

1813

The Massachusetts Society for the Suppression of Intemperance is formed February 12 at the Hall of the Union Bank in Boston.

"The Society for the Reformation of Morals" is organized at New Haven, Conn.

Rev. Heman Humphrey, D.D., publishes in the "Panoplist" a series of six articles on the subject, "Causes, Progress, Effects and Remedy of Intemperance in the United States."

The General Association of Connecticut in June takes further and stronger action against intemperance.

In April temperance societies are organized at Brunswick, Topsham and Harpswell, Maine.

Local temperance societies, auxiliary to the Massachusetts Temperance Society, are organized in that state in North Yarmouth, Charleston, Franklin, Danvers, Bradford, Dedham, Byfield, Bridgewater and other towns.

Rev. Nathaniel S. Prinne of Cambridge, Washington County, N. Y., organizes the farmers of his congregation into a temperance society.

A system of excise is inaugurated by Congress, including licenses on retailers of "wines, spirituous liquors and foreign merchandise." These taxes are to cease one year after the termination of the War of 1812.

The Act of Congress of August 2 contains the provision that no license shall be granted to any person to sell wines, distilled spirituous liquors, or merchandise, who is prohibited to sell the same, by any state.

1814

The following article is inserted in the Book of Discipline of the Church of the United Brethren in Christ: "Article II. Every member shall abstain from strong drink, and use it only on necessity as medicine."

Dr. Jacob Ide of Medway, Mass., makes his famous plea for total abstinence.

Hon. Samuel Dexter, president of the Massachusetts Society for the Suppression of Intemperance, and who had been Secretary of War and of the Treasury, calls attention to the appalling increase in the use of ardent spirits.

The General Convention of Universalists votes to request societies not to permit liquors at subsequent meetings of those bodies.

A large number of local temperance societies are organized in Massachusetts as auxiliaries to the Massachusetts Temperance Society.

An additional tax of 50 per cent is levied upon

retail liquor dealers by the Act of Congress on December 23.

1815

Congress enacts a law providing that any one establishing a still in the Indian country shall be fined $500 and shall forfeit the still.

Rev. Justin Edwards of Andover urges the necessity of temperance.

1816

Rev. Justin Edwards of the Congregational Church in Andover, Mass., preaches a strong temperance sermon.

The "Christian Disciple" publishes a series of articles on the "Causes, Delusions and Cure of Intemperance."

Dr. Appleton, president of Bowdoin College, at the anniversary of the Massachusetts Society for the Suppression of Intemperance, delivers a strong address in the interest of the temperance reform.

The African Methodist Episcopal Church is organized by Rev. Richard Allen and Rev. Absalom Jones, and provides against "drunkenness and the drinking of spirituous liquors unless ordered to do so by a physician."

The General Conference of the Methodist Episcopal Church passes a resolution introduced by Rev. James Axley, declaring that "no stationed or local preacher shall retail spirituous liquors without forfeiting his ministerial character amang us."

Congress by the Act of April 29 partially removes the taxes on retail liquor dealers.

1817

Rev. Samuel Worcester, D.D., of Salem, Mass.,

speaking before the annual meeting of the Massachusetts Temperance Society, estimates that there are 80,000 drunkards in the United States and that the annual drink bill of Massachusetts is $2,000,000.

Many vessels along the coast of New England adopt the policy of total abstinence from all ardent spirits during their voyages.

All taxes laid upon retail liquor dealers are removed by the Act of Congress of December 23.

1818

By the Act approved April 14 Congress authorizes the President to "make such alterations in the component parts of the ration as due regard to the health and comfort of the army and economy may require."

The Secretary of War, John C. Calhoun, calls for a report from the Surgeon General as to the propriety of furnishing a substitute for the spirit ration. The report when made is averse to any change in the spirit ration.

In order to prohibit the habitual use of ardent spirits among the people Secretary Calhoun prohibits the use of liquor altogether in the United States Army.

Selectmen, overseers of the poor, tithing men and retailers of Northampton, Mass., in a meeting together resolve to discourage intemperance and not to permit spirituous liquors to be sold or drunk in their respective stores.

Forty auxiliary local temperance societies have been organized in Massachusetts in five years.

A temperance society is organized in Hector, N. Y., the preliminary meeting of which is held in a bar-room. The manner of keeping the record of the signers of two kinds of pledges used by this society originates the term "T-totalers" or "Tee-totalers." (Rev. Joel Jewell, elected secretary in 1827, placed before each member's name on the roll the initial letters "O. P." or the letter "T," the former meaning "Old Pledge," which was a pledge against the use of ardent spirits, and the latter "Total," which referred to the new pledge against the use of all intoxicating liquors.)

An address issued by the Legislature of Vermont to the inhabitants of that state urges temperance upon the people.

1819

"The New York Society for the Promotion of Internal Improvement" delivers a strong address against the policy of taxing and trying to regulate the liquor traffic as one tending to protect rather than to diminish the traffic.

The National Committee and Council of the Cherokee Nation, at Newton, Ga., the capital, passes their first Prohibition law, providing that "no person or persons, not citizens of the nation, shall bring into this nation or sell any spirituous liquors." As all the liquor-sellers are whites, this act amounts to total Prohibition of liquor selling within the jurisdiction of the nation.

1820

On August 10 George Gibson, Commissary General of Subsistence, sends to all assistant commissary generals a letter stating that it is his own wish and the wish of Mr. Calhoun, Secretary of War, to dispense with the spirit ration, and offering the troops the contract price thereof in money.

The first treaty made with the Indians by the Federal Government, which contained a definite provision eliminating the liquor traffic, is made with the Choctaw Nation.

The Cherokee Nation extends the Prohibition of liquor selling by forbidding the sale of liquors by negro slaves.

Rev. Joshua Leavitt of Stratford, Conn., through the columns of the Christian Spectator, urges total abstinence from all ardent spirits.

A temperance society is formed at Charlotte, N. C., which is maintained until 1836. This society is organized and promoted by Presbyterians.

1821

The following action is taken by the General Conference of the Church of the United Brethren in Christ: "Resolved, that neither preacher nor lay member shall be permitted to carry on a distillery; that distillers be requested to cease the business; that the members of the General Conference be requested to lay this resolution before the several annual conferences; that it shall then be the duty of the preachers to labor against the evils of intemperance during the intervals between this and the next General Conference, when the subject shall again be taken up for further consideration."

Maine requires selectmen to post in all places where liquor is sold the names of all persons reported to be drunkards or tipplers.

The Baltimore Yearly Meeting of Friends places in its discipline an article on moderation and temperance emphasizing the "unnecessary use of intoxicating liquors of every description."

The Tennessee Legislature repeals all laws prohibiting the sale of ale, beer, cider and methylin by retail.

1822

Rev. Dr. Justin Edwards, pastor at Andover, Mass., preaches two powerful temperance sermons at funerals which were the direct result of intemperance, and advances the idea that the only means of preventing sober men from becoming drunkards is by entire abstinence.

1823

Dr. Justin Edwards reports the First and Second Baptist Churches of Boston as having no member engaged in the liquor traffic and the Boston Baptist Bethel as having sustained a Monday evening temperance meeting every week for more than 40 years.

Rev. William Metcalfe of the Bible Christian Church publishes a tract on "the duty of entire abstinence from all intoxicating drinks." Concerning the accursed beverages he says, "We should not even hear their names."

The Massachusetts Society for the Suppression of Intemperance issues an arousing appeal penned by Henry Ware, Esq., of Boston, warning the public against the evils of the liquor traffic and urging legislative action.

The annual consumption of ardent spirits in the United States increases to 7½ gallons per capita. A Boston editor writes a vigorous editorial on the subject.

Rev. Eliphalet Nott, D.D., publishes a volume of sermons on the evils of intemperance.

The Massachusetts Society for the Suppression of Intemperance is reorganized and adopts a more aggressive program.

1824

The Russian-American treaty of April 17 prohibits the sale of intoxicants to the natives of the Alaska Territory.

The Cherokee Nation passes several measures making more stringent their laws against liquor selling in their territory.

1825

In this year, according to Rev. Lyman Beecher, at an ordination in Plymouth, Conn., "besides food, is a broad sideboard covered with decanters and sugar and pitchers of water."

Shrewsbury, Mass., with 1,400 population, consumes 120 hogsheads of rum in a year.

New York State reports 1,149 distilleries within her borders.

Fitchburg, Mass., with a population of 1,900, consumes 100 hogsheads of rum in a year.

Rev. Justin Edwards issues a pamphlet entitled "A Well Conducted Farm," which is a description of the farm of I. V. S. Wilder, Esq., of Bolton, conducted on strict temperance lines.

A meeting of leading temperance advocates is held at Andover, out of which a series of movements of great importance to the temperance reform begins.

Dr. Justin Edwards takes measures looking to a call for the friends of the temperance cause to meet in Boston, Mass., early in the next year.

King Kamehameha II. inaugurates a total abstinence campaign in Hawaii.

CHAPTER IV

THE PERIOD OF ORGANIZATION—1826–1851

THE YEAR 1826 marks the beginning of the period of organized temperance effort of a general character in the United States. Prior to 1826 numerous local societies and one or two state organizations had been created and had played their part in the progress of the temperance movement. There had indeed been one or two attempts to inaugurate temperance movements which would have more than a local or state significance, but no such effort proved successful until the organization of the American Temperance Society, later known as the American Society for the Promotion of Temperance, which was born at Boston, Massachusetts, on February 13, 1826.

The first organized temperance movement on record was that created by more than 200 farmers in Litchfield county, Connecticut, in 1789. This society was organized as "an association to discourage the use of spirituous liquors." To this end the farmers constituting the members of the society pledged themselves to do away with the use of distilled liquors in the harvest fields and among farm laborers. The use of intoxicating liquors by farm hands and in all coöperative farm efforts was such a generally accepted custom in New England at that time that the action of the Litchfield farmers was considered fanatical in the extreme, but the effect of the movement in the country surrounding Litchfield was marked in the sentiment which manifested itself in that particular section during the forty years immediately following the birth of the farmers' organization. It was at Litchfield that the crusade for temperance reform in New England, inaugurated by the church, began in 1810, and it was from this same Litchfield that the voice of that great pioneer reformer, Doctor Lyman Beecher, sounded forth the call to the church and the moral forces of New England which aroused out of lethargy the Christian people, stripped the liquor traffic of its cloak of respectability, and laid the foundation of the temperance work of a century. It was at Litchfield that Doctor Beecher preached the famous six temperance sermons, which were heard around the world.

The next organization of record was a total abstinence society organized by Micajah Pendleton in the Shenandoah Valley, Virginia, in 1804. The year following the organization of this Virginia abstinence movement witnessed the organization of an association among journeymen and other laborers engaged in the manufacture of paper in the city of Philadelphia, the object of which was to promote temperance among workers.

The famous "Billy Clark" society, known as the Union Temperance Society of Moreau and Northumberland, was organized at Saratoga, New York, in 1808. This society, while local in its scope and organization, nevertheless attracted such attention that immediately following its birth numerous similar societies were brought into existence in other counties and municipalities of New York state. The Clark society, while not the first organized temperance movement, was probably more important and more far-reaching in its influence than any of those which sprang into existence before 1808. That influence was such, in fact, that Saratoga became the Mecca of early temperance reformers and many of the most important general temperance conventions of the early days were held at that place, which was generally recognized as the place where aggressive, organized effort against the liquor traffic in the United States had its beginning.

The Massachusetts Society for the Suppression of Intemperance, which was the first state organization of record, was organized in Boston on February 12, 1813. While this society was active at first and while about forty local auxiliaries to this state organization were formed between 1813 and 1818, the organization itself soon fell into a state of inactivity. The society was reorganized in 1823, but never assumed the kind of aggressive leadership needed even in that day in the state of Massachusetts, although it continued in existence for a century.

During this period of the awakening of the church, hundreds of local temperance societies sprang into existence in response to the demand for aggressive Christian service, which was the natural outgrowth of the fervor which attended the great revival of religion during that period, and in response to the demand for aggressive and organized activity which the church's awakened conscience on the liquor question made necessary. The American Temperance Society of 1826, in fact, was nothing more nor less than the voice and conscience of the church expressing itself in militant organized form. The leaders of that organization and those that followed in the movement for a quarter of a century were almost entirely of the church, and even in the case of the few non-church members who became active in the reform during the following twenty-five years, their spirit and motives were born in the atmosphere and under the peculiar moral influences of the church.

Had the temperance reform in America waited for a non-church or a non-Christian leadership, the temperance revolution of the past century would yet remain to be accomplished. No close student of the philosophy of history during the nineteenth century and the first twenty years of the twentieth century could reasonably arrive at any other conclusion than that the motive, the genius and dynamic force of the temperance reform, regardless of whatever form it may have assumed or through whatever particular organizations it may have expressed itself, nevertheless has been the product of the Christian church. It would be as reasonable to declare that the power which moves the electric railway car comes from the trolley wire and not from the dynamo in the power-house, as to say that the temperance revolution owes its success to this or that organized temperance movement rather than to the church.

Every successful temperance movement of the last century has been merely the instrument—the machinery and equipment—through which the fundamental principles of the Christian religion have expressed themselves in terms of life and action. The permanent success or failure, moreover, of any temperance reform organization for a hundred years, has been measured and is easily indicated by the distance which separated the motive and guiding principle of any such organization from the soul of the church.

The movement inaugurated in 1826 was electric in its effect throughout the country. Almost immediately state and local auxiliaries by the hundreds sprang into existence, bound together by a common purpose and a common program. Within a year after the organization of the American Temperance Society there had been formed 222 local auxiliaries in the states of Maine, New Hampshire, Vermont, Massachusetts, Rhode Island, Connecticut, New York, New Jersey, Pennsylvania, Delaware, Maryland, Virginia, North Carolina, Kentucky, Ohio and Indiana. By 1829 the number of auxiliary locals had increased to about 1,000, eleven of which were state organizations. By 1831, state organizations had been created in all but five states, and 2,200 local societies had been formed with a membership aggregating 170,000. The number of local organizations had increased to 3,000 by 1832, and in 1833 the number was estimated at 5,000, with a total membership of 1,250,000. Two years later there had been formed 8,000 local temperance societies throughout the United States.

The first national temperance convention was held in the city of Philadelphia in 1833. By action of this convention a general temperance union was created, consisting of the officers of the American Temperance Society and the officers of twenty-three state temperance societies in their associated capacity. This, however, proved to be an organization in name only, until 1836, when a second national convention was called to meet at Saratoga, New York, at which the movement was reorganized and the name changed to the American Temperance Union. Two years later at the second annual meeting of the American Temperance Union, the Union declared for total abstinence from all intoxicants including fermented as well as distilled liquors. Immediately after the taking of this advance step by the American Temperance Union, local organizations throughout the nation by the thousands reorganized on the basis of total abstinence and by the year 1839 it was estimated that more than 350,000 had signed the total abstinence pledge.

The decade immediately following 1840 witnessed the founding of more temperance organizations of a general and national character than any other similar period in the history of the United States. The Washingtonian movement was organized in the city of Baltimore in 1840. The Martha Washington movement followed in 1841. The first local society of the Sons of Temperance came into existence in 1842, in which year also the order of Rechabites was first introduced into the United States, and the Congressional Temperance Society of 1833 was reorganized on a basis of total abstinence. The first state division of the Sons of Temperance was organized in New York state in 1843, and the national division came into existence the following year. The Order of Templars of Honor and Temperance was created and became operative in 1845, while the National Temple of Honor and Temperance and the Cadets of Temperance organized under the direction of the Sons of Temperance came into existence in 1846. The following year witnessed the organization of the Society of Good Samaritans. The Order of Templars of Honor and Temperance was reorganized on a life pledge basis in 1848, and the important

Father Mathew movement had its beginning in 1849. By 1850 the order of the Sons of Temperance had extended its organization work throughout the country to such a degree that there were recorded in that year 36 grand chapters, 5,894 subordinate divisions, with a total membership of 245,233.

Most of the temperance organizations which came into existence between 1840 and 1850 operated in the form of lodges with paying members, each of whom was compelled to take the pledge upon initiation. The most successful of these lodges was the order of the Sons of Temperance, which reached a point of greater influence and larger membership than any other similar organization of the century, with the single exception of the Independent Order of Good Templars which came into existence in 1851 and which exercised such a great influence in state and local temperance campaigns of the fifties and sixties, and out of which came the leaders who organized the National Temperance Society and the Prohibition party.

The influence of the efforts of the various temperance organizations which came into existence between 1826 and 1851 can never be estimated. These movements swept the country until almost every town and community had one or more auxiliary local orders. The movement for the organization of these local societies grew into a mighty moral crusade throughout the nation, in which churches and moral societies of almost every character joined.

The American Society for the Promotion of Temperance, however, later organized into the American Temperance Union, was in reality the outstanding temperance movement of the period, occupying as it did the place of leadership for the larger part of that eventful quarter of a century, creating public sentiment and directing a nation-wide campaign of education along temperance lines, which formed the foundation for the great state-wide Prohibition crusade of the fifties.

Among those who were the leaders in the temperance reform of this period, in addition to those already named, there appear such names as John B. Gough, William Lloyd Garrison, Lewis Cass, John Hawkins, John Marsh, William E. Channing, Edward C. Delavan, Father Theobald Mathew, William Goodell, Nathaniel Hewit, Thomas P. Hunt, and Charles Jewett. Anything like a record of the services which these men rendered to the cause of temperance reform in the United States would easily require a large volume.

The following chronology covers the principal items of interest in connection with the temperance reform during the period.

CHRONOLOGY OF THE TEMPERANCE REFORM FOR THE
PERIOD 1826–1851
1826

Dr. Lyman Beecher preaches his six famous temperance sermons at Litchfield, Conn.

Rev. Calvin Chapin, D.D., on January 1, begins the publication in "The Connecticut Observer" of a series of 33 temperance articles under the general subject, "The Infallible Antidote."

The conference called by Dr. Justin Edwards meets in January and agrees to form a strict temperance organization. A committee is appointed to draft a constitution and correspond with temperance advocates throughout the country.

"The National Philanthropist" is established in Boston and its motto is, "Temperate drinking is the down-hill road to intemperance." The editor is Rev. William Collier.

Dudley, Mass., with 1,800 inhabitants, consumes 10,000 gallons of rum in a year.

A young men's temperance society is organized at Providence, R. I., with 250 members. A similar organization is effected at Andover.

Dr. Gamaliel Bradford, in an address before the Massachusetts Society for the Suppression of Intemperance, urges the establishing of inebriate asylums.

As a result of the efforts of Dr. Justin Edwards and others "The American Temperance Society," later known as "The American Society for the Promotion of Temperance," is organized at Boston, Mass., on February 13 with Hon. Marcus Morton of Boston as president. Rev. Nathaniel Hewitt of Boston is engaged as a special evangelist of the society and goes across the Alleghanies and down through the Carolinas urging the people to organize against the liquor traffic.

Resolutions are considered in the House of Representatives declaring that it is expedient to increase the duty on all imported spirits and to levy an excise on domestic liquors. The matter is referred to a committee which reports favorably, but the excise recommendation fails of passage by Congress.

The Baptist Church establishes a temperance and

Prohibition publishing house which is the first such establishment in the United States.

The Virginia Society is founded by Rev. Abner Clopton among Baptist ministers of Charlotte county, Va., the members pledging themselves to use spirituous liquors as medicine only.

1827

A temperance society organized in Virginia declares against the intemperate use of spirituous liquors, the election of drunkards as legislators, the employment of intemperate physicians, and the use of spirituous liquors on funeral occasions.

The Massachusetts Medical Society resolves: "To discourage the use of ardent spirits" and "to discontinue the employment of spirituous preparations whenever they can find substitutes."

The General Assembly of the Presbyterian Church strongly pronounces in favor of the temperance reform, declares for total abstinence and for co-operation with other bodies for the promotion of temperance.

The General Synod of the Reformed Dutch Church recommends that the ministry, consistories and congregations promote the cause of temperance.

The General Convention of Vermont makes a strong pronouncement against intemperance.

The Park Street Church of Boston goes on record in favor of abstinence from spirituous liquors.

Rev. Thomas P. Hunt administers his total abstinence pledge to numerous children in New York.

The Medical Society of New Hampshire adopts a resolution declaring it to be the profound conviction of its members that water is "the only proper beverage for man."

Wilbraham, Mass., with 2,000 inhabitants, consumes 8,000 gallons of rum in a year.

Salisbury, Conn., has 34 families who consume 29½ gallons of rum each in a year.

Two discourses on intemperance by Rev. J. G. Palfrey, D.D., of Boston, are published, as is also a pamphlet by Reuben Muzzey, M. D., of New Hampshire, entitled "The True Nature of Alcohol."

A total abstinence society is organized at Ludlowville, N. Y.

Hon. Jonathan Kittredge, an able lawyer of Canaan, N. H., on January 8 delivers an address on "The Effects of Ardent Spirits" before a public meeting in the town of Lyme, N. H.

Prof. Reuben D. Muzzey of Dartmouth Medical College delivers a famous address against the liquor traffic before the New Hampshire Medical Society.

The General Synod of the Reformed Dutch Church in America resolves to "discourage the indiscriminate use of ardent spirits in family and in social circles."

One of the Choctaw districts in the Indian Territory prohibits the introduction and sale of ardent spirits.

"The Morning Star," a religious publication of the Free Baptist Church, begins the publication of a temperance department, strongly urging the importance of total abstinence.

A report of the trustees of the almshouse for the city and county of Baltimore, Md., shows that of the 623 adults committed to the institution in the

year 1826 there were 554 who were placed in the
institution on account of poverty produced by excessive drunkenness.

The first criminal code is enacted by the chief
of Hawaiian Island tribes against murder, theft,
retailing ardent spirits, Sabbath breaking and gambling.

The Massachusetts and New Hampshire Medical
Societies pass resolutions against the use of distilled
liquors.

At the first anniversary of the American Temperance Society reports show the organization of thirteen temperance societies in Maine, twenty-three in
New Hampshire, seven in Vermont, thirty-nine in
Massachusetts, two in Rhode Island, thirty-three in
Connecticut, seventy-eight in New York, six in New
Jersey, seven in Pennsylvania, one in Delaware, one
in Maryland, five in Virginia, two in North Carolina, one in Kentucky, one in Ohio and two in Indiana, making a total of 222 local societies in the
Union.

Thirty thousand men during the year pledge
themselves to total abstinence from ardent spirits
through the efforts of the American Temperance
Society.

The Massachusetts Temperance Society goes on
record as against efforts to prohibit the use of wine,
as unreasonable and impolitic and suggests that
wine of the milder kinds may be an important instrument in promoting the suppression of intemperance.

1828

The Connecticut State Medical Association declares in favor of Temperance Reform.

Rev. Albert Barnes of Morristown, N. J., publishes twelve essays on intemperance.

The General Synod of the Reformed Dutch Church in America recommends to ministers, churches and individual Christians to promote the cause of temperance by the formation of societies and recommends total abstinence from liquor except as a medicine.

The General Synod of the Cumberland Presbyterian Church recommends the discontinuance of the use of ardent spirits.

Twelve Essays on Temperance by Rev. Albert Barns, D.D., of Philadelphia, are published. Similar pamphlets are published by Rev. W. B. Sprague, D. D., of West Springfield, Mass., Rev. Heman Humphrey, D. D., and Samuel Natt, of Galway, N. Y.

Under the leadership of Rev. Wilbur Fisk, D. D., the General Conference of the Methodist Episcopal Church adopts strong resolutions on temperance and urges total abstinence.

Because of the remarkably effective temperance agitation over the country many taverns are compelled to close for want of patronage and several distilleries are closed for want of a market for their product.

The Free Baptist Church in General Conference adopts the total abstinence pledge, and appoints a committee on temperance. All members are advised to abstain from the use of ardent spirits except as medicine.

A total abstinence society is organized at Lansing, N. Y.

The Associate Reformed Synod of New York of the United Presbyterian Church characterizes intemperance as "the greatest evil in our country."

The first Woman's Temperance Society is organized in the state of Ohio.

The first Prohibition legislation is enacted by the Chickasaw Nation.

A perpetual charter is granted to the Boston Beer Company.

1829

The New York State Temperance Society is organized at Albany on January 17, largely through the instrumentality of Mr. Edward C. Delavan.

February 22 is set apart by the temperance people of the country as a day of fasting and prayer for the temperance cause.

The Connecticut State Temperance Society is organized on May 20 as a result of a meeting held at Hartford; President Jeremiah Day of Yale College is made chairman, Rev. Dr. E. John Marsh, secretary, and Dr. Calvin Chapin, chairman of the executive committee.

A remarkable address delivered by Dr. John Marsh at a meeting of the Windham County, Conn., Temperance Society is printed and circulated to the number of 150,000 copies.

A half-dozen strong temperance documents are published by the press and are widely read.

Rev. Justin Edwards, D. D., is permanently appointed corresponding secretary of the American Society for the Promotion of Temperance.

The Journal of Humanity, a temperance periodical edited by Rev. Edward W. Hooker, is established by the society at Andover, to succeed "The National Philanthropist," which has been removed from Boston to New York.

The selectmen of each town in the state of Maine are authorized to decide whether or not liquor selling shall be permitted.

The Presbyterian Church appoints a day of fasting and prayer in the interest of the temperance reform.

Troy, N. Y., with a population of 10,000, consumes 73,959 gallons of rum.

William Lloyd Garrison is appointed editor of the National Philanthropist.

The New Hampshire Temperance Society is organized.

As a result of the organized efforts of the temperance reformers more than 1,000 temperance societies have been created. Of these 62 are in Maine, 46 in New Hampshire, 56 in Vermont, 169 in Massachusetts, 3 in Rhode Island, 133 in Connecticut, 300 in New York, 21 in New Jersey, 53 in Pennsylvania, 1 in Delaware, 6 in Maryland, 52 in Virginia, 15 in North Carolina, 14 in Georgia, 8 in Alabama, 30 in Ohio, 9 in Kentucky, 5 in Tennessee, 4 in Mississippi, 13 in Indiana, 1 in Illinois, 3 in Michigan and 1 in Missouri. There are 11 state societies.

The Pennsylvania State Temperance Society is organized.

A pledge of total abstinence from distilled spirits is drawn up in the Cherokee language and widely circulated by Indian societies among the Cherokees.

The Seneca chiefs of Ohio join in a petition to the President asking for the removal of their people to the West, where they can live well and be out of reach of the white men's strong drink.

The introduction and sale of ardent spirits is prohibited in all the districts of the Choctaw Nation.

A young people's temperance society with a total abstinence pledge is organized on August 22 at Hector, N. Y.

As a result of three years' activity of the American Temperance Union, 400 merchants have relinquished the traffic in liquor, 50 distilleries have closed, the number of local temperance societies has increased to 1,000, 11 being state societies; the pledged membership of these societies has increased to 100,000, of whom 1,200 have been drunkards.

February 22 is set apart as a day of fasting and prayer on account of intemperance.

1830

A prize of $250 offered for the best essay on the question as to whether church members should use or traffic in distilled liquors is awarded to Prof. Moses Stuart of Andover Theological Semniary, who in his essay takes strong ground against the use or trafficking in licenses by church members.

Maine has thirteen distilleries with an annual output of 1,000,000 gallons of rum. Three hundred thousand gallons of rum, cider and fermented liquors are imported.

The Reformed Dutch Church recommends the

formation of total abstinence societies in all local congregations.

The first annual report of the New Hampshire Temperance Society declares that there are 80 auxiliary local societies in New Hampshire with more than 8,000 members.

The per capita consumption of distilled spirits in the United States is 6 gallons per annum.

The Presbyterian Church takes a strong stand for total abstinence and declares for the limiting of the sale of liquor to "the druggist shop."

The first annual report of the New York Temperance Society at the convention held in Albany, January 19, indicates 300 local societies in the state and a membership of 40,000.

The Methodist Protestant Church organizes. In its constitution and discipline it declares against the use, manufacture and sale of liquor as a beverage.

The first annual report of the Connecticut State Temperance Society mentions 17 auxiliary societies in the state with a membership of 22,532.

The State Temperance Society of Pennsylvania is organized.

It is estimated that 60,000 men are enrolled in the temperance societies over the country.

The Methodists decide to form total abstinence societies on the several circuits of the church.

General Lewis Cass of Michigan, afterward Secretary of War, delivers a strong temperance address at Detroit, Mich.

The primitive temperance societies organized among the Iroquois Indians are organized after the white man's style into formal societies with written constitutions. Branch societies are formed on different reservations and for a number of years annual conventions are held.

John H. Eaton, Secretary of War under President Jackson, makes an attack upon the spirit ration of the army, recommending its abolition. He presents the statistics of desertion during seven years, and states that nearly all who deserted in 1829 did so through drink. He also presents a number of reports from army chiefs recommending the abolition of the spirit ration.

Secretary of War Eaton, under the authority of President Jackson, issues a department order, on November 30, discontinuing the regular spirit ration and making stringent rules for the government of sutlers in selling spirits to the troops. Not more than two gills of ardent spirits may be sold to any soldier per day, and no spirits are to be sold save on the written permission of the commanding officer; no liquor is to be sold before noon, or on credit.

The provision against the liquor traffic, inserted in the treaty made in 1820 with the Choctaw Nation, is strengthened by the treaty with the Choctaw Nation of September 15.

The Connecticut State Medical Society appoints a committee to report on the need of a special asylum for medical treatment of inebriates.

1831

General Lewis Cass (afterward Secretary of War), Dr. Hossack of New York, and Dr. Sewall of Washington, D. C., strongly endorse the temperance movement.

Dr. Justin Edwards visits Washington and by permission addresses the American Congress in the Capitol on the subject of temperance. He also visits other cities on his tour and organizes ten societies with an aggregate membership of more than 1,000.

Through the generosity of Mr. Edward C. Delavan of Albany, N. Y., a wealthy gentleman who has become greatly interested in the temperance movement, Dr. Hewitt is sent as a temperance missionary to England.

By the close of the year state temperance societies have been organized in all the states except Maine, Alabama, Louisiana, Illinois and Missouri. A total of 2,200 societies have been organized with an aggregate membership of 170,000.

The first annual report of the Pennsylvania Temperance Society recommends the abandonment of fermented liquor as well as spirituous liquors.

Dr. James Kirk of Scotland finds alcohol in the brain of a dead debauchee and burns it in a spoon.

Under the administration of Kuakini as Governor of Oahu, a native temperance society is formed at Honolulu with a membership of one thousand.

The Presbyterian General Assembly strongly urges upon the church the immorality of the liquor traffic and its inconsistency with the Christian religion.

No-license is adopted in those parts of Massachusetts where the Pilgrims landed; two counties and several towns exclude the traffic.

The Secretary of the Navy expresses his conviction that the use of ardent spirits is one of the greatest curses, and declares his intention to recommend a change with regard to it in the navy.

In September the "Western Cherokees" who had voluntarily emigrated west of the Mississippi, pass a law prohibiting the selling of ardent spirits within five miles of the national council.

1832

Congress gives the soldiers the right to draw coffee and sugar instead of the spirit ration.

Indiana enacts a local option law providing for remonstrances in townships or towns.

Dr. Francis Wayland, president of Brown University, becomes one of the leading American advocates of the temperance cause.

The General Assembly of the Presbyterian Church denounces the use of ardent spirits even in moderation.

The Board of Health of Washington, D. C., acting under an opinion of Attorney General Wirt, issues the following proclamation: "That the vending of ardent spirits, in whatever quantity, is considered a nuisance and, as such, is hereby directed to be discontinued for the space of ninety days from this date. James Larnard, secretary."

The General Conference of the Methodist Episcopal Church adopts ringing resolutions in behalf of the temperance movement and appoints a committee on temperance.

Twenty-one state and 3,000 auxiliary temperance societies in the United States have been organized prior to this date. Almost 1,000 of the auxiliary societies are in New York State.

A congressional temperance meeting is held in the national capital which results in the organization of the Congressional Temperance Society the next year.

There are 2,000 places in the state of Maine where liquor is sold.

The State Temperance Society of Maine is organized.

Seventy-five of the eighty physicians in Boston sign a declaration against the use of ardent spirits by men in health.

The commissioners of Athens, Ga., acting under state authority, impose a license tax of $500 on venders of intoxicating liquors.

Daniel Webster makes an address before a meeting of the Congressional Temperance Society in Washington on January 13, moving a resolution that the efforts of the temperance societies of the United States have had the effect of diminishing crime and benefiting conditions.

General Lewis Cass, Secretary of War, a life-long abstainer, strengthens the order issued by Secretary of War Eaton, by absolutely forbidding the sale of spirits by sutlers, and substituting coffee in lieu of spirits in the ration. The "fatigue ration" is declared not to be within executive discretion.

The Navy Department tries the experiment of having a vessel manned by a crew without the usual supply of rum.   The vessel itself is named Experiment.

At a conference of the Free Baptist Church held at Meredith, N. H., a temperance society is organized.   Members pledge themselves not to drink liquors, nor to vend them, nor to sell them to employees or friends, and to use their influence to prevent drinking.   Clergymen who are members pledge themselves not to ordain to the ministry any man who drinks liquors or advocates their use as a beverage.

The restraints upon the manufacture, sale and use of liquor are relaxed in Hawaii on the accession of a new king.

Secretary of War General Lewis Cass issues an order on November 2, forbidding the introduction of ardent spirits into any fort, camp, or garrison of the United States, and prohibiting their sale by any sutler to the troops.   He also provides a substitute for the army liquor ration allowing eight pounds of sugar and four pounds of coffee in place of 100 liquor rations.

The Secretary of the Navy discourages the use of spirits in the navy by directing that coffee, tea, sugar or money may be offered to the seamen in place of the liquor ration.

1833

The Congressional Temperance Society, composed entirely of members of Congress and of the executive officers of the government, is organized at Washington, D. C., on February 26, with Secretary of War Lewis Cass of Michigan as president.

The Temperance Society of the New York College of Surgeons and Physicians is organized.

A delegated convention (the first such national convention) representing the temperance societies of all the states as well as some English societies, meets in the First Presbyterian Church of Philadelphia, May 24-27, with 440 delegates present. Nineteen states and territories are represented. An immediate result of this convention is the organization of a national society under the name "United States Temperance Union" (later called the American Temperance Union), composed of the members of the American Temperance Society of Boston and the officers of the several state temperance societies.

The Governor of Massachusetts presides over the state temperance convention held at Worcester, Mass.

State temperance conventions are held at Hartford, Conn.; Milledgeville, Ga.; Columbus, Ohio; Utica, N. Y.; Jackson, Miss.; and Richmond, Va.

The Georgia Legislature grants the right of local option on the liquor question to the inferior courts of Liberty and Camden Counties whereupon the city of Athens, where the State University is located, and the whole of Liberty County with a population of more than 8,000, go under Prohibition.

Judge Platt, eminent jurist of New York, gives it as his opinion that, "Wherever public opinion and the moral sense of our community shall be so far corrected and matured as to regard them in their true light and when the public safety shall be thought to require it, dramshops will be indictable at common law as public nuisances."

The Sixth General Conference of the United Brethren Church makes it an offense punishable with expulsion, for an exhorter, preacher or elder to manufacture or sell ardent spirits. A year is given to those so engaged to close the business.

Florida enacts a license law providing that applications for license shall be signed by a majority of the registered voters in the election district where application is made.

Dr. Wayland, president of Brown University, in a letter to Dr. Justin Edwards, stands for legislative action and Prohibition of the liquor traffic.

The State Temperance Society of Mississippi recommends abstinence from vinous as well as ardent spirits.

Dr. Woodward of the Worcester, Mass., insane asylum, urges that inebriety be regarded as a disease and that a special hospital be established for treatment of the same.

A total abstinence society is formed at Andover, Mass.

The Seventh-Day Baptists stand for total abstinence.

The United Presbyterian Church urges upon the membership of the church the formation of temperance societies.

The Ohio Conference of the African M. E. Church goes on record as in favor of temperance societies which the conference declares to be especially important to the colored people.

Twenty-five members of the Twenty-second Congress sign a paper agreeing to associate in the formation of the Congressional Temperance Society. Some of the signers are Theodore Frelinghuysen, John Davis, Samuel Bell, Gideon Tomlinson, Horatio Seymour, Felix Grundy, G. M. Dallas, W. W. Ellsworth and William Hendrickson. On the evening of February 26 the society is organized in the U. S. Senate chamber, with Hon. William Wilkins chairman of the meeting; Hon. Lewis Cass, Secretary of War, is chosen the first president; Hon. Walter Lowrie, secretary of the Senate, as secretary. The object of the society is declared to be "By example and kind moral influence, to discountenance the use of ardent spirits and the traffic in it throughout the community."

It is estimated that there are more than 5,000 local temperance societies in the United States, with an estimated membership of 1,250,000, of whom 10,000 have been drunkards; about 4,000 distilleries have been discontinued and 6,000 merchants have given up the sale of ardent spirits, while over 1,000 vessels have abandoned the use of strong liquors.

The members of the Massachusetts Legislature form a legislative temperance society, with the governor of the colony as the president.

Luther Jackson, Esq., of New York, publishes at his own expense a pledge afterward adopted by the American Temperance Society, as follows: "We whose names are hereunto annexed, believing that the use of intoxicating liquors as a drink is not only needless but hurtful to the social, civil and religious interests of men; that they tend to form intemperate appetites and habits; and that while they are continued the evils of intemperance can never be done away, do therefore agree that we will not use them or traffic in them; that we will not provide them as articles of entertainment or for persons in our employment, and that in all suitable ways we will discountenance the use of them in the community."

A state temperance convention is held in Utica, N. Y.

The Connecticut Temperance Society has a state convention in Middletown on December 3.

A state temperance convention is held in Columbus, Ohio, on the 18th of December, at which the Governor of the state presides.

The State Temperance Society of Mississippi holds a convention in Jackson, Miss., on Christmas Day.

1834

Edward C. Delavan, an ex-wine merchant of Albany, N. Y., draws up the following declaration against strong drink, to which he afterwards secures the signatures of Presidents Jackson, Madison, John Adams, Van Buren, Tyler, Polk, Taylor, Fillmore, Pierce, Buchanan, Lincoln and Johnson: "Being satisfied from observation and experience, as well as from medical testimony, that ardent spirits, as a drink, is not only needless but hurtful, and that entire disuse of it would tend to promote the health, the virtue and the happiness of the community, we hereby express our conviction that should the citizens of the United States, and especially the young men, discontinue entirely the use of it they would not only promote their own personal comfort but the good of our country and the world."

The first state temperance convention ever held in Missouri is called at St. Louis.

Maine holds a state temperance convention and organizes for aggressive work against the drink traffic.

The Twenty-third Congress of the United States passes an act prohibiting the introduction or sale of spirituous liquors and wine into the Indian countries to be supplied to Indians by gift or otherwise.

The New York Temperance Society declares for total abstinence.

The Presbyterian General Assembly declares that the traffic in strong drink is morally wrong.

The Philadelphia Conference of the African M. E. Church resolves, "That it shall be the duty of all the preachers of this conference to strictly recommend the temperance cause in their circuits or stations."

The New York Conference of the African M. E. Church resolves, "That we will make use of all disciplinary measures, both by precept and example, to promote and extend the temperance cause."

By the act approved June 30 it is forbidden to set up or continue any distillery within the Indian country, under a penalty of $1,000.

The first anniversary of the Congressional Temperance Society is held in the Representatives' Hall, the attendance having outgrown the limited dimensions of the Senate Chamber.

The state temperance convention held at Frankfort, Ky., on January 7 recommends that all new temperance societies should agree to abstain from wine as well as spirits.

Important state temperance conventions are held in Vermont, January 15; Maine, February 5; New Jersey, February 12; New York, February 19; Pennsylvania, March 4; and in Missouri and Delaware in May.

1835

Dr. Humphrey of Amherst College, Judge Pratt and Hon. Theodore Frelinghuysen, later a candidate for Vice President on the ticket with Henry Clay, strongly advocate a movement against the license system of the country.

Congress, with the cordial approval of President Andrew Jackson, enacts a law prohibiting the selling of liquors to Indians in Indian countries, under penalty of $500.

The Presbyterian General Assembly meeting in Philadelphia strongly declares against the traffic in ardent spirits.

The grand jury in New York City, attributing two-thirds of the crime and pauperism of New York to the influence of intoxicating liquors, places the following declaration on record: "It is our solemn impression that the time has now arrived when our public authorities should no longer sanction the evil complained of by granting licenses for the purpose of vending ardent spirits, thereby legalizing the traffic at the expense of our moral and physical power."

Rev. Dr. George B. Cheever of Salem, Mass., is committed to jail for libel because of a publication under the title, "Deacon Giles' Distillery," which a certain Deacon Story claims was intended to personate him and accordingly sues the preacher.

Mr. Edward C. Delavan of Albany, N. Y., having charged the brewers of Albany with using water for malting purposes drawn from a pond which is practically a sewer for the city of Albany, is sued for libel on a number of counts asking $300,000 damages. He is compelled to give bail in the sum of $40,000 to keep out of jail. Later Mr. Delavan is victorious in the suit.

A New Jersey association of Baptist Churches declares that "it is morally wrong in all, but especially in a professor of religion to manufacture, vend or use liquors (intoxicating or alcoholic) as a common article of luxury or living;" it also declared for total abstinence and expulsion of members who make, sell or use intoxicating liquors as a beverage.

The temperance convention at Boston, Mass., declares against all intoxicating liquors.

The annual report of the American Society for the Promotion of Temperance is devoted chiefly to the nature of alcohol and abstinence from all intoxicating liquors is avowed.

The Pennsylvania Conference of the Evangelical Association passes uncompromising resolutions against the liquor traffic; it declares for total abstinence, the instruction of the youth, favors Constitutional Prohibition, opposes its members signing license petitions or the renting of property for the sale of liquors, and declares against the use of fermented wine at the Lord's Supper as "contrary to the total-abstinence principles of our church."

It is estimated that in the United States more

than 8,000 temperance societies have been formed; more than 4,000 distilleries have been stopped; more than 200,000 persons have ceased to use any kind of intoxicating liquor; about 2,000,000 have ceased to use distilled liquors, 1,500,000 of whom are enrolled members of temperance societies.

Prof. Reuben D. Muzzey, M. D., distinguished medical man and professor of anatomy and surgery, Dartmouth College, decares that "So long as alcohol retains a place among sick patients so long will there be drunkards."

The General Convention of Universalists declares for the suppression of intemperance in all its forms.

A petition signed by six chiefs and several thousand natives is presented to King Kamehameha III. of Hawaii, asking for the total Prohibition of the liquor traffic.

A great temperance meeting is held in Honolulu and a committee of natives draw up a memorial to prohibit the liquor traffic. A law is passed imposing a fine for disorderly conduct due to drunkenness.

1836

In spite of the fact that 1,774 ministers in the annual conferences of the Methodist Church have voted for the reinstatement of John Wesley's rule against the use, buying or selling of distilled liquors, and in spite of the further fact that a motion to carry out this mandate in the General Conference is approved by a vote of 76 to 38, the presiding Bishop declares the motion lost because the affirmative vote is not two-thirds of the entire membership of the General Conference.

The Second National Temperance Convention is held at Saratoga, N. Y. The pledge of the society is changed from abstinence from "alcoholic liquors or ardent spirits" to abstinence from "all intoxicating liquors." The society is reorganized as the American Temperance Union with Hon. John H. Cooke of Virginia as president and Edward C. Delavan of Albany, N. Y., as chairman of the executive committee.

The Reformed Presbyterian Synod unanimously resolves that "as the liquor traffic is always damaging to our fellow-men, it is recommended that our members totally abstain from the traffic."

Most temperance societies in the United States revise their pledges to include all kinds of intoxicating liquors as well as spirits.

The National Cherokee Temperance Society is formed and branches are organized in numerous towns and villages.

1837

The charter of Mercer University, in Georgia, prohibits liquor houses on the lands of the institution.

The Maine Temperance Union is organized.

The Free Baptist Church condemns the dealers in intoxicating drinks as responsible for all evils growing out of the traffic, and urges legislation against the traffic.

The Seventh General Conference of the United Brethren Church advises all members, both clerical and lay, to abandon the manufacture and sale of ardent spirits.

The Legislature of Massachusetts confers upon

county commissioners the right to refuse the granting of licenses.

The Journal of the American Temperance Union is first published.

The State of Tennessee abolishes all special taxes on the sale of liquors and provides for dealing with such sale "as in other cases of misdemeanor."

Dr. Channing of the Unitarian Church at the council of the Massachusetts Temperance Society, held at the Odeon in Boston, delivers a memorable address on intemperance, explaining the grave danger to youth.

The conference of the Free Baptist Church, held at Greenville, R. I., resolves to save inebriates from drinking, help others from falling and urges the example of total abstinence.

Two thousand temperance societies have been formed in New York State

1838

Rhode Island and New Hampshire adopt local option for towns on the question of liquor license.

Each soldier in the United States Army is given the option of drawing coffee and sugar, or the money equivalent, instead of a gill of spirits a day.

The Legislature of Tennessee repeals all license laws and provides that all persons retailing liquors shall be fined at the discretion of the court.

The Legislature of Massachusetts passes the "fifteen-gallon law," which prohibits the sale of ardent spirits in less quantities than 15 gallons at a time.

The American Temperance Union in its annual report cheerfully acknowledges that the temperance reformation is the "fruit of the gospel," and urges the church to stronger action against the drink evil.

At the second meeting of the American Temperance Union the principle of total abstinence is strongly avowed.

The Yale College Temperance Society is organized.

Senator Daniel Webster presents a petition from army officers asking Congress to abolish the "fatigue ration" of spirits.

Congress by Act of July 5 substitutes coffee "in lieu of spirit or whisky" and abolishes the army spirit ration.

A joint standing rule is adopted by Congress that "no spirituous liquors shall be offered for sale or exhibited within the Capitol or on the public grounds adjacent thereto."

1839

The State of Connecticut enacts a local option law, leaving the licensing of liquor dealers optional with the towns.

Mississippi enacts what is commonly known as "the gallon law," which is intended to suppress tippling.

Illinois passes a local option law which provides for Prohibition in all cities and towns where the majority of the adult male citizens sign a petition for it.

It is estimated that 350,000 persons in the United States have signed the pledge.

Fifteen strong temperance journals are being published in the United States.

The following temperance newspapers are being published in the United States: "The Journal of the American Temperance Union." Philadelphia; "The Temperance Gazette," Augusta, Maine; "Temperance Journal," Boston, Mass.; "The Temperance Herald," Providence, R. I.; "The Temperance Star," Montpelier, Vt.; "The Temperance Recorder," Albany, N. Y.; "The Temperance Reporter," Trenton, N. J.; "The Temperance Recorder," Philadelphia; "The Standard," Wilmington, Del.; "The Temperance Herald," Baltimore, Md.; "The Western Temperance Journal," Cincinnati, Ohio; "The Temperance Herald," Jackson, Mich.; "The Temperance Advocate," Indianapolis, Ind.; "The Temperance Herald," Alton, Ill.

The state temperance societies of Maryland, Wisconsin, Texas and Iowa go on record in favor of abstinence from all forms of intoxicating liquors.

Dr. Percy proves by experiments that alcohol causes death by its specific effect upon the nerve centers and not by coagulating the blood.

"The Youths Temperance Advocate" is established, with Dr. John Marsh as editor.

Most of the temperance societies having disbanded in New York State, 1,200 societies with a membership of over 130,000 are formed with total abstinence as the principal foundation.

A great temperance meeting is held in Faneuil Hall, Boston, on July 4.

The members of the Cherokee Nation, driven from Georgia, meet at Tahlequah, Indian Territory, to draft a constitution and a code of laws. The sixteenth law, adopted on September 26, prohibits the introduction or vending of ardent spirits within the territory of the nation.

King Kamehameha III. is compelled by the presence of a French warship to sign a treaty admitting French wines and brandy into the island of Hawaii.

1840

The Washingtonian Temperance Movement is inaugurated at Baltimore, Md., by a Baltimore drinking club of six men—W. K. Mitchell, a tailor; J. F. Hoss, a carpenter; David Anderson and George Steers, blacksmiths; James McCarley, a coachmaker; and Archibald Campbell, a silversmith—who are induced to change their habits by the address of a temperance lecturer.

The State Temperance Society of Pennsylvania declares for total abstinence from all intoxicating liquors.

Another law is enacted in Hawaii for the Prohibition of the manufacture of intoxicating liquor.

The Massachusetts "fifteen-gallon law" is repealed.

Reports show 10,306 distilleries operating in the United States, 200 of which are in New York.

The Washingtonians report 34,000 signatures to the pledge in New Jersey and Delaware; 6,000 in Boston; New Orleans, 6,000; Mobile, 2,000; Ohio, 60,000; Kentucky, 30,000; Pennsylvania, 29,000; Baltimore, 4,600. It is estimated that in the United States 150,000 men take the pledge.

1841

The National Temperance Convention meets at Saratoga.

The Eighth General Conference of the United

Brethren Church prohibits any clerical or lay member from manufacturing or selling any ardent spirits under penalty of expulsion.

The Martha Washington temperance societies for women are organized and result in strengthening the Washingtonian movement.

The Cherokee National Council of Indian Tribes prohibits the sale of intoxicating liquors within the territory of these tribes, under penalty of the destruction of all liquors seized.

The local option law of Rhode Island is repealed.

The General Conference of the Free Baptist Church, held at Topsham, Maine, condemns the use of fermented wines and advises their rejection from the sacrament.

The Reformed Presbyterian Church prohibits any of its members from engaging or continuing in the liquor traffic, and sessions are urged to remove the evil from the church as speedily as possible.

The Third National Temperance Convention is held at Saratoga Springs, N. Y.

1842

Abraham Lincoln addresses the Washingtonian Society at Springfield, Ill., urging a temperance revolution.

John B. Gough signs the temperance pledge at Worcester, Mass., on October 31.

The Legislature of Connecticut wipes out all restrictive laws against the liquor traffic.

The State Temperance Societies of Mississippi, New Jersey, North Carolina and Virginia declare for total abstinence from all intoxicating liquors.

The Order of Sons of Temperance is organized

by sixteen strong-souled, earnest men, who meet in Tee-totalers' Hall, New York, on Thursday evening, September 29. This organization is designated as New York Division No. 1, Sons of Temperance.

A report made to the American Temperance Union states that in the few years ending in 1842 widespread temperance propaganda has been carried on in marine circles, especially on merchant vessels. The spirit ration is abandoned on merchant ships, coasters and whalers everywhere. Sailors' homes, Bethel churches and mariners' temperance societies are formed. At Charleston, S. C., 400 sailors sign the pledge. In New York City 1,400 seamen do likewise. The entire crew of the United States frigate Columbia sign the pledge in a body, with Captain Parker, the chaplain and the purser in the lead. Practically the entire crew of the Ohio do the same.

Congress reduces the rum ration of the navy to one gill per day, and forbids that being issued to persons under 21 years of age. It also allows the alternative of half a pint of wine, butter, meal, raisins, dried fruit, pickles, molasses, or the value in money.

Kamehameha, King of Hawaii, places himself at the head of an active propaganda movement for total abstinence.

An agreement is made between the Russian-American Company and the Hudson Bay Company which prohibits entirely the selling or giving of rum to the natives of Alaska.

The Independent Order of Rechabites is introduced into the United States from England.

The Congressional Temperance Society is reorganized with "total abstinence" provisions for all members and the president is Hon. George N. Briggs; vice presidents, Hon. Messrs. Thomas W. Gilmer of Virginia, Thomas Henry of Pennsylvania, S. S. Bowne of New York, T. F. Marshall of Kentucky, Edmund Deberry of North Carolina, H. M. Watterson of Tennessee, J. T. Mason of Maryland, Calvary Morris of Ohio, and John Mattocks of Vermont; secretary, I. M. Howard, of Michigan. Among the members at the time of this new departure are Messrs. Calhoun of Massachusetts, Hall of Vermont, Giddings of Ohio, Morgan of New York, Choate of Massachusetts, Wise of Virginia, and many others.

1843

Oregon passes a law prohibiting the sale of intoxicating liquors to Indians.

John B. Gough begins to lecture in Massachusetts for 75 cents a night.

In June the city of New York resolves not to provide intoxicating liquors at the reception to the President of the United States. The same action is taken in Boston at the Bunker Hill celebration.

The Grand Division of the Sons of Temperance of New York is legally constituted. Daniel H. Sans is elected and installed Grand Worthy Patriarch.

A Grand Council Fire is held at Tahlequah (Indian Territory) on July 3 and a solemn anti-liquor compact formed by representatives of the Cherokees, Creeks and Osages.

1844

Governor George N. Briggs is made Governor of Massachusetts. He is a strong promoter of total abstinence and does not serve liquors in the Governor's mansion.

The Territorial Legislature of Oregon enacts a general prohibitory law.

The National Division of the Sons of Temperance is instituted, with jurisdiction over six grand divisions, 71 subordinate divisions and about 6,000 members.

The first known effort to induce the young to join an organization and take the pledge of total abstinence is made at a quarterly session of the Grand Division of the Sons of Temperance of New York, January 9.

The Hawaiian Total Abstinence Union is organ·ized.

1845

The Order of the Templars of Honor and Temperance is organized.

John B. Gough is ensnared by a trick of his enemies and becomes intoxicated.

In more than 100 towns in Massachusetts the traffic in ardent liquors has ceased.

The records of the Sons of Temperance show that at the end of this year the order has 14 grand divisions, 650 subordinate divisions and 40,000 members. It is recommended by the National Division that the members of the order support public temperance meetings throughout the country.

Huntsville, Ala., places a license tax of $2,500 on the retail sale of intoxicating liquors.

The New York State Legislature enacts a local option law governing the sale of intoxicating liquors. The law provides for elections in the month of May and applies to all towns and cities of the state outside of New York City.

The first General Eldership of the Church of God held at Pittsburgh, Pa., adopts strong temperance resolutions.

The prohibitory law of Oregon is strengthened.

The local option law is re-enacted in Rhode Island.

Michigan enacts a local option law.

The liquor dealers employ Rufus Choate and Daniel Webster to defend their interests before the courts. Three test cases in which the defendants have been convicted of violating the state laws restricting or forbidding the selling of liquor are appealed to the United States Supreme Court.

A Temple of Honor is established December 5 and is called "Marshall Temple No. 1, Sons of Temperance."

William A. McKee of Philadelphia emphasizes temperance juvenile organization before a session of the Grand Division of the Sons of Temperance. In November, at a meeting of Morning Star Division No. 66, the Sons of Temperance, definite steps are taken to organize a society for the young. The pledge prohibits the use of tobacco and profanity as well as the use of liquors.

1846

The Democratic Legislature of Maine enacts a

law prohibiting the sale of liquor by any except those designated by selectmen.

Vermont enacts a local option law.

Pennsylvania enacts a no-license law which is later declared unconstitutional by the Supreme Court.

The membership of the Sons of Temperance is reported to be 100,000, which shows an increase of 60,000 in one year.

Dr. J. E. Turner of Maine urges the necessity of establishing a special asylum for the treatment of inebriety.

A separate order called the "National Temple of Honor of the United States" is organized November 5, after unsuccessful efforts to connect with the Sons of Temperance.

The Legislature of Ohio grants the privilege of township local option to ten counties of the state.

The Maryland Legislature enacts a law preventing the clerk of Montgomery county from issuing licenses on certain roads without an order by one of the judges of the court.

The first organization of the Cadets of Temperance, Germantown, Pennsylvania, section No. 1, is organized December 6.

Rufus Choate delivers an address in the Massachusetts Senate in behalf of measures to restrict the liquor traffic.

England forces the King of Hawaii to allow the importation and sale of English liquors in the islands.

1847

All but one county of Iowa votes for Prohibition

under the local option law passed by the first Legislature after statehood.

The famous liquor cases from Massachusetts, New Hampshire and Rhode Island are decided by the United States Supreme Court against the liquor traffic.

Congress makes more stringent the law against the introduction of liquors in Indian countries and the gift or sale of the same to Indians.

The Delaware Legislature votes to submit to the people the question of license or no license.

A civil damage anti-liquor law is proposed in the Massachusetts Legislature but fails of passage.

The Order of Good Samaritans is founded in New York.

The New York Legislature repeals the law passed in 1845.

The Grand Division of the Sons of Temperance of New Brunswick is enthusiastically organized. A deputy is commissioned to introduce the order into Great Britain, which is done in London on November 19.

A Grand Section of the Cadets of Temperance is organized at Philadelphia on February 22.

The township local option provisions enacted by the Ohio Legislature in 1846 are repealed.

New Jersey enacts a township local option law.

Chief Justice Taney in a decision of the Supreme Court states that "Although the gin sold was an import from another state, Congress has clearly the power to regulate such importations, . . . yet as Congress has made no regulation on this subject.

the traffic in the article may be lawfully regulated by the state as soon as it is landed in its territory, and a tax imposed upon it, or a license required, or a sale altogether prohibited, according to the policy which the state may suppose to be its interest or duty to pursue."

Senator William H. Seward of New York presents petitions to Congress asking for the abolition of the spirit ration.

Congress enacts that "no annuities, moneys or goods shall be paid or distributed to Indians while they are under the influence of any description of intoxicating liquor."

1848

The Methodist Episcopal Church at the first General Conference after the division of the church, held in Pittsburgh, Pa., reinstates the original rule of John Wesley against "drunkenness, buying or selling spirituous liquors or using them except in cases of extreme necessity." This is done in harmony with action taken in the annual conferences where the vote stood 2,017 for the rule and 21 against.

The Supreme Court of Delaware declares the prohibitory law unconstitutional.

The Philadelphia Yearly Meeting of Friends urges abstinence from all intoxicating liquors.

Maryland enacts a law closing saloons on Sunday.

The Legislature of New Hampshire submits to the people the question of the expediency of a law prohibiting the sale of intoxicating liquors except for mechanical and medicinal purposes; three-fourths of the votes cast on this question are in favor of the law.

New Jersey enacts a law closing saloons on Sunday.

The Templars of Honor and Temperance make the pledge to total abstinence binding for life, this being the first order to make such requirement.

1849

The General Conference of the United Brethren Church forbids the use as well as the manufacture and sale of intoxicating liquors by any and all members.

Father Mathew arrives from Ireland on July 2, and begins his pledge-signing crusade. President Tyler gives a banquet at the White House to Father Mathew and the Senate votes the extraordinary distinction of admitting him to the bar of the Senate.

The Legislature of Iowa passes a law leaving the granting of liquor licenses to the board of supervisors in each county, which in effect repeals the county option law.

A prohibitory measure stronger than previous ones passes the Legislature of Maine, but is vetoed by Governor Dana.

Neal Dow is elected Mayor of Portland, Maine.

New Hampshire enacts a law prohibiting the granting of licenses to sell wines and spirituous liquors except for medicinal, mechanical and chemical purposes. The bill is approved July 7.

The prohibitory liquor law of Oregon is repealed.

The vote on the liquor question at the polls in Vermont results in a majority against license of 12,000.

The New Jersey Legislature confirms and makes more stringent the Sunday closing law.

The Court of Appeals in Maryland sustains the Sunday closing law.

Wisconsin by a vote of 13 to 3 in the Senate and 29 to 21 in the House enacts a law permitting no man to vend or retail spirituous liquors until he shall have given bond to pay all damages the community or individuals may sustain by such traffic, to support all paupers, widows and orphans and pay the expenses of all civil and criminal prosecutions growing out of or justly attributed to such traffic.

General Cary, chief officer of the National Division of the Sons of Temperance, says, "We must have a nobler, higher, holier ambition than to reform one generation of drunkards after another. We must seal up the fountain whence flows the desolating stream of death."

George W. Crawford, Secretary of War, issues an order dated September 21 forbidding sutlers from selling ardent spirits or other intoxicating drinks, under penalty of losing their situations.

1850

At the fourth annual meeting of the Sons of Temperance in Boston on June 11, there are representatives from 36 grand chapters, 5,894 subordinate divisions and 245,233 paying members.

The Neal Dow Prohibition measure presented to the Legislature of Maine is lost by a tie vote in the Senate.

The annual per capita consumption of distilled spirits in the United States is $2\frac{1}{2}$ gallons.

Michigan adopts a constitutional amendment prohibiting the issuing of liquor licenses in the state.

Wisconsin enacts a civil damage anti-liquor law.

A very stringent temperance bill is passed by the House of Representatives in Massachusetts, but fails to pass the Senate.

The people of Vermont decide against license by an aggregate majority of nearly 8,000 votes. A short prohibitory law is enacted.

A prohibitory bill is introduced in the New York Legislature, but does not come to a vote.

A temperance measure is defeated by a small majority in the Legislature of Indiana.

Wisconsin enacts a law which provides for the enforcement of the law enacted the previous year.

A new departure in the establishment of the degree in Temperance Society is made by the Templars of Honor and Temperance.

A law is enacted fining the natives of Hawaii $200 or two years' imprisonment for buying or selling spirituous liquor.

The Government of the United States makes a treaty with King Kamehameha III. of Hawaii, by the terms of which he is forced to allow the introduction and sale of intoxicating liquors.

The Cherokee Temperance Society reaches a membership of 1,752.

CHAPTER V.

THE FIRST STATE-WIDE PROHIBITION WAVE—
1851–1869

FOR SEVERAL years prior to 1851, agitation for Prohibition in several states had compelled action by the state Legislatures, notably in Oregon Territory, Delaware, Maine, New Hampshire and Michigan.

The first state or territorial Prohibition law on record was the law enacted in 1843 by the Territorial Legislature of Oregon, which law was repealed in 1848. Three years after the Oregon law was enacted, the Democratic Legislature of Maine in 1846 enacted a law providing for Prohibition throughout the state. This law was weak and difficult of enforcement. A stronger law was passed by the Legislature of 1848 but was vetoed by the governor. Another effort to enact a stronger prohibitory law in Maine was defeated in 1850 by a tie vote in the Senate.

The Legislature of Delaware passed a prohibitory law in 1847, which was declared unconstitutional by the Supreme Court of the state in the following year. The New Hampshire Legislature submitted to the people of the state in 1848 the question of the advisability of enacting a prohibitory law, with the result that three-fourths of the votes cast at the election expressed the desire of the people that such a law be enacted. The Legislature of 1849 accordingly prohibited the granting of licenses to sell wines and spirituous liquors except for medicinal, mechanical and chemical purposes. The state of Michigan in 1850 adopted a constitutional amendment prohibiting the issuing of retail liquor licenses in the state.

The effect of these several campaigns for state-wide prohibitory legislation was to turn the attention of the organized temperance forces throughout the United States toward state Prohibition, and a campaign to this end in practically every state in the Union was organized in 1851. That year, therefore, marks the beginning of the period of aggressive organized effort throughout the states for prohibitory legislation.

Between 1851 and 1856 the Legislatures of practically all the states were compelled to wrestle with the Prohibition question. The Dow Prohibition law in the state of Maine was enacted that year. It was re-enacted with increased penalties in 1855, was repealed in 1856, and re-enacted in 1857. The constitution of Ohio was amended in 1851 so as to prohibit the licensing of the liquor traffic throughout the state. This provision of the constitution, however, was never fully enforced and in later years the constitutional amendment was circumvented by acts of the Legislature placing a tax upon the traffic, which in reality was nothing more nor less than a license fee. The Legislature of Illinois passed a prohibitory law in 1851, which did not stand the test of the courts. The Illinois Legislature in 1855 submitted Prohibition to a vote of the people, with the result that the law was rejected.

The first prohibitory law in Rhode Island was enacted in 1852. It was declared unconstitutional by the

Supreme Court in 1853, whereupon the Legislature of the state, in session the same year, passed another prohibitory provision. The same was submitted to a vote of the people and was ratified the same year. Another prohibitory law was enacted by the Legislature of Rhode Island in 1855 and was repealed in 1863. The state of Vermont, which by a majority of 8,000 votes had refused to enact a license provision in 1850, passed a prohibitory law in 1852 and the same was ratified by vote of the people in 1853. The Territorial Legislature of Minnesota enacted a prohibitory measure in 1852, as did also the Legislature of the state of Massachusetts. Some of the provisions of the Massachusetts law were declared unconstitutional in 1854. The law was revised the following year in order to stand the test of the courts and remained on the statute books until it was finally repealed in 1868. The Connecticut Legislature enacted a prohibitory law in 1853, but the same was vetoed by the governor. Another prohibitory statute was enacted the following year.

The first prohibitory measure in Indiana was passed by the Legislature in 1853 and declared unconstitutional by the Supreme Court of the state. Another similar effort of the Legislature in 1855 met with the same result. A prohibitory law was passed by the Legislature of the state of Pennsylvania in 1846 but was declared unconstitutional by the court. Eight years later, in 1854, the Legislature submitted the question to a vote of the people, with the result that Prohibition was rejected by a majority of approximately 3,000 out of a total vote of 300,000. Another prohibitory law enacted in Pennsylvania was repealed in 1856. After several efforts in different Legislatures in New York state, a prohibitory law was enacted in 1854 by a goodly majority of both houses of the Legislature, but the same was promptly vetoed by the governor. The following year another prohibitory law was enacted by the Legislature only to- be declared unconstitutional by the Supreme Court and repealed in 1856. The New York Legislature of 1860 passed a prohibitory measure which required the action of the next Legislature. When it came up for action in the next Legislature it passed the Senate but was defeated in the House of Representatives.

The Legislature of Michigan in 1853 enacted a state prohibitory law and then promptly repealed the same, later in the same year submitting the question to a popular vote with the result that Prohibition was rejected. In 1855, however, the Legislature enacted a state-wide prohibitory statute without a referendum. The Legislature of New Hampshire, which had enacted a prohibitory law against wines and spirits in 1849, enacted full Prohibition in 1855, as did also the Legislature of the state of Delaware. The Delaware law however, was repealed in 1857. The Iowa Legislature in 1855 passed a resolution providing for state Prohibition and submitted the same to a vote of the people. The amendment was adopted by a good majority, but was later thrown out by the courts on a technicality. The Wisconsin Legislature, catching the spirit of Prohibition which was sweeping the country, passed a prohibitory law in 1855, but the same was vetoed by the governor. The Legislature promptly passed another prohibitory law which met the same fate. The Territorial Legislature of Nebraska enacted Prohibition in 1855.

The failure of state-wide Prohibition in most of these states and the lack of stability and permanency in the Prohibition movement, which had promised so much between the years of 1851 and 1856, was due to many causes, several of which stand out in bold relief. In the first place, just at the time when Prohibition activity and Prohibition legislation was at its height, the attention of the moral reform forces of the nation was turned to the slavery question, which reached its crisis in the war of 1861-1865. The general demoralizing effect of the war itself upon most questions of public morality was also a significant factor in turning the tide which had been running so strongly in the direction of temperance reform. The internal revenue plan which was adopted as a war measure but which indirectly turned over the policy of the government on the liquor question to the dictation of financially and politically powerful liquor interests which promptly sprang into existence as a direct result of that policy, was one of the very strongest factors in saddling the liquor traffic on the nation for long years after the war.

Another factor which was undoubtedly responsible to a considerable degree for wrecking the Prohibition movement and causing the prompt repeal of prohibitory laws that had been enacted in the several states, was the partisan political turn which the Prohibition movement took in the fifties. In most of the states, in fact, the question of Prohibition became a party issue, being championed by one political party and opposed by another, thus dividing to a great degree those whose sympathies were in favor of Prohibition but whose allegiance to party ties and whose party loyalty in those stirring times was regarded as a virtue of more importance even than their temperance proclivities.

While all these and other causes tended to check the Prohibition movement and promote wholesale reaction in states which had adopted prohibitory laws, it is undoubtedly true that the greatest and most important factor in the recession of the Prohibition wave was that of the general attitude of the temperance public which lost interest in the fight when Prohibition laws had been placed upon the statute books and the exciting campaigns for these laws were over. This loss of interest resulted in apathy on the part of great numbers of those who had been intensely interested in the Prohibition campaigns and a natural falling off of financial support and active coöperation with the organized temperance movements which had succeeded in such a remarkable way in bringing the sentiment of the country to the point of demanding Prohibition legislation, and upon which fell the growing burden of insuring enforcement and permanency of the laws.

The educational value of the Prohibition campaigns for the decade preceding the war of 1861-1865 was tremendous. Prohibition became the burning question of the day—a subject of conversation everywhere. Thus, in spite of what might have been only a temporary recession of the wave of Prohibition activity, there had been laid a strong foundation for the crystallizing of the widespread sentiment which existed, into public opinion strong enough to demand and secure the enforcement and the permanency of prohibitory laws. Had there been an organized movement, ready to grasp the opportunity presented and thus conserve the remarkable results of a half century of temperance work and church activity for sobriety, the story of the state-wide Prohibition wave of 1851-1869 might have been a different story.

Had the American Temperance Union retained the strength and virility which characterized it in the fourteen years following 1826, it would undoubtedly have been able to meet the situation and turn the tide at the close of the war in such a way as might have promptly retrieved the defeat which came to the Prohibition forces during the war period. In fact, it might easily have made the war itself the occasion for a sweeping Prohibition victory. The weakness of the temperance forces, however, due to the apathy of the temperance public, together with the lack of financial support and coöperation, made it impossible for even the strongest temperance movement of the day to cope with the new phase of the problem which presented itself. Even that part of the failure which was due to the efforts to make Prohibition a partisan political issue might have been overcome, since the general trend of the movement represented by the American Temperance Union was toward non-partisan coöperative effort in behalf of temperance reform. This fact is evidenced by the action of the convention of 1853, which was recorded as the first world's temperance convention but which in reality was only a great national convention of the temperance forces of the United States. It is a significant fact that that convention, representing the Prohibition forces of the nation, in the very midst of the numerous fights for state-wide Prohibition in 1853, recorded the conviction of its great body of delegates in the following resolution, "that while we do not desire to disturb political parties, we do intend to have and enforce a law prohibiting the liquor manufacture and traffic as a beverage, whatever may be the consequences to political parties, and we will vote accordingly." The following further resolution by that important convention is also significant: "Resolved, that the cause of temperance is a question altogether separate and apart from the question of women's rights, land reforms or any other, and that it must stand or fall upon its own merits."

Rev. John Marsh, D.D., for thirty years the corresponding secretary of the American Temperance Union, in his "Temperance Recollections," referring to this remarkable convention and the resolutions from which the above quotations are taken, discloses the fact that in the discussion of the resolutions the question arose in the convention as to the advisability of mingling temperance and politics, whereupon one of the delegates, the Rev. John Pierpont of Boston, made the following declaration: "We ask at the hand of our civil Legislatures a prohibitory law which we can not get except at the hands of political action. It is, therefore, to me absurd to renounce or reject all pretensions to mingle in politics. We mean to carry it to the polls and to carry the polls in our favor. We do it upon the principle that it is a moral question, paramount in God's eye to questions of office-holding, of finance and of policy. We have up to this time been timid before politicians. We have said, 'We did not mean you.' We say now, 'We do mean you and will put you down if you do not give us what we ask.' These are our sentiments."

The words of John Pierpont in the great temperance convention of 1853 were prophetic. They directly suggested the secret of success in the fight for Prohibition in a free government. They set forth in terse terms the platform on which Federal Constitutional Prohibition became a reality sixty-six years later. If they had formed the foundation of action by a strong temperance organization in 1853, the Prohibition movement of the fifties might have been a tide instead of a wave.

The successful outcome of the anti-slavery movement might easily have made the organization equipment of that movement an asset of first value in an aggressive fight for Prohibition, but leadership was lacking. The strongly organized temperance movement that had brought the temperance sentiment almost to the pinnacle of power had been crippled and was rapidly disintegrating, so that systematic propaganda effort was impossible.

The difference between the follow-up efforts of the government in military operations necessary to settle a great moral question by force of arms, and the follow-up efforts of the forces for Prohibition is shown in a most striking way by the post-war activities of that remarkable period. For long years after the war was over, the Federal government of the United States took every precaution and spent millions upon millions of dollars to conserve the victories of the war and to insure permanence of that for which the Union forces fought. Many historians, in fact, agree today that those efforts were too strong and too drastic. On the other hand, however, the forces upon whom the Prohibition movement relied, considered that the fight was over in state after state, when prohibitory laws were enacted, and the absolutely essential features of conservation and development were lacking.

The internal revenue bulwark of the liquor interests, which had been reluctantly agreed to by President Lincoln, could probably have been successfully stormed and taken had the organized temperance forces been kept intact after the Prohibition victories of the fifties and during the period of the war. The internal revenue act was purely a war measure, and the system which it created did not become thoroughly entrenched in governmental policy until many years after the war was over. The American Temperance Union, with the splendid organization which it had builded in the first half of the period of organized activities, might have rallied the moral forces of the nation in a successful fight against it, had the Union been kept intact and been able to operate at this crucial period as it had operated in previous years.

In short, the record of the temperance reform movement during that trying period of American history strongly indicates that had the temperance public been fully awake to the conditions and the opportunities of their day, National Prohibition of the liquor traffic in America might have been permanently established in the United States fifty years before the Prohibition amendment was finally made a part of the Federal Constitution. The Eighteenth amendment to the constitution might have been the sixteenth.

Among those whose names stand out with peculiar

luster in connection with the temperance movement of this period are: Abraham Lincoln, who as a member of the Sons of Temperance strongly advocated abstinence and Prohibition; Major J. B. Merwin, who as a representative of President Lincoln preached t he gospel of temperance to the soldiers in the camps during the Civil War; Wendell Phillips and Henry Ward Beecher, who had been so prominent in the anti-slavery movement and who when the success of that cause was assured became aggressively active in the temperance reform; Doctor Justin Edwards, who preached the gospel of temperance in most of the states; and Horace Greeley, whose paper, both in editorial and news columns, helped to promote the movement for temperance reform.

The following chronology covers the principal items of interest in connection with the temperance reform during this period.

CHRONOLOGY OF THE TEMPERANCE REFORM FOR THE PERIOD 1851–1869

1851

The Independent Order of Good Templars is organized at Saratoga, N. Y.

Illinois adopts State-wide Prohibition.

The Sons of Temperance report a membership of 250,000, "men only, 21 years of age, nearly all legal voters."

The National Temperance Convention meets at Saratoga, N. Y.

The State of Ohio votes an additional section in

the Constitution forbidding the licensing of the liquor traffic.

The Dow Prohibition law passes the Maine House by a vote of 86 to 40 and the Senate by a vote of 18 to 10, and is signed by the Governor on June 2. The law provides for the confiscation of liquors stored for sale.

Missouri enacts a local option law.

Father Mathew sails for Ireland on the steamer Pacific, embarking at Philadelphia on November 8, after an extended and eminently successful tour throughout the United States.

Templars of Honor and Temperance are reported as having been established in nearly every state and in the Canadas.

1852

Abraham Lincoln joins the Sons of Temperance at Springfield, Ill.

A prohibitory law is passed in Rhode Island by a Democratic Legislature on May 2.

Horace Greeley declares for the destruction of the liquor traffic.

The Massachusetts Legislature enacts the "Maine Law" in its most stringent form.

Vermont enacts a state-wide prohibitory law on December 20.

Louisiana enacts a local option law.

The General Conference of the Methodist Church endorses the action of "civil rulers to interpose the authority of the state for the protection of society against what we hold to be an enormous social wrong, the manufacture and sale of intoxicating liquors."

The Territorial Legislature of Minnesota adopts Prohibition and the same is ratified by the people.

A Prohibition law similar to the Maine law is adopted by Massachusetts on May 22.

The Seventh-Day Baptists pass resolutions of deep interest in the movement for State Prohibition in a number of the commonwealths.

The ninth session of the National Division of the Sons of Temperance delivers its first pronuncia mento on Prohibition.

1853

The prohibitory law of Rhode Island is declared unconstitutional, whereupon the Legislature passes another prohibitory law meeting court objections, which law is submitted to a vote of the people and ratified.

The Vermont prohibitory law is ratified by direct vote of the people.

John B. Gough makes a temperance lecture tour of England.

The Connecticut Legislature passes a prohibitory law which is vetoed by Governor Seymour.

The Indiana Legislature passes a prohibitory law with a provision that it be submitted to a vote of the people; the court declares the law unconstitutional because of the submission clause.

The Legislature of Wisconsin votes to submit a prohibitory liquor law to the people. No such law, however, is drafted.

The General Conference of the Free Baptist Church resolves "that the traffic in intoxicating liquors is, in its nature, nearly allied to theft and robbery," and stands for the principle of the Maine law.

Thomas L. Carson of New York State, in the interests of enforcement of anti-liquor laws, establishes a paper called "The Carson League."

A civil damage anti-liquor law is enacted in Indiana.

Rhode Island enacts a stronger prohibitory law. The question of the repeal of the law is submitted to the people with the result that the law is sustained.

The Michigan Legislature enacts a state-wide prohibitory statute, which is promptly repealed.

Michigan submits Prohibition to a popular vote.

The Illinois prohibitory law is repealed and license provisions re-enacted.

The Free Baptist Church declares against the liquor traffic, endorses the Maine prohibitory law, and declares it to be the duty of all Christians to vote only for men who are in favor of Prohibition.

A World's Temperance Convention is held in Metropolitan Hall, New York, September 6-10.

The Democratic party of Maine having decided to oppose Prohibition, Anson P. Morrill bolts the party and runs for Governor of the state on a Free Soil and Prohibition platform.

The question of Prohibition becomes an issue in the election in Washington, D. C., and the dry ticket wins in the election by a vote of 1,963 to 991.

J. S. Lainhoff of The Good Samaritans becomes dissatisfied with certain accounts issued by the grand section, is defeated for office and withdraws his section and organizes the "Junior Templars."

1854

Texas submits the question of the sale of liquors to the counties.

Connecticut passes a prohibitory law with the provision for town agents to sell liquors for sacramental, chemical and medicinal uses.

Some of the provisions of the Massachusetts prohibitory law are declared unconstitutional by the court.

Mississippi enacts a local option law.

The manufacture, sale or introduction of liquor is prohibited west of the Mississippi river in Minnesota within the limits of the territory purchased under the Sioux treaties.

Myron H. Clark, a Whig, is elected Governor of New York on a Prohibition platform.

The New York Legislature charters the first company organized to establish an asylum for inebriates.

A Prohibition law is passed in the New York Legislature by a vote of 21 to 11 in the Senate and 78 to 42 in the House, but the measure is vetoed by Governor Seymour.

The Prohibition law submitted to a vote of the people in Pennsylvania is defeated by a majority of 3,000 in a total vote of 300,000.

A civil damage anti-liquor law is enacted in Ohio.

The General Assembly of the Presbyterian Church declares for prohibitory laws.

The General Eldership of the Church of God strongly approves of the movement to secure prohibitory laws in all the states.

An effort is made at Cincinnati to establish a national section of the Cadets of Temperance on September 13, but the organization effected soon disbands.

1855

The militia of Illinois is called out in the city of Chicago to suppress a riot occasioned by the agitation of the license question.

The militia is called out in Maine to prevent a crowd from taking possession of certain liquors held by the officials.

Pennsylvania prohibits the sale of liquors to be drunk on the premises.

The prohibitory law of Massachusetts is thoroughly revised to stand the test of the courts.

The prohibitory law of Maine is re-enacted by the Legislature and its penalties increased.

Another prohibitory law is passed in Rhode Island.

New Hampshire enacts a State Prohibition law similar to that of the State of Maine.

The Legislature of Iowa submits State Prohibition to a vote of the people; the law is adopted by a majority of 2,910. The submission clause is declared unconstitutional, but the rest of the law is upheld.

The Indiana Legislature passes a State Prohibition law which is made void by the Supreme Court.

The sale of liquor to Indians is prohibited in Washington territory.

The Illinois Legislature enacts a prohibitory dram drinking law which is rejected by vote of the people.

Prohibition is adopted by the Legislature of Wisconsin, but the measure is twice vetoed.

Delaware enacts a prohibitory law.

Michigan enacts Prohibition, without a referendum.

The Synod of the Moravian Church declares for all proper measures for the suppression of intemperance.

A prohibitory law is adopted by the Legislature of New York by a joint vote of 101 to 56 and becomes a law on April 9. The same is declared unconstitutional by the courts.

The Territorial Legislature of Nebraska enacts a prohibitory law.

The Right Worthy Grand Lodge of the Independent Order of Good Templars is organized as the supreme head of the order, by the representatives of ten Grand Lodges, which meet for the purpose at Cleveland, Ohio.

The new national division of the Sons of Temperance of Great Britain and Ireland is organized on April 26.

Many Sons of Temperance advocates, after great victories achieved, become indifferent to enforcement of law and the cause suffers thereby.

1856

The local option law of Texas is repealed by the enactment of a license law.

The Maine prohibitory law is repealed by the enactment of a license provision.

The Chickasaw Nation prohibits intoxicating liquor within its territory.

The Sons of Temperance inaugurate the movement for National Constitutional Prohibition. (The amendment is adopted 63 years later.)

The prohibitory law of Pennsylvania is repealed.

The prohibitory law of New York is repealed.

A new temperance society is organized in Boston.

Rev. John Chaney of Farmington, Maine, is mobbed in his own town for starting a temperance movement.

The prohibitory law of Rhode Island is strengthened.

1857

The Sons of Temperance in New York endorse the scheme for a constitutional amendment prohibiting the liquor traffic.

The Supreme Court of Iowa declares the state prohibitory law unconstitutional on a technicality, whereupon the State Legislature enacts a statutory state-wide prohibitory provision.

The Philadelphia Yearly Meeting of Friends advises women Friends to exclude liquors from the social circle.

New York enacts a complete license law.

The Choctaw Nation prohibits intoxicating liquor within its territory.

The Prohibition law of Delaware is repealed.

The State of Maine re-enacts a state prohibitory law.

The Reformed Presbyterian Church declares that the sale and use of intoxicating liquors as beverages deserves church discipline and directs sessions to act accordingly.

1858

Iowa passes the so-called "wine and beer clause" in the law permitting the sale of such liquors made from Iowa products.

The Maine Legislature submits a prohibitory amendment to a vote of the people, who adopt the law by a vote of 28,864 to 5,942.

The United Presbyterian Church is organized and in the first General Assembly resolves against the liquor traffic and liquor drinking.

Indiana repeals the prohibitory law of 1855, which had been declared unconstitutional.

The first session of the Right Worthy Grand Lodge of the Independent Order of Good Templars meets in Hamilton, Canada.

The Seventh-Day Baptists pronounce the liquor license system to be immoral in its tendency and destructive to the best interests of the community, and urge the enactment of prohibitory laws.

The New York Witness publishes, May 29, an interesting history of the temperance movement.

The prohibitory law of Nebraska is repealed by the enactment of a license provision.

1859

Kansas enacts a law prohibiting the sale of liquor to drunkards and also to married men against the known wishes of their wives.

The General Assembly of the United Presbyterian Church opposes the manufacture and vending of intoxicating liquors and urges total abstinence.

Louisiana prohibits the licensing of free negroes to keep coffee houses, billiard tables or retail stores where spirituous liquors are sold.

1860

President-elect Abraham Lincoln declines a request to furnish liquors to the national committee sent to inform him of his nomination to the Presidency; he returns unopened the hampers of wines and liquors sent to him.

The General Conference of the Methodist Episcopal Church protests against the renting of buildings for the sale of intoxicating drinks and the practice of selling grain where it is known to be used for the manufacture of such liquors, and urges all ministers and members to co-operate for securing in their several states the Prohibition of the traffic in intoxicating liquors.

The Legislature of New York passes a provision for Constitutional Prohibition which requires action by the next session.

The results of investigations on alcohol by Lallemand, Perrin and Duroy are first published.

There are 1,269 breweries in the United States, which produce 3,812,346 barrels of beer.

1861

The New York Senate by a vote of 69 to 33 approves the joint resolution providing for a constitutional prohibitory amendment.

President Lincoln signs an act of Congress forbidding the selling or giving of intoxicating drinks to soldiers.

Generals Butler, McClellan and Banks issue orders expelling all liquors from their respective commands.

A gill of whisky is allowed by Congress to each man in the navy in case of excessive fatigue and exposure.

Aggressive efforts to place Prohibition in the revised Constitution of New York State fail.

Congress greatly increases the tax on intoxicating liquors by an elaborate tax system.

The Legislature of Alabama enacts sixteen local prohibitory laws and repeals several such laws formerly enacted.

The Revised Army Regulations, issued by Secretary of War Simon Cameron, August 10, re-establish a ration of one gill of whisky per man daily, in case of excessive fatigue or severe exposure.

The disaster of Bull Run is credited largely to account of drunkenness.

An elaborate system of liquor taxation is enacted by a special session of the Thirty-seventh Congress.

1862

A joint resolution passed by both houses of Congress provides that any officer found guilty of habitual drunkenness shall immediately be dismissed from the service.

The Act of March 19 provides for a board of officers to prepare a list of articles to be sold by sutlers, and further provides "that no intoxicating liquors shall at any time be contained therein, or the sale of such liquors authorized."

General McClellan on June 19 issues an order for the immediate discontinuance of the spirit ration, and for hot coffee to be served after reveille.

General Benjamin F. Butler first prohibits the presence in camp of any intoxicating liquor whatever, and forbids all use of it in his own quarters.

Messrs. Sargent, Harrison and Woodruff, members of the United States House of Representatives, propose amendments to the internal revenue measure in Congress which would limit the licensing of the liquor traffic to territory where the state and local authorities recognize the traffic as a lawful one.

United States Senator Henry Wilson of Massachusetts, on May 27, attacks the principle of licensing the retail liquor traffic, in the Senate, stating that "no man in this country should have a license from the Federal Government to sell intoxicating liquors. . . . The Federal Government ought not to derive a revenue from the retail of intoxicating drinks." This attack by Senator Wilson is seconded by Senator Pomeroy of Kansas.

Senator Charles Sumner suggests an amendment to the license and internal revenue measure of 1862, providing that no liquor license shall be granted within any state or territory where liquor is not licensed by local laws.

Congress by Act of February 13 makes it a crime punishable by fine and imprisonment to sell liquors to Indians under the care of a superintendent or an agent, whether on or off the reservation.

An internal revenue tax measure, including taxes on liquors, is inroduced in the House of Representatives of the United States by Anson P. Morrill of Maine.

Senator William Pitt Fessenden of Maine, a champion of Prohibition, chairman of the Ways and Means Committee, sponsors an internal revenue measure in the Senate. The measure is passed by Congress and approved on July 1.

Congress, on July 14, forbids the sale of liquor to soldiers and volunteers in the District of Columbia.

In July Congress abolishes entirely the naval spirit ration.

The United States Brewers' Association is organized on November 12 in the city of New York.

Congress passes a law declaring that the spirit ration in the navy shall cease forever after September 1.

1863

The prohibitory law of Rhode Island is repealed by the enactment of a license law.

A demand of the United States Brewers' Association causes the government to reduce the tax on beer from $1 to 60 cents a barrel.

A million copies of an address prepared by E. C. Delavan of New York and endorsed by such men as General Winfield Scott and General Dix, are distributed among the troops through the army posts.

1864

The Binghamton, N. Y., asylum for inebriates, said to be the first of its kind, is established through the efforts of Dr. J. E. Turner of Maine.

Dr. B. W. Richardson begins his research on effects of alcohol on the human system.

The Synod of the Moravian Church strongly urges efforts for the uprooting of the evil of intemperance.

The United Presbyterian General Assembly insists that the rule of total abstinence be enforced "as rigorously as the honor of religion and the cause of temperance demands."

The internal revenue measure is amended three times, raising the tax on whisky to 60 cents, $1.50 and $2, respectively. The effect of this measure is to increase distillation enormously, speculation runs riot and vast fortunes are made.

Congress enacts a drastic search and seizure law to prevent the selling of intoxicating liquors in Indian countries.

1865

The Presbyterian General Assembly declares that liquor makers and sellers shall be excluded from membership in the church.

The fifth National Temperance Convention at Saratoga, N. Y., composed of 325 delegates from 25 states, resolves to form a national society and establish a publishing house under the name of "The National Temperance Society and Publication House," with headquarters in New York City.

The Order of Friends of Temperance is organized.

When the Civil War closes and 200,000 Union soldiers assemble for review in Washington, D. C., no liquor is allowed to be sold in the national capital and drunkenness is entirely absent from the celebration.

Local option is added to the license law of Connecticut.

The second session of the Right Worthy Grand Lodge of the Independent Order of Good Templars is held in London, Canada.

"The Youth's Temperance Advocate" is merged into "The Youth's Temperance Banner."

The special revenue commission reports to Congress as follows: "The immediate effect of the enactment of the first three and successive rates of duty was to cause an almost entire suspension of the business of distilling, which was resumed again with great activity as soon as an advance in the rate of tax in each instance became probable. The stock of whisky and high wines accumulated in the country under this course of procedure was without precedent, and Congress, by its refusal to make the advance in taxation in any instance retroactive, virtually legislated for the benefit of the distillers and speculators rather than for the Treasury and the Government."

David A. Wells, Commissioner of Internal Revenue, states in a public address that "By statistical reports it has been proven that 6,000,000 barrels of beer are brewed annually, while only 2,500,000 pay tax."

The native Legislature of Hawaii repeals the law which forbids the selling of liquor to natives. King Kamehameha V. vetoes the measure.

1866

The Legislature of Maryland passes a bill to enforce strict observance of Sunday.

The Kansas Legislature enacts a state prohibitory statute.

The General Synod of the Lutheran Church endorses the efforts for the suppression of intemperance.

More stringent provisions are added to the liquor tax law in Ohio.

The Seventh-Day Baptists declare vigorous war against intemperance.

The Alabama Legislature enacts several local Prohibition laws.

The National Division of the Sons of Temperance abolishes all restrictions on the entrance of colored people into the order, by an ordinance adopted at Montreal.

The office of sutler is abolished by the Act of Congress approved July 28; trading posts are established instead.

The Internal Revenue Act of 1862 is amended, by the Act of July 13. so as to change the "license" of the retailer into a "tax" and merely issue a receipt for the money. The rate for retail liquor dealers is fixed at $25 and for retail dealers in malt liquors at $20.

The special commissioner of revenue reports to Congress that many and perhaps the majority of the leading distillers of the country are satisfied with the present excise system and strongly adverse to any alteration of it.

In February an official report is presented in Congress showing that the effect of the license regulations has been to greatly increase the retail price of whisky.

1867

The state temperance convention in Pennsylvania declares for independent voting on the liquor question.

The Congressional Temperance Society is revived by Senator Henry Wilson of Massachusetts.

The National Brewers' Congress at Chicago declares for personal liberty, and against all candidates, of whatever party, who are in any way disposed toward the total abstinence cause.

The Maine Legislature passes a law providing for the enforcement of Prohibition by the appointment of a state constable.

Kansas enacts Prohibition for the unorganized counties of the state.

A committee of the Massachusetts Legislature under the leadership of ex-Governor Andrew makes an investigation of the liquor traffic in the state.

The Massachusetts State Board of Charities declares that intemperance is the chief reason for pauperism.

Additional restrictions are placed in the Ohio liquor tax law.

The inebriate asylum at Binghamton, N. Y., is deeded to the State of New York, to become a general insane asylum.

An inebriate asylum is established by Dr. Blanchard in Brooklyn, N. Y.

The Chicago Washingtonian Home is opened.

The Pennsylvania Grand Lodge of Good Templars at Pittsburgh, on June 17, declares in favor of voting for temperance candidates.

Connecticut enacts a license law and holds the same in suspense until the next session of the Legislature, which fails to concur.

The Pennsylvania State Temperance Convention, held at Harrisburg in February, declares for a nonpartisan attitude toward candidates favorable to the liquor interests.

Major General Halleck recommends to General U. S. Grant that the newly-acquired Territory of Alaska be declared to be "Indian country" in order to prevent the introduction of intoxicating liquors.

The Secretary of the Treasury on June 5 issues instructions to prevent the shipment of ardent spirits to the Territory of Alaska.

1868

The National Temperance Convention is held in Cleveland, Ohio.

The General Conference of the Methodist Episcopal Church reaffirms its strong position in favor of the temperance reform, declaring against all classes of intoxicating liquors and recommends the appointment of preachers in the Annual Conference to devote themselves exclusively to the temperance reform.

The Massachusetts prohibitory law is repealed largely as a result of the investigation of 1867, with many misleading conclusions reached as a result.

The General Synod of the Lutheran Church declares against the licensed traffic in intoxicating liquors.

The Legislature of Tennessee prohibits the granting of licenses within six miles of a blast furnace.

C. H. Van Wyck, chairman of the committee on retrenchment, makes a report to Congress in which he touches on the extensive frauds in the collection and payment of taxes on intoxicating liquors, and states that an honest payment of the tax on whisky would realize $200,000,000, whereas but little over $25,000,000 is received.

Congress authorizes the President of the United States to prohibit the liquor traffic in the Territory of Alaska.

Congress adopts the recommendation of the revenue commission and reduces the tax on spirits from $2 to 50 cents.

CHAPTER VI

THE years following the close of the war of 1861-1865 were not such as to encourage the friends of temperance reform. The American Temperance Union, which had been the great central temperance organization for almost forty years, had been greatly weakened by reason of the numerous temperance organizations which sprang into existence between 1840 and 1852, all of which tended to take from the Union financial support and constituency.

While this was true to a greater or lesser degree of all the new temperance organizations and societies, it was especially true in regard to the Independent Order of Good Templars, which was organized in 1851 and which gradually developed into a movement with a larger membership and a far greater influence than any of the numerous similar movements which had preceded it.

The American Temperance Union, as an organization, was on the decline before the Independent Order of Good Templars was formed. After the formation of that order the Union continued to lose financial support and coöperation even more rapidly than before and the effect of the war period was such as to complete the work of disintegration, so that the Union went out of existence in 1865 or rather what was left of it was merged into a new organization similar in

method and purpose known as the National Temperance Society, the prime mover in the organization of
which was the Hon. William E. Dodge, ex-member
of Congress from New York state.

The Prohibition movement had suffered a very decided reaction, and the temperance leaders were put to
their wits' end to know just what to do and how to
turn the tide. Most such leaders, in that day, were
connected in one way or another with the Good Templars, which by 1867 had acquired a membership of
almost half a million. The National Temperance
Society, which had been organized in 1865, was
rapidly growing into a position of strength and influence as a literature distributing agency, but it had
not yet become a strong political force.

Under such circumstances it was perfectly natural
that the initiative in connection with any new con-
certed effort of the temperance forces should arise in
the Independent Order of Good Templars.

The National Grand Lodge of the Good Templar
order, which met at Detroit in May, 1867, took up the
question of political activity in behalf of temperance
reform. A committee appointed for the purpose
brought in a report which was not satisfactory. After
considerable discussion, Mr. J. A. Spencer brought in
a substitute for the committee report, recommending
the "formation of political leagues for the support of
present party candidates who are out and out Prohibitionists, and who will enforce the laws against the
liquor traffic, and to nominate and support candidates
of their own where acceptable candidates are not presented by the party."

This substitute was accepted by the committee and

adopted as the expression of the convention. It is of interest to note that the attitude thus taken by the Independent Order of Good Templars in 1867 was in part practically the same as that taken by the Anti-Saloon League more than a quarter of a century later. Had the Good Templars stuck to the doctrine thus enunciated and had they succeeded in organizing a political movement of a non-partisan character, the course of the Prohibition movement during the next quarter of a century might have been different. This, however, was not to happen.

The Prohibition Party

The annual convention of the National Grand Lodge of the Independent Order of Good Templars met in Richmond, Ind., in 1868 and adopted the following resolution: "Whereas, We are convinced of the absolute necessity of political action in order to the uniform and ultimate success of the temperance reform, and whereas it is evident that neither of the now existing parties will formally adopt our principles, therefore resolved, that we recommend to the temperance people of the country the organization of a new political party whose platform and principles shall contain prohibition of the manufacture, importation and sale of intoxicating liquors to be used as a beverage."

On July 24, 1869, at Mansfield, Ohio, there was formed a state Prohibition party which nominated a ticket. This was the first such active party organization, although a party under the name had been organized in Illinois in 1867 and a similar party had been organized in Michigan the same year. Neither the Illinois nor the Michigan parties, however, had gone so far as to place a ticket in the field.

The National Convention of the Grand Lodge of Good Templars held at Oswego, N. Y., in May, 1869, completed the arrangements for the formation of a national Prohibition party by appointing a committee which was instructed to summon a national convention for that purpose. The Good Templar committee call was issued and as a result a convention of five hundred delegates met in Chicago September 1, 1869, and organized the National Prohibition Party. Thus was born the movement which was destined to place a Prohibition party ticket in the field in every presidential election for the next half century.

The first national Prohibition party ticket was put in the field in the presidential campaign of 1872. It was headed by John Black, who received a total of 5,607 votes for President. Four years later, in 1876, the party ticket headed by Green Clay Smith received 9,737 votes. Hon. Neal Dow was the presidential candidate of the party in 1880, receiving 10,366 votes. Hon. John P. St. John as a candidate in 1884 received 151,809 votes. Clinton B. Fisk, who was the standard-bearer in 1888, received 249,945 votes. John Bidwell, who was the candidate in 1892, received a total of 270,710 votes, which was the largest number ever cast for a presidential candidate on the Prohibition ticket either before or after that date.

Joshua Levering in 1896 received 132,871 votes, while the "Broad-Gauge" faction, which split off from the Prohibition party that year and formed the National party, polled a total of 13,757 votes. John G. Woolley, the presidential candidate of the party in

1900, polled 209,936 votes, while the Union Reform party, which was the successor to the National party, polled 5,690 votes. Silas C. Swallow, the standard-bearer of the party in 1904, polled 258,536 votes. Eugene Chafin, who was the candidate of the party in the presidential elections of both 1908 and 1912, received 253,840 votes in the campaign of 1908 and 208,923 votes in the campaign of 1912, while J. Frank Hanly, who headed the ticket in 1916, received 220,506 votes. The name of the party was changed in 1876 to "The National Prohibition Reform Party." Frances E. Willard and others in 1881 formed the "Home Protection Party," which was merged with the National Prohibition Reform party in 1882 under the name of "The Prohibition Home Protection Party." At the national convention of 1884, however, the old name was revived and from that time on the party went under the name of the National Prohibition Party.

The National Prohibition party marked an epoch in the history of the temperance reform movement in America. It pioneered the path of political activity for the Prohibition movement, and although it failed to accomplish its original purpose it certainly helped to clear the way for the non-partisan political activity which in later years succeeded in securing what the party as such could not secure. The Prohibition party, moreover, sounded the alarm against the growing liquor traffic. Its clarion call for aggressive political action was largely responsible for breaking down the ancient doctrine that the temperance movement and political activity should be kept separate, which doctrine had been preached by temperance advocates for half a century. In this respect, in fact, the Prohibition party jumped from one extreme to the other. The organized temperance movements prior to 1869 had been both non-partisan and non-political. The efforts of many of the leaders of the American Temperance Union and the Good Templars of the fifties and sixties were to evolve a movement that would be political and yet non-partisan. The Prohibition party was an attempt at both political and partisan action.

The experience of the Prohibition party demonstrated the fact that even friends of Prohibition and Christian voters who are favorable to Prohibition refuse nevertheless to leave the political party with which they are affiliated and vote for a new party, although that party may advocate the thing in which they believe. This fact undoubtedly had its effect upon the men who later saw the possibilities and opportunities for a great non-partisan political movement which would enable men to remain in their own political parties and yet give political expression to their Prohibition sentiments.

The founders of the Prohibition party were not politicians; they were crusaders. They did not draw the line of distinction between principle and policy as applied to party government in the United States. Partyism, in the very nature of the case, is opportunism. Principle is something different. Great fundamental principles do not originate and are not developed in political party councils. They originate outside such councils and through the process of agitation and education they gradually grow into what becomes so acceptable to the public that parties finally declare for them in order to attract the many rather than the few.

Political parties are of many ideas; champion many causes, selected with a view to those most likely to attract the largest number of voters. The Prohibition party, on the other hand, was in reality a movement with one idea. Many of the national platforms of the Prohibition party committed it to numerous propositions other than Prohibition, but the one thing which counted with those who voted the ticket and the one policy of the platform which was the keystone of the arch, was Prohibition.

Political parties are. not consistent; they change front, often standing openly for that which they had previously disavowed. The Prohibition party has been consistent. The one principle for which it stood in 1869 has been upon its banners in every campaign. The Prohibition party was born with one idea. It was launched for one purpose. It was committed to one great fundamental principle. Its leaders never knew the meaning of policy, prudence, or diplomacy. It never changed its fundamental platform. For more than fifty years it held the banner of Prohibition in every national election, reminding friend and foe alike that whatever might be its fate as a party, the liquor problem would never be settled until it was settled by Prohibition.

The Prohibition party was a demand to right a great wrong by political revolution rather than by political evolution. Strictly speaking, the Prohibition party was a political party in name only. It was not a party; it was a crusade.

THE WOMAN'S CHRISTIAN TEMPERANCE UNION

The Woman's Crusade of 1873 and the organization

of the Woman's Christian Temperance Union in 1874 marked the entrance into the active movement for temperance reform of the women of America. Just twenty years before the Woman's Crusade, at the great temperance convention in New York city, women had been practically read out of the Prohibition movement. The action of the Independent Order of Good Templars, however, which opened its doors to women as well as men, similar action on the part of the Sons of Temperance and other temperance organizations as well as the general tendency of the times, gradually developed the demand for the assistance of women in the fight against the liquor traffic which up to 1873 had not proved so successful that the man-controlled movements prior to that time could boast of any particular monopoly of successful operations.

The Woman's Crusade has been generally recognized as having been started in Hillsboro, Ohio, on December 24, 1873. It was the direct result of a meeting held in Hillsboro and addressed by Dr. Dio Lewis on the night of December 23. Doctor Lewis, then on the lecture platform, had spoken in Hillsboro the night before and had been persuaded to stay for a second address in which he told of the unsuccessful effort of his mother and some of her friends to get rid of the saloon in their community by prayer and visitation. His story appealed to the women of Hillsboro who decided to attempt such a movement, and the following day saw the Christian women of that village, headed by Mother Thompson, begin what was destined to sweep the country as a mighty moral crusade, and out of which was to spring in the following year the Woman's Christian Temperance Union.

On the evening of December 14, just nine days before Doctor Lewis' remarkable meeting in Hillsboro, he had made a similar appeal at Fredonia, New York, with the result that a hundred women of that city, under the leadership of Mrs. Barker, began a praying crusade to close the saloons. A similar movement was also started in Jamestown, New York, after an address by Doctor Lewis on December 17.

The principal point of difference between these efforts in New York and the one at Hillsboro, Ohio, was that the initial New York crusade did not succeed in closing the saloons in Fredonia and Jamestown, while the Hillsboro movement did succeed in a most remarkable manner.

The story of the crusade as it rapidly spread into other towns and cities in Ohio and later into the cities and towns of other states is one of the most interesting and inspiring stories of all reform history, while the history of the great women's organization of which the Crusade was the forerunner reads like a book of chapters from the Acts of the Apostles.

From the time of the birth of the Woman's Christian Temperance Union at the convention in Cleveland in 1874 until the presidential campaign of 1880, the society was a non-partisan organization. There had been no connection whatsoever between the Union and the Prohibition party. The women, however, had been led to believe that the presidential candidate on the Republican ticket in 1880, James A. Garfield, was a true friend of the temperance cause. After the election and inauguration, however, Miss Willard called upon the President at the White House. The reception which Miss Willard received on that occasion led her to believe that neither the President nor the party which he represented were vitally interested in the Prohibition movement. Consequently, upon her return to Chicago she set about the work of organizing a new political party, and in 1881 with the coöperation of others launched the "Home Protection Party," which was later merged into the National Prohibition party.

In 1883, largely as a result of the efforts of Miss Willard, who had become national president in 1879, the Woman's Christian Temperance Union in its annual convention in Detroit passed the following resolution: "Resolved, That we lend our influence to that party, by whatever name called, which shall furnish the best embodiment of Prohibition principles and will most surely protect our homes. Resolved, That effort be made to secure in each state and territory, nonpartisan Prohibition conventions of men and women before the party nominating conventions of 1884 are held. At such conventions, efforts shall be made to unite electors in declarations that they will vote with no party that has not Prohibition in its platform. These conventions shall adjourn to meet after the last nominating convention has been held."

This resolution was presented to the four party conventions in 1884, but the appeal was rejected in all cases except that of the National Prohibition party which met at Pittsburgh and in which the resolution was cordially received and promptly adopted. At the national convention of the Woman's Christian Temperance Union which met in St. Louis later in the year

1884, the Union endorsed and pledged itself to support the Prohibition party, by a vote of 195 to 48.

Opposition to committing the Woman's Christian Temperance Union to partisan activity was led by Mrs. J. Ellen Foster, the president of the Iowa State Woman's Christian Temperance Union, a close personal friend of Miss Willard, and one of the strongest leaders in the national organization. In the national convention of the Union at Philadelphia in 1885 the party resolution was adopted by a vote of 245 to 30, Mrs. Foster presenting at the time a protest signed by herself and 26 other members of the organization. The vote on a similar resolution at the Minneapolis convention in 1886 was 241 to 42, at which time the Union passed a by-law providing that thereafter in national conventions the vote on any resolution as to the attitude of the Woman's Christian Temperance Union toward political parties should be decided without discussion. This action was rescinded two years later.

Mrs. Foster offered a resolution at the Nashville convention declaring that the Woman's Christian Temperance Union is non-sectarian in religious matters and non-partisan in political work, but the resolution was defeated. In the campaign of 1888 Mrs. Foster and the representatives of the so-called "Anti-Saloon Association" requested the Republican party to insert a temperance plank in its national platform, with the result that the following plank was adopted: "Resolved, That the first concern of all good government is the virtue and sobriety of the people and the purity of the home. The Republican party cordially sympathizes with all wise and well-directed efforts for the promotion of temperance and morality." In this campaign Mrs. Foster became the chairman of the Woman's National Republican committee.

Mrs. Foster with several other women of the Iowa delegation walked out of the convention of the Woman's Christian Temperance Union in 1889 and organized, the following year, the Non-Partisan Woman's Christian Temperance Union, which for many years was conducted as a separate society, but which after the death of Mrs. Foster was reunited with the mother organization. From 1884 until after the death of Miss Willard, the Woman's Christian Temperance Union continued to be a partisan organization, throwing its influence and support in every possible way to the Prohibition party.

In 1901 when the national convention of the Union met at Fort Worth, Texas, a resolution expressing sympathy and coöperation with the Prohibition party aroused such opposition that it was finally withdrawn and the following resolution substituted: "We desire to express gratitude to the men who at the ballot box represent the principles we are working to see incorporated in the government." This resolution was adopted. From that time forward the activities of the Woman's Christian Temperance Union as an organization were recognized generally as being of a non-partisan character.

The Woman's Christian Temperance Union was one of the most remarkable temperance organizations of the century. Its contribution to the temperance reform can never be fully estimated. The Woman's Christian Temperance Union pioneered the movement for equal suffrage which was destined not only to play a great part in numerous state and local Prohibition campaigns, but which in its final consummation as a part of the Federal Constitution so soon after the success of the National Prohibition movement was destined to insure the permanency of that movement, since with the women of the nation enfranchised the repeal of the Eighteenth Amendment to the Constitution is next to impossible. The Woman's Christian Temperance Union was the real pioneer of the general movement that in less than half a century has shown such remarkable results in the effort to purify the politics of the nation. It enlisted the Christian women of the nation in moral warfare not only against the saloon, but against impurity and corruption in politics by bringing to bear an organized public sentiment that compelled action.

The Woman's Christian Temperance Union through the leadership of Mrs. Mary H. Hunt was largely responsible for securing scientific temperance instruction in the public schools in most of the states between 1882 and 1888, which resulted in bringing up a generation of men as well as women schooled in the knowledge of the evil effects of alcohol upon the human body and mind. But for this remarkable achievement, the Prohibition victories of the first two decades of the twentieth century would have been practically impossible.

The organization of the Woman's Christian Temperance Union demonstrated for the first time in history the possibilities of organized Christian womanhood in a crusade in behalf of moral reform. Aside from the church itself, of which it was the child, the

Woman's Christian Temperance Union without question, in most respects, proved to be one of the greatest moral forces in social reform that the world has ever seen.

THE SECOND STATE PROHIBITION WAVE

Between the years 1880 and 1890 what has been known as the second great state-wide Prohibition wave swept the country. During this eventful period not so many states adopted Prohibition as had done so in the first state-wide Prohibition movement of the fifties, yet it is safe to say that more states were actively involved in the movement and more state legislative bodies were called upon to vote directly upon the Prohibition question than during the former period. Moreover, a larger number of state legislatures submitted the question of Prohibition in the form of state constitutional amendments and the question was voted on directly by the people in more states than during any similar period in the nation's history. The question, in fact, was a very prominent one in the legislative sessions of three-fourths of the states and territories.

The state-wide Prohibition movement of the eighties started in the state of Kansas, the legislature submitting the question in 1879 and the people adopting the amendment in the fall election of 1880. The legislature of Iowa, by favorable action in the two successive sessions of 1880 and 1882 submitted a prohibitory amendment to a vote of the people. The amendment was adopted only to be declared unconstitutional by the courts. A similar amendment submitted to a vote of the people in North Carolina in 1881 was rejected at the polls by a substantial majority.

A resolution to submit a prohibitory amendment was defeated in the Ohio legislature in 1882 but was passed in 1883 and the same was submitted to the voters of the state during the same year along with another constitutional amendment providing for license, the no-license provision of the state constitution adopted in 1851 still being in force. Accordingly at the general election in Ohio in the fall of 1883 the people had an opportunity to express themselves both ways, with the result that the license amendment was lost by almost 100,000 majority, while the prohibitory amendment received 323,189 votes in favor and 240,975 against its adoption. While on the face of the returns the prohibitory amendment had more than 82,000 majority in its favor it failed of enactment by virtue of the provision which required a majority of all votes cast at the election.

The Maine legislature submitted a prohibitory amendment to the people in 1883. The vote was taken in 1884 with the result that the amendment was adopted and has remained in the constitution of that state to the present time. Rhode Island, moreover, again adopted constitutional Prohibition in 1886. The question, however, was submitted by the legislature again in 1889 with the result that the amendment was repealed by vote of the people.

An effort to secure a prohibitory amendment resolution in the legislature of Michigan in 1881 failed of the necessary two-thirds vote although the vote in the House was 63 to 33 and the vote in the Senate 21 to 10. A similar resolution was defeated in 1883, but the legislature of 1887 submitted the amendment which, however, was rejected by the people at the polls.

A prohibitory amendment resolution passed the lower house of the Texas legislature in 1881, but failed to pass the Senate. A similar resolution was defeated in 1883 but was successful in the legislature of 1887. When the question came up for ratification by the people at the polls, however, the amendment was defeated by a large majority. In the state of Pennsylvania the lower house of the legislature voted to submit an amendment in 1881. Failure in the Senate, however, delayed submission until 1889, when the amendment went to the people who in turn defeated it by a majority of more than 188,000 votes.

Submission of an amendment failed for lack of four votes in the West Virginia legislature in 1881. In 1883 a similar resolution passed the House but was defeated in the Senate. The legislature of 1888 took favorable action but the amendment was defeated by vote of the people.

A prohibitory amendment resolution passed the Arkansas House of Representatives in 1881 but met defeat in the Senate. The Indiana legislature of 1882 voted to submit the question, but the necessary action of the succeeding legislature of 1883 was not completed on account of the failure of the measure to pass the Senate after it had been adopted by the House.

The question was up in the Illinois legislature in 1882 and a resolution to submit a prohibitory amendment passed the lower house but failed of passage in the Senate. The same thing happened in Missouri in 1882 and again in 1883. A similar fate, moreover, befell a similar resolution in the New Jersey legislature in 1883.

The legislative contests for submission in the states of Wisconsin in 1881, in Minnesota in 1883, and in Vermont in 1883, were not successful, the amendment resolution in each case being defeated. In the state of Nebraska, however, the submission resolution, though defeated in 1882 and 1883, was finally successful in 1889, but the amendment was rejected by the people at the polls.

The legislature of Oregon by favorable action in the sessions of 1885 and 1887 submitted an amendment which was rejected by the people in the fall of 1887. A similar situation was presented in the state of Tennessee where the legislature of 1884 and 1886 voted for submission and the people rejected the amendment when it came to a vote in 1887.

Vermont and New Hampshire both continued under statutory Prohibition during this entire period. The Vermont law was strengthened in 1881. A prohibitory amendment submitted in New Hampshire in 1889 was rejected by vote of the people. North Dakota and South Dakota both adopted constitutional Prohibition in 1889, while the people of the state of Washington rejected a constitutional provision the same year.

A very interesting situation developed in New York state, the legislatures of 1888 and 1890 having voted to submit a prohibitory amendment which, however, was never submitted because the Attorney General of the state ruled that a Prohibition bill would need to be submitted to the people and the proposed prohibitory bill failed to pass the legislature.

The Connecticut legislature in 1880 voted for submission, but the measure failed of the necessary favorable action in the session of 1882 for lack of a

majority in the Senate. A similar resolution passed
the legislature of Massachusetts in 1887 and again in
1889, after having failed in 1881. The amendment,
however, was lost at the polls, the people casting a
large majority against its adoption. The territory of
Alaska was placed under Prohibition in 1884 by
President Grover Cleveland.

As a result of the campaigns for Prohibition during
the decade, only six states emerged at the end of the
period with Prohibition laws or constitutional Prohibition amendments. These states were Maine, Kansas,
North Dakota, South Dakota, Vermont and New
Hampshire. Prohibition in Iowa had not been repealed, but it had been practically nullified in about
one-third of the counties of the state by the so-called
"Mulct Law." It is an interesting coincidence that at
the close of this period, after the state-wide Prohibition wave of the eighties, there was the same number
of Prohibition states as there was at the close of the
period which witnessed the first Prohibition wave.
Three of these stood the test of both periods. They
were Maine, New Hampshire and Vermont. Kansas,
North Dakota and South Dakota took the place of the
three that went back to license during the period beginning 1869.

It is also interesting to note that three of this latter
list of Prohibition states repealed Prohibition within
slightly more than a decade after the close of the
period. South Dakota enacted a local option feature
patterned after the Iowa "Mulct Law" in 1897; Vermont went back to local option in 1902 and New
Hampshire followed Vermont in 1903. The states of
Maine, Kansas and North Dakota, however, stood

firm until National Prohibition went into effect in 1920.

The failure of Prohibition in three-fourths of the states in which the state-wide fights took place during the decade following the accomplishment of the Prohibition victory in Kansas, was due to many causes. The Woman's Christian Temperance Union, the Prohibition party, the National Temperance Society, the Good Templars, and other active temperance agencies of the period, had created a remarkable sentiment favorable to Prohibition. At no time perhaps in the history of the movement had the agitation of the liquor question reached such a high pitch as at the very time when these state-wide contests were taking place. That party prejudice which was so dominant during the entire period, divided the temperance forces and prevented the full coöperation of those favorable to prohibitory legislation, goes without saying. Moreover, the lack of organization at the polls to see that the Prohibition vote reached the ballot box and that the Prohibition count was registered in each precinct after the ballots had been cast, must also be taken into account as an important factor in accounting for the failure of Prohibition at the polls in so many states. Evidences later bore out the theory of the friends of Prohibition at the time that wholesale fraud in city after city and state after state was responsible for counting out the prohibitory amendments in many states.

The most important factor, however, was that while there was plenty of organized activity in agitational and educational work there was no organized movement through which the temperance forces could work together in state-wide campaigns and at the polls.

The Prohibition wave of the eighties is accounted for largely by reason of the activity in politics of the growing liquor interests and the arrogant dictation by those interests in state and local governments. The Prohibition wave of the eighties in fact may be said to have been a great revolt against liquor domination in politics, but when it came to handling the Prohibition campaigns, polling the vote and seeing that it was properly counted, there was no organized force on the Prohibition side sufficient to match the political liquor machines which through all these campaigns were in good running order.

While the Prohibition party and the Woman's Christian Temperance Union held the center of the stage during most of this period, other temperance organizations rendered valuable assistance in connection with the campaign of education which characterized the years between 1869 and 1893. The National Temperance Society and Publication House, established in New York in 1865, was a non-partisan organization. Its efforts, however, were not along political lines so much as they were along lines of education through the distribution of literature, the effort to secure scientific temperance instruction in the public schools, the publication of temperance lesson books, and the effort to secure systematic temperance instruction through the Sunday School Lesson Committee. The records of the Society show that during this period it succeeded in distributing throughout the country almost one million dollars' worth of temperance literature in the form of books, pamphlets, leaflets and tracts. The effort of the National Temperance Society, moreover, to secure at the hands of

Congress a Commission of Inquiry was one of the interesting contests of the period. Five times this measure was passed by the United States Senate but failed to come to a vote at any time in the House of Representatives.

The Good Templar order, after its organization in 1851, gradually grew in influence and numbers until it was estimated near the close of this period that it had succeeded in pledging more than two million persons to total abstinence.

The Catholic Total Abstinence Union which was organized in 1872 showed a very remarkable increase in numbers and influence during the 20 years immediately following its birth. This society helped to crystallize much of what had been done by Father Mathew and it has continued to do a large work in the way of organizing the temperance sentiment of the Catholic Church.

The Francis Murphy pledge-signing movement of the seventies, the National League for the Suppression of the Liquor Traffic, the Sons of Temperance, as well as the Templars of Honor and Temperance, the numerous "Cold Water Armies" and the Bands of Hope, all played a helpful and important part in the general temperance movement of the period.

Mrs. Lucy Webb Hayes, moreover, as the "First Lady of the Land" during part of this period, made an important contribution to the temperance movement by banishing intoxicating liquors from the White House in 1878 and keeping them from the White House table during the four years of the Hayes administration.

Among the beacon lights of this period, each of

whom played no mean part in the struggle and many of whom were the great personalities around which the movements of the period centered, are the names of Neal Dow, Frances E. Willard, Francis Murphy, Mother Thompson, Mother Stewart, Lucy Webb Hayes, Anna Shaw, Mary A. Livermore, Annie Wittenmeyer, Mary T. Lathrop, Mary C. Leavitt, Ellen M. Foster, John P. St. John, Sam Jones, Senator William H. Blair, Henry A. Reynolds, Dr. Dio Lewis, H. K. Carroll, W. E. Dodge, John B. Finch, Clinton B. Fisk, John Russell, Gideon T. Stewart, and many others.

The following chronology covers the principal items of interest in connection with the reform movement of the period.

CHRONOLOGY OF THE TEMPERANCE REFORM FOR THE PERIOD 1869–1893

1869

The National Temperance Convention, held at Chicago, Ill., is attended by more than 500 delegates; the Prohibition party is organized September 1-2.

Massachusetts enacts a state prohibitory law.

Vermont enacts a civil damage liquor act.

The General Assembly of the Presbyterian Church recommends total abstinence.

The New York law is so amended as to give license to ale and beer sellers who do not keep hotels.

The National Grand Lodge of the Independent Order of Good Templars advocates the calling of a convention "at an early day" for the formation of a political party committed to the Prohibition of the liquor traffic.

By a constitutional amendment the Legislature of Texas is given the power to prohibit the sale of liquor in the immediate vicinity of any college or seminary of learning if not at the Capital or at the county seat.

The state Prohibition party of Ohio is organized at Mansfield, Ohio, on July 24. The adherents of the new party cast 679 votes in the fall election.

1870

The Legislature of Maine passes a bill to increase the effectiveness of the prohibitory law.

Ohio passes the Adair law, making the liquor seller and owners of premises jointly responsible for injury caused by liquor.

The American Association for the Cure of Inebriates is organized.

The Royal Templars of Temperance is organized at Buffalo, N. Y.

The Minnesota Legislature passes a local option law.

The Prohibition party receives 3,712 votes in Illinois, 8,692 in Massachusetts, 2,170 in Michigan, 1,167 in New Hampshire, 1,459 in New York, and 2,812 in Ohio.

New York does away with the county excise boards, and excise commissioners in each city, town and village are granted the authority to grant liquor licenses.

P. De Marmon, M. D., of King's Bridge, N. Y.,

before the New York Medical Association on February 18, says, "Within a year I have seen three cases of poison by alcohol in children—that having drunk large quantities of whisky, two of them died."

The prohibitory law of Massachusetts is so amended as to exclude from its operation ale, porter and beer.

The Reformed Dutch Church strongly urges total abstinence.

Iowa passes a mongrel local option law, which is declared unconstitutional by the State Supreme Court.

The New Hampshire prohibitory law is strengthened by the Legislature.

The Legislature of Alabama enacts seventeen local Prohibition laws.

Juvenile societies under the name of "Cold Water Templars" are organized by the Independent Order of Good Templars.

The National Temperance Society publishes the temperance catechism and the catechism on alcohol.

President Grant issues an order forbidding the importation of distilled spirits into Alaska.

Standing upon the proposition for laboring "unceasingly for the promotion of the cause of temperance—morally, socially, religiously and politically," the Royal Templars of Temperance establish the first supreme council February 16.

1871

Francis Murphy delivers his first temperance sermon.

The United Friends of Temperance organize in Nashville, Tenn.

The Prohibition party vote in the several states is as follows: Massachusetts, 6,598; New Hampshire, 314; New York, 1,820; Ohio, 4,084; and Pennsylvania, 3,186—a total of 16,002.

A law is passed prohibiting the sale of intoxicating liquors near the line of the Northern Pacific Railroad during the construction thereof.

Several townships in New Jersey are granted local option by special acts of the Legislature.

The General Synod of the Lutheran Church adopts resolutions favoring thorough temperance education from the platform, press and pulpit, and stands for "judicious legislation" on the liquor question.

The Indiana Yearly Meeting of Friends appoints a standing committee on temperance.

A great temperance wave begins to sweep over the country. Pledges are signed by tens of thousands.

The Catholic temperance societies of Connecticut are organized into one union.

The General Assembly of the United Presbyterian Church strongly urges renewed action against the growing evil of intemperance.

1872

Temperance Republicans throughout the country resent the resolution passed in the National Republican platform declaring for personal liberty.

The Prohibition party convention in session at Columbus, Ohio, nominates James Black of Pennsylvania for President and John Russell of Michigan for Vice President.   The total vote for the Prohibition party is 5,607.

New York passes a local option law for towns only, but the measure is vetoed by the Governor.

Thirty-two local Prohibition acts are passed by the Legislature of Alabama, prohibiting the sale of liquor within certain distances from towns, churches, schools and factories.

The Legislature of Iowa restricts the sale of liquors and limits the number of licenses.

The Legislature of Maine amends the prohibitory law so as to forbid the sale of liquor and wine made from home-grown fruits.

The National Conference of the Unitarian Church declares that "it is a duty to do everything possible to arrest and destroy this mighty foe of civilization" (the liquor traffic).

A bill providing for a commission of inquiry on the liquor question is presented and considered by the Forty-second Congress.

Wisconsin enacts a license law with a civil damage provision.

The General Conference of the Methodist Episcopal Church recommends the use of unfermented wine at the sacrament and declares for Prohibition.

The Prohibition law of Connecticut is repealed by the enactment of a license law.

The Western Indiana yearly meeting appoints a special committee on temperance.

Pennsylvania enacts a county local option law under which 67 counties later vote for Prohibition.

The Indiana Yearly Meeting of Friends petitions the Legislature to enact Prohibition laws.

The Gardner Reform Club is formed in Gardner, Maine, on January 22.

The Catholic Total Abstinence Union of America is formed on February 22 at the national convention called to meet in Baltimore, Md.   One hundred and twenty-five societies are represented in this first convention.

The second national convention of the Catholic Total Abstinence Union is held in Cleveland, Ohio, October 10.

The Franklin Home for inebriates is opened in Philadelphia.

The National Temperance Society petitions Congress for Prohibition in the District of Columbia and the territories.

By the Act of Congress on December 24, collectors of internal revenue are required to keep for public inspection a list of those who pay special taxes within their respective districts.

The chief of police of Boston in his annual report says that "the 'beer drunk' is the worst drunk of all."

1873

Francis Murphy of Maine inaugurates the Blue Ribbon temperance movement.

Mississippi enacts a local option law.

Alabama enacts, by special legislation, local option law provisions for many towns in the state.

The Tennessee Legislature passes a strong local option law by a large majority in both houses, but the measure is vetoed by the Governor.

Indiana passes the Baxter license law.

The Maine law is strengthened.

The Georgia Legislature passes five local liquor laws affecting six counties and three other places.

The New York Legislature passes the landlord and tenant bill and a civil damage bill for the regulation of the liquor trade.

Kentucky adopts a local option law, with the result that of 259 towns ordering elections 207 vote against license.

The Alabama Legislature enacts 41 local Prohibition measures.

The National Temperance Convention meets at Saratoga, N. Y.

The Maryland Legislature, by special act, grants local option to five counties and a number of districts in other counties.

The Prohibition law of Massachusetts is repealed.

North Carolina enacts a local option law.

The Minnesota Legislature enacts a law which provides for a special tax on saloonkeepers, the money realized from the tax to be applied toward a fund for the erection of an inebriate asylum at Rochester.

Several additional towns in New Jersey secure local option by special acts of the Legislature.

On December 14, Dr. Dio Lewis speaks in Fredonia, N. Y., and tells how his mother and her friends prayed for the liquor dealers who were destroying their homes. As a result 100 women under the leadership of Mrs. Judge Barker start a praying crusade to close the saloons. The movement, however, is not successful.

On December 17 a similar crusade is inaugurated

in Jamestown, N. Y., but the effort fails to secure the closing of the saloons.

On the evening of December 22 Dr. Dio Lewis speaks at Music Hall in Hillsboro, Ohio. On December 23 Dr. Lewis speaks again in Hillsboro on intemperance, relating how women in eastern states attempted to close saloons by visitation. The audience takes a vote to try the plan. Seventy-five women thus inspired to action start the Woman's Crusade on the following day which results in the closing of the saloons. The movement rapidly spreads.

The American Synod of the Moravian Church opposes "all traffic in intoxicating drinks and the use as a beverage of hard cider, beer, ale, whisky, wine, brandy, gin, rum, patent bitters, etc."

The New York Legislature re-enacts the old local option law of 1846, but the measure is vetoed by Governor Dix.

The General Council of the Reformed Episcopal Church resolves that "it marks with pleasure the progress of the temperance revival throughout the country."

Governor Dix of New York, in his message to the Legislature, calls attention to the alarming increase of murders and says that they are traceable to the "drinking saloons."

The Attorney General of the United States renders an opinion to the effect that Alaska is to be regarded as Indian country and that no spirituous liquors or wines may be introduced therein without an order from the War Department.

The Sundry Civil Appropriation Act in Congress of March 3 forbids the sale of spirits or wine in Alaska and prohibits the erection of distilleries therein. Jurisdiction in liquor cases is conferred upon the United States courts.

The third national convention of the Catholic Total Abstinence Union is held in New York City on October 8.

The National Temperance Society begins agitation for a commission of inquiry on the liquor problem.

1874

The Woman's Crusade against the saloons of southern Ohio continues with remarkable success.

The Legislature of Rhode Island passes a law prohibiting the sale of intoxicating beverages and a constabulary act for its enforcement.

Georgia prohibits the liquor traffic in 40 counties unless two-thirds of the property-holders agree thereto in writing. At the same session the Legislature extends local option to 13 other counties and 25 other smaller localities.

Oregon prohibits the sale of liquor unless a majority of the legal voters shall petition therefor.

Christian women at Chautauqua, N. Y., decide to call a national convention of temperance women, which convention meets on November 17 in Cleveland, Ohio, at which convention the Woman's Christian Temperance Union is organized on November 19.

The Legislature of California enacts a local

option law for townships and incorporated cities, but it is declared unconstitutional by the courts.

A constitutional amendment in favor of license in the state of Ohio is voted down by 6,286 majority.

The North Carolina Legislature strengthens its local option law.

A whisky ring composed of distillers and government officials assumes national proportions, robbing the government and disgracing the administration.

The Bangor Reform Club for reformed drinking men is organized at Bangor, Maine, by Dr. Henry A. Reynolds and adopts a red ribbon as its badge.

The old prohibitory law of Indiana, which has never been operative on account of conflicting court opinion, is repealed by the enactment of a license law.

Arkansas enacts a local option law which applies to townships, incorporated towns and city wards.

The Women Crusaders at Washington C. H., Ohio, on the coldest day of the winter, locked out of a saloon they attempted to enter, stand all day on the street holding religious services. The next day they build a "tabernacle" in the street in front of the saloon and continue their "watching and praying." Before night the sheriff closes the saloon.

State organizations of the W. C. T. U. are formed in Maine, New York, New Jersey, Pennsylvania, Maryland, Ohio, Indiana, Illinois, Michigan, Wisconsin, Iowa and Nebraska.

Kentucky enacts a general local option law.

The Society of Friends, although standing for temperance from the beginning (about 1660), appoints a committee to "put forth earnest efforts to suppress the traffic in intoxicating drinks."

By virtue of the operation of the local option law in Pennsylvania the number of breweries is reduced from 500 to 346 in two years.

New York State makes the excise boards in towns elective.

Alabama enacts seventy local Prohibition measures, the areas affected being two to twelve miles in diameter.

The New England Yearly Meeting of Friends appoints a temperance committee to help fight the evils of intemperance.

The Prohibition law of Hawaii, promulgated by the native rulers, is repealed and free reign given to the liquor and gambling interests, under the rulership of King Kalekaua.

The War Department issues regulations under which intoxicants may be introduced into Alaska, for certain purposes, but these privileges are grossly abused and later withdrawn.

I. D. Hastings of Wisconsin is sent by the Independent Order of Good Templars to visit the Sandwich Islands, Australia and New Zealand in the interest of the Prohibition movement.

The fourth national convention of the Catholic Total Abstinence Union is held in Chicago on October 7.

The first statistical study of inebriates is made at the Binghamton, N. Y., asylum.

The Legislature of Alabama enacts a regular local option law authorizing the Probate Judges of seventeen counties to grant local option privileges upon petition of any freeholder, the same to apply to territory within certain distances of any place within the said counties.

The Seventh-Day Baptist convention declares for the entire suppression of the use of intoxicating liquors.

The National Conference of the Unitarian Church declares strongly against the liquor traffic.

The United States Senate by a vote of 26 to 21 passes a bill providing for a commission of inquiry on the liquor traffic.

Forty thousand sign the pledge in Pittsburgh under Francis Murphy.

Dr. James Edmunds in a lecture in New York declares "Alcohol is in no sense a food, but a poison."

The Woman's State Temperance Alliance is formed in Wisconsin.

Minnesota enacts a high license law.

1875

The whisky frauds in Western States are exposed, showing a loss to the government by corruption of $1,650,000.

The second Woman's National Temperance Convention meets in Cleveland, Ohio.

The Rhode Island Legislature repeals the constabulary prohibitory law and passes an act of regulation.

The Constitution of the State of Texas is changed so as to guarantee local option.

The National Temperance Society convention meets in Chicago.

Masachusetts enacts a license law which includes a local option provision.

The Michigan prohibitory law is repealed.

Tennessee prohibits liquor licensed places "within four miles of any chartered academy," further providing that any common or district school may be chartered as an academy. The law does not apply to chartered cities or chartered villages.

State organizations of the W. C. T. U. are formed in Vermont, Massachusetts, Rhode Island and Connecticut.

The first "Red Ribbon" Reform Club is organized in Massachusetts at the city of Salem, September 19.

The eighth convention of the National Temperance Society is held in June at Chicago.

Alabama adds 7,000 members to the I. O. G. T. in two years.

The local option law of Pennsylvania is repealed, license and regulation taking its place.

The official organ of the Woman's Christian Temperance Union is established under the name of "The Christian Temperance Union." Mrs. Jennie F. Willard of Chicago is the editor.

An amendment to the constitution of the Independent Order of Good Templars is adopted which gives to colored people the right to have subordinate and grand lodges of their own.

The fifth national convention of the Catholic Total Abstinence Union is held in Cincinnati, Ohio, on October 6.

The National Temperance Society begins the publication of Independent Temperance Lesson Leaves.

Daniel H. Pratt, Commissioner of Internal Revenue, states that the government has been robbed of $4,000,000 through the connivance of officials.

Congress places in the hands of the President, instead of the Secretary of War, the power to make and publish regulations for the government of the army in accordance with existing laws.

The eighth National Temperance Convention is held at Chicago, June 3, and Mr. A. Powell, secretary of the National Temperance Society, offers a resolution calling for a national prohibitory amendment. In November the board of managers of the society send a memorial to Congress petitioning for such an amendment to the Federal Constitution.

1876

General O. E. Babcock, private secretary to President Grant, is tried and acquitted of complicity in the whisky frauds.

The Vermont Legislature enacts a law providing for the abatement of law violating saloons as nuisances.

The second national convention of the Prohibition party is held in Cleveland, Ohio, and nominates Clay Green Smith of Kentucky for President and Gideon T. Stewart of Ohio for Vice President. In the election 9,737 votes are recorded from 18 states.

The Woman's Christian Temperance Union holds its annual convention at Newark, N. J.

An investigation in the city of Philadelphia reveals the fact that intoxicating liquors are sold at 8,034 places in the city and that of the 8,034 liquor sellers there are 2 Chinamen, 18 Italians, 140 Spaniards, 160 Welshmen, 205 white Americans, 265 Negroes, 285 French, 497 Scotch, 568 English, 2,179 Germans, 304 Irish, and 672 whose nationality is unknown.

Hon. Henry W. Blair, member of Congress from New Hampshire, on December 27 presents in the National House of Representatives a bill providing for the submission to the states of a prohibitory amendment to the Federal Constitution, and makes a speech supporting the resolution.

About 70 reform clubs are reported to be in existence in the state of Massachusetts.

A state organization of the W. C. T. U. is formed in New Hampshire.

The United States Senate by a vote of 73 to 20 again passes a bill providing for a commission of inquiry.

Mississippi repeals a proviso which requires the signatures of a majority of the women of a given district before licenses can be granted.

By a majority of 8,078 in a total vote of 113,200, the people of Michigan repeal the no-license constitutional provision.

At Philadelphia the International Medical Congress, which is the highest medical body in the world, holds its sessions and takes a strong position against alcohol as a food.

A woman's International Temperance convention is held in Philadelphia, June 12-14.

The name of the official organ of the Woman's Christian Temperance Union is changed from "The Christian Temperance Union" to "Our Union."

The Right Worthy Grand Lodge of the Independent Order of Good Templars is held in May at Louisville, Ky. The representatives from Great Britain, Nova Scotia, Newfoundland, two lodges from Indiana, one from Ohio and one from Iowa secede from the order and form another organization, because of the change in the constitution of the order admitting negroes to membership.

The sixth national convention of the Catholic Total Abstinence Union is held in Philadelphia on July 4. A delegation of total abstaining Indians take part in the parade.

The National Temperance Society suffers from a falling off of financial support.

Representatives of nine grand sections of the Cadets of Temperance meet June 16 in Independence Hall, Philadelphia, and effect another national organization, but it soon disbands.

The Congressional Temperance Society, after some years of lack of interest, is rejuvenated.

1877

The Temperance Society of the Blue Cross is organized.

The Citizens' League of Chicago is organized for the purpose of saving young men from intemperance. This league is organized as a result of the part played by drink in the railroad riots in Chicago.

The national convention of the Woman's Christion Temperance Union is held at Chicago.

A national conference of the Prohibition party is held in New York City.

In state elections Iowa casts 10,545 Prohibition party votes, while Massachusetts casts 16,354.

Maine declares wine and cider intoxicants when used for tippling purposes and prohibits all intoxicating liquors except cider, thus closing all the breweries in the state.

The "Four Mile Law" of Tennesse is enacted.

The state of Virginia levies a tax of 2½ cents on each drink of ardent spirits and a half cent on each drink of beer, a bell punch register being provided for registering all drinks.

Similar laws are enacted in Texas and Louisiana, but fail to accomplish their purpose in all three instances.

The General Conference of the United Brethren Church strongly declares for total abstinence, Prohibition and the electing of temperance men to office.

The General Council of the Reformed Episcopal Church declares its sympathy with the temperance movement.

The General Assembly of the United Presbyterian Church stands for "entire Prohibition" of the liquor traffic by the state.

A constitutional prohibitory amendment to the State Constitution of Michigan is defeated at the polls by a vote of 178,636 for and 184,251 against.

Two hundred thousand in Michigan sign the temperance pledge during the year.

The license law of New York is amended and made more stringent.

The National Temperance Society memorializes the International Sunday School committee requesting quarterly temperance lessons.

The "Law and Order Movement" originates in Chicago.

A local option bill for towns and cities passes the Massachusetts Legislature, but is vetoed by Governor A. H. Rice.

A state organization of the W. C. T. U. is formed in Minnesota.

The General Synod of the Reformed Dutch Church appoints a special committee on temperance.

The Royal Templars of Temperance is organized.

The New Hampshire prohibitory law is strengthened and extended.

Justice Bradley of the United States Supreme Court, in rendering the decision in the case of Beer Company vs. Massachusetts, states: "If the public safety or the public morals require the discontinuance of the manufacturing or traffic, the hand of the Legislature can not be stayed from providing for its discontinuance by the incidental inconvenience which individuals or corporations may suffer. All rights are held subject to the police power of the state."

Mrs. Rutherford B. Hayes, wife of President Hayes, banishes intoxicating liquors from the White House at Washington.

The Woman's Christian Temperance Union adopts a report calling for temperance lessons in the Sunday Schools, and appoints a committee to urge the introduction of temperance teaching in the schools and colleges.

The seventh national convention of the Catholic Total Abstinence Union is held at Buffalo, N. Y., on August 8.

The Society for the Prevention of Crime, largely aimed at the liquor traffic, is organized by Rev. Dr. Howard Crosby in the city of New York in the month of March.

The National Conference of the Unitarian Church

urges greater activity in fighting the beverage liquor traffic.

"The Sunday School Temperance Army" is organized at Philadelphia by Rev. George Sigler, of the Church of God.

Under a new basis of organization, on February 3, Central Council No. 1 of the Royal Templars of Temperance is instituted with ten members. Twenty councils in the state of New York and one in Pennsylvania are reported at the end of the year.

1878

As a result of the operation of local prohibitory laws 30 counties in Georgia are under Prohibition.

The General Assembly of the Cumberland Presbyterian Church strongly declares for temperance reform and against the granting of liquor licenses.

The United States Senate by a vote of 29 to 19 passes for the third time a bill providing for a commission of inquiry on the liquor question.

The Western Indiana Yearly Meeting of Friends favors a Constitutional Prohibition amendment for Indiana.

A General Convention of the "Disciples of Christ" at Cincinnati, Ohio, declares unequivocally for the banishment of intemperance.

State W. C. T. U. organizations are formed in Kansas and Arkansas.

The Temperance Lesson Book, by Dr. G. W. Richardson, of England, is published and introduced into the United States for use in the public schools.

The eighth national convention of the Catholic Total Abstinence Union is held in Indianapolis, Ind., on August 28.

The Walnut Lodge Hospital for inebriates is opened at Hartford, Conn.

Delegates from the General Assembly of the United Presbyterian Church are sent to the different denominations to secure their assistance in a united effort to combat the evil of intemperance.

Deputy Customs Inspector Isaac D. Dennis, at Wrangell, Alaska, inaugurates a campaign against the use of liquors, and breaks up the liquor trade for a short time.

The National Woman's Christian Temperance Union meets in convention at Baltimore, Md.

The Grand Council of the Royal Templars of Temperance of the State of New York is instituted in Buffalo, January 15.

1879

On March 28 Congress, at the urgent request of the distillers, extended the bonding period for liquors to three years.

Frances E. Willard is elected president of the Woman's Christian Temperance Union, which holds its national convention in Indianapolis.

The Michigan Legislature defeats a state prohibitory measure by a vote of 50 to 37 and enacts a liquor tax law.

The ninth national convention of the Catholic Total Abstinence Union is held in Detroit, Mich., on September 17.

At a session of the Sons of Temperance the National Mutual Relief Society is organized, June 25.

The Grand Council of the Royal Templars of

Temperance of the State of Pennsylvania is instituted in Meadville. During the year the order is established in six other states.

The United States House of Representatives by a vote of 128 to 99 creates the House Committee on the Alcoholic Liquor Traffic.

The Kansas Yearly Meeting of Friends appoints a committee to assist in securing State Constitutional Prohibition for Kansas.

The Kansas Legislature by a vote of 37 to 0 in the Senate and 88 to 32 in the House submits a prohibitory amendment to the Constitution.

The National Liquor Dealers' Association is organized at Cincinnati, Ohio, November 20 and 21.

"The Business Men's Moderation Society" is formed in New York City on March 11.

The General Synod of the Lutheran Church declares for the Prohibition of the sale of intoxicating liquors.

Vermont enacts a law to "abate and suppress nuisances."

Hyde Park, Mass., through the local school board, includes the teaching of scientific temperance in the regular public school instruction.

The California State W. C. T. U. is organized.

1880

The Massachusetts anti-screen law for saloons becomes operative.

The Iowa Legislature votes to submit a prohibitory amendment to a vote of the people. The measure requires favorable action by the next Legislature.

The third national convention of the Prohibition

party meets in Cleveland, Ohio, nominating Neal Dow of Maine as a candidate for President and H. A. Thompson of Ohio as a candidate for Vice President. The party received in the election a total vote of 9,678 in 16 states.

The National W. C. T. U. meets in annual convention in Boston, Mass. It creates a department of scientific temperance instruction for the public schools. This department is placed under the direction of Mrs. Mary H. Hunt.

The Prohibition law of Vermont is made more stringent by the passage of a "nuisance act."

Progressive Section No. 1, consisting of girls, is organized by the Cadets of Temperance.

The Royal Templars of Temperance organize grand councils in two more states.

Distilled liquor is introduced in the Hawaiian Islands by some escaped convicts from Botany Bay.

Henry H. Reuter, president of the United States Berwers' Association, at the annual convention in Buffalo says "The State of Maine, with only seven barrels last year and 7,031 barrels the year previous to that, has now disappeared entirely from the list of beer-producing states."

B. Kelly, United States Pension Agent at Topeka, compiles a statement of the paupers and criminals of the 106 counties of Kansas, which shows 44 without a pauper, 37 without a criminal in jail.

A special meeting of the National Liquor Dealers' Association is held in Cincinnati January 21 and 22 for the purpose of planning to secure important changes in revenue laws.

Two liquor bills under the titles of "Alcohol Leakage Bill" and the so-called "Carlyle Bill" are enacted by Congress as a result of an active effort on the part of the liquor interests.

The second annual meeting of the National Distillers and Spirits Dealers' Association is held in Cincinnati, Ohio, October 13 and 14, at which 380 firms from almost every state in the Union are represented.

The census shows four times as many drinking places as churches, nine times as many liquor sellers as ministers, and twelve times as much paid for liquor as for the gospel in the United States.

The people of Kansas adopt a prohibitory amendment to the Constitution by a vote of 92,302 to 84,304 on November 2, at the time of the presidential election.

The Loyal Temperance Legion is organized under the auspices of the W. C. T. U.

State organizations of the W. C. T. U. are formed in Delaware and Colorado.

The General Conference of the Methodist Protestant Church declares for State Prohibition.

The Nebraska prohibitory law is repealed.

The Woman's Christian Temperance Union organizes a Sunday School department under the superintendency of Miss Lucia E. F. Kimball, of Illinois.

A complete prohibitory law is proposed in the Connecticut Legislature but not finally enacted.

Miss Julia Coleman's book, "Alcohol and Hygiene," is published for use in the public schools by the National Temperance Publishing House.

The Woman's Christian Temperance Union appoints a special committee on Young Ladies' Leagues.

The tenth convention of the Catholic Total Abstinence Union is held at Scranton, Pa., on October 4.

The North Georgia Annual Conference of the Methodist Episcopal Church, South, appoints a temperance committee.

1881

The first high license law in the country is enacted by the Nebraska Legislature.

The Brewers' Congress opposes woman suffrage.

The lower house of the Delaware Legislature passes a local option measure which is defeated in the Senate. The Senate passes a prohibitory measure which is defeated in the House.

The Maryland Legislature enacts local option provisions for several counties under which three counties vote against license, thus making ten entire Prohibition counties in Maryland.

A local option law is defeated in the Indiana Senate by three votes.

Wisconsin enacts an anti-treating law.

Many parishes in Louisiana vote for Prohibition under the local option law.

Washington Territory enacts a Sunday closing law.

The prohibitory law of Vermont is amended and strengthened by the addition of a "nuisance act," a property owners' liability provision and another provision compelling fines to be assessed against sellers of liquor so as to provide $1 a day for the families of those who are committed to jail for crimes committed under the influence of liquor.

An effort to enact a prohibitory law in Rhode Island fails, but the Legislature enacts a law prohibiting the sale of liquor within 400 feet of any public school. A search and seizure law is also enacted.

The Connecticut local option law is amended and strengthened.

Fifty-four counties in Alabama are under Prohibition by special local option enactments.

A local option bill passes the Florida House, but is defeated by the Senate.

An effort to repeal the "Four-Mile Law" in Tennessee is defeated. A law against selling liquor to minors is enacted.

Kentucky passes a law prohibiting the sale or giving away of liquors on Sunday.

A prohibitory law passed by the Legislature of North Carolina by a vote of 46 to 15 in the House and 32 to 10 in the Senate is submitted to the people and defeated by a vote of 48,370 for and 166,325 against, the colored vote being almost solidly against Prohibition.

A prohibitory amendment resolution passes the Texas Senate by a vote of 23 to 7, but fails by 7 votes in the House.

The Arkansas House passes a prohibitory amendment resolution by a vote of 66 to 47, but the measure is defeated in the Senate.

The Cumberland Presbyterian Church, in an assembly orders that "our people be advised to favor the passage of prohibitory laws and that they vote for men who will both make and execute such laws."

The third annual meeting of the National Distillers and Spirits Dealers' Association is held in Chicago October 12 and 13, and a pro-liquor program for congressional legislation is agreed upon.

The Pennsylvania House passes a prohibitory amendment resolution by a vote of 109 to 59, but the measure is defeated in the Senate.

Kansas enacts a law enforcement code for the purpose of putting in operation the prohibitory constitutional amendment.

A constitutional amendment resolution in Michigan receives 63 yeas and 33 nays in the House and 21 yeas to 10 nays in the Senate, thus failing in the House for lack of a two-thirds vote.

The Philadelphia Yearly Meeting of Friends appoints a temperance committee to assist in the temperance movement.

The Church Temperance Society of the Protestant Episcopal Church is organized in New York City in April.

The vote by which a proposed prohibitory law is defeated in the lower house of the Massachusetts Legislature is 73 to 95.

The International Sunday School Committee is memorialized by a petition containing several thousand names, requesting quarterly temperance lessons.

The United Brethren General Conference takes a firm stand for Constitutional Prohibition in every state and in the United States.

The Treasury Department issues instructions to

allow the importation of beer and wine into Alaska, alleging that distilled spirits only are prohibited.

President R. B. Hayes, on February 22, issues an order "to prevent the sale of intoxicating liquors as a beverage, at the camps, forts and other posts of the army."

The National Temperance Convention meets at Saratoga, N. Y.

The National Brewers' Congress meets in Chicago and goes on record as opposed to woman suffrage.

The national convention of the Woman's Christian Temperance Union is held in the city of Washington, D. C.

The eleventh national convention of the Catholic Total Abstinence Union is held in Boston on August 1. A membership of 26,000 in 524 societies is represented in the convention.

As a memorial to her stand on the temperance question, especially in the White House, and at the suggestion of President Frederick Merrick, of the Ohio Wesleyan University, Miss Frances E. Willard presents a picture of Mrs. Lucy Webb Hayes to be hung in the East Room of the White House. The picture is received by President Garfield on March 5, the day after his inauguration.

Governor St. John of Kansas is re-elected on the temperance issue by a majority of 52,000—a larger majority than that ever before given to a Governor.

A local option law for towns and cities is enacted in Massachusetts.

The Kentucky State W. C. T. U. is organized.

The Presbyterian Church appoints a permanent committee on temperance.

The Royal Templars of Temperance organize grand councils in three more states.

1882

The Mississippi Legislature passes a law against the selling or giving away of intoxicating liquors within five miles of the University of Mississippi.

The W. C. T. U. holds its national convention at Louisville, Ky.

The Downing high license law is enacted by the Missouri Legislature.

On May 24 a national convention of brewers, distillers and liquor dealers is held in the city of Chicago for the purpose of "resisting sumptuary legislation" and organizing a national movement of all those interested in the liquor business, which shall be known by some such name as the "National Personal Liberty League."

The National Distillers and Spirits Dealers' Association meets in Cincinnati September 21 and reorganizes under the name of "The National Spirits and Wine Association of the United States."

A convention of liquor dealers is held in Turn Hall, Boston, to organize against the temperance movement.

The first annual meeting of the "National Protective Association" is held in Milwaukee in October, at which the name of the association is changed to "The Personal Liberty League of the United States." Branch leagues are organized in the leading states, cities and towns of the United States for the purpose of influencing the elections in November, 1882.

The Iowa Legislature, by a vote of 65 to 24 in the House and 35 to 11 in the Senate, passes a resolution submitting a Prohibition amendment to a vote of the people, the preceding Legislature having also passed the same resolution. The vote taken on June 27th results in a Prohibition victory by a vote of 155,436 to 125,677.

The Supreme Court of Iowa declares the prohibitory amendment null and void because of a discrepancy in the wording of the resolutions which passed two successive Legislatures.

The Indiana Legislature passes a resolution submitting a prohibitory amendment to a vote of the people. The same resolution must pass the succeeding Legislature before a vote can be taken.

Arkansas passes a law providing that whenever a majority of the adult inhabitants within three miles of any "institution of learning" petition for the Prohibition of the sale of liquor, Prohibition becomes effective.

Sixty-two of the 74 counties in Arkansas vote for Prohibition in the September elections.

The lower house of the Mississippi Legislature passes a local option bill, which is defeated in the Senate.

Ohio passes the Pond bill imposing a tax on liquor sellers of $100 to $300. The Sunday closing law is strengthened.

The license law of Virginia is changed so as to make the granting of licenses by judges optional.

Several provisions are added to the anti-liquor

legislation of South Carolina. The majority of the rural sections of the state grant no license.

A local option measure of general application throughout the entire state is defeated in the Georgia House of Representatives by three votes. More than half the state is under Prohibition by virtue of the special local option provisions granted by the Legislature from time to time.

A proposed prohibitory law is defeated in the Massachusetts House of Representatives by a vote of 110 to 110.

Massachusetts enacts a law removing screens from licensed places, closing interior passages between tenement houses and saloons, and prohibiting saloons within 400 feet of any school house on the same street.

The Connecticut Legislature enacts a law authorizing the use of temperance text-books in the public schools where the majority of the voters in a district favor the plan.

Maryland provides local option for three additional counties and eleven districts in other counties.

The Quadrennial Convention of the Christian Church declares against the "crime of crimes" (the liquor traffic), stands for Constitutional Prohibition and for the election of men and parties in favor of these principles.

A prohibitory constitutional resolution is defeated in the Nebraska Legislature by a small majority.

The Ohio House passes a prohibitory amendment resolution by a vote of 77 to 16, but the measure is defeated in the Senate.

The Association of Norfolk County, Mass., of the

Unitarian Church, passes vigorous resolutions against the use of intoxicants and favors legislation "looking to the total suppression of the manufacture or sale of intoxicating liquors for use as a beverage."

Two joint resolutions submitting a Constitutional Prohibition amendment are introduced in the United States Senate by Senator Plumb of Kansas and Senator Blair of New Hampshire, and referred to the Committee on Education and Labor.

Governor St. John of Kansas is renominated by a vote of 200 to 87 in the convention, but is defeated at the polls by 8,000 majority, largely as a result of the opposition of most of the people to a third term.

The Methodist Episcopal Church, South, makes sweeping declarations against the liquor traffic and stands unreservedly for Prohibition.

Bishop Ireland delivers a notable sermon and scathingly arraigns intemperance in the Cathedral at St. Paul, Minn., on August 2.

State organizations of the W. C. T. U. are formed in the states of West Virginia, Missouri, Texas and Dakota Territory.

The United States Senate, by a vote of 34 to 19, passes for the fourth time a bill providing for a commission of inquiry on the liquor traffic.

Hon. George G. Vest, at Booneville, Mo., makes a strong speech defending so-called "sumptuary" or Prohibition legislation.

Vermont, New Hampshire and Michigan enact scientific temperance laws for public school instruction.

The Connecticut Legislature passes a prohibitory

amendment resolution which is to be submitted to the next session.

The official organ of the Woman's Christian Temperance Union is consolidated with "The Signal," of Chicago, under the name of "Our Union Signal."

The Right Worthy Grand Lodge of the Independent Order of Good Templars meets in Charleston, S. C., in May.

The twelfth national convention of the Catholic Total Abstinence Union is held in St. Paul, Minn. Archbishop Ireland delivers the address of welcome.

The Citizens' Law and Order League of Massachusetts is organized in May.

The Convention of the Christian Church adopts a report declaring for "total abstinence upon the part of all persons from intoxicating liquors of every kind, and Prohibition of the traffic as such, by statutory and constitutional enactment."

The army canteen has its beginning at Vancouver Barracks, in Washington Territory. No beer nor any other form of intoxicants is allowed in this canteen.

The Sons of Temperance report 73,000 members, 1,468 divisions, a gain of 33,200 members and 319 divisions in three years.

The Royal Templars report 455 select councils, membership of 18,173, a primary membership of 1,175, making a total of 19,348 members. During the year the order is instituted in Virginia, South Carolina, New Brunswick and Ontario.

King Kalakaua, of Hawaii, repeals the Prohibition law of Hawaii, thus allowing the sale of liquor to Hawaiians made free, as to other races.

Under the leadership of the Sons of Temperance the New York State Prohibitory Association is organized.

1883

The World's Woman's Christian Temperance Union is organized at the national convention of the W. C. T. U., held at Detroit, Mich.

The Missouri Legislature enacts the Downing high license law.

The Illinois Legislature passes the Harper high license law.

A petition containing the names of 50,000 voters in Massachusetts is presented to the Legislature of that state, asking for the submission of a prohibitory constitutional amendment.

The Brewers' and Maltsters' Association inaugurates a non-partisan movement in defense of the liquor business.

The Scott law taxing the liquor traffic is passed in Ohio.

The Ohio Legislature passes two forms of constitutional amendments, one providing for license and the other for Prohibition. Both are submitted to a vote of the people. A majority of all votes cast at the election is required to pass either. Both fail, the license amendment by 270,807 votes and the prohibitory amendment by 37,467 votes. The Prohibition amendment has a majority of 82,000 of the votes cast on that issue.

The Oregon Legislature passes a prohibitory amendment resolution by a vote of 52 to 6 in the

House and 18 to 10 in the Senate.   It must pass another Legislature before it goes to the people.

The New Jersey Senate passes a prohibitory constitutional amendment resolution by a vote of 11 to 10, but the measure fails in the House by a vote of 27 to 29.

The General Assembly of the Cumberland Presbyterian Church goes on record in favor of Prohibition of the manufacture, sale and use of intoxicating liquors.

A prohibitory amendment resolution passes the West Virginia House by a vote of 49 to 14, but fails in the Senate.

The Indiana House passes a resolution submitting a prohibitory amendment to the people, but the resolution is defeated in the Senate.

The Genessee Yearly Meeting of Friends appoints a special temperance committee.

An effort to resubmit Prohibition to a vote of the people in Kansas is defeated by an overwhelming majority in the Legislature.

Michigan and New Hampshire enact laws providing for the teaching of scientific temperance in the public schools.

The Law and Order League of the United States is organized at Tremont Temple, Boston, on February 22, by the representatives of 27 Law and Order Leagues.

New York removes the right of summary arrests for the violation of the liquor laws.

Michigan enacts an anti-liquor civil damage law.

The Seventh-Day Baptists demand the entire Prohibition of the liquor traffic.

The Templars of Temperance is organized in New York City on June 16.

The thirteenth national convention of the Catholic Total Abstinence Union meets in Brooklyn, N. Y., on August 2.

The National Temperance Hospital is established by the Woman's Christian Temperance Union.

The Right Worthy Grand Lodge of the Independent Order of Good Templars meets in Chicago in May.

The national convention of the Woman's Christian Temperance Union, held at Detroit, Mich., decides to present a memorial to each of the national political conventions to adopt platforms declaring for a national prohibitory amendment to the Federal Constitution.

Miss Frances E. Willard and Miss Anna A. Gordon visit all the states and territories in the interest of the National Woman's Christian Temperance Union.

The Royal Templars of Temperance establish organizations in Georgia, Iowa, Nebraska and the Provinces of Quebec and Manitoba.

1884

Congress prohibits the importation of intoxicating liquors into Alaska.

The National Democratic Convention adopts a liquor plank in its platform.

A petition containing 106,000 signers is presented to the Massachusetts Legislature asking for the submission of a prohibitory amendment.

The third plenary council of Roman Catholic

prelates at Baltimore, Md., declares against the liquor traffic.

The Church Temperance Society of New York reports that 633 political conventions and primaries out of a total of 1,002 are held in saloons and that the boodle board of 22 aldermen contains 12 saloon-keepers and 4 saloon politicians.

The fourth national convention of the Prohibition party meets in Pittsburgh, Pa., and nominates John P. St. John of Kansas and William Daniel of Maryland for President and Vice President. In the election the party received 150,626 votes from 34 states.

The national convention of the W. C. T. U. is held in St. Louis, Mo.

The General Conference of the Methodist Episcopal Church adopts a resolution calling upon the friends of temperance to celebrate in 1885 the centennial of the temperance movement in America, it having been begun with the publication of Dr. Benjamin Rush's pamphlet against the use of ardent spirits.

The Tennessee Legislature passes a resolution submitting a prohibitory amendment to a vote of the people with the provision that the resolution shall be submitted to the next Legislature to be elected, and that it shall be published for six months prior to the election at which the members of the succeeding Legislature are to be elected.

The Southern Baptist Convention adopts stringent resolutions against "The use, manufacture or sale of intoxicating liquor as a beverage; the renting of property where liquor is to be manufactured or sold; condemning the sale of fruits and cereals for making liquors and the signing of whisky petitions or going on the bonds of liquor sellers, and declaring for Constitutional Prohibition."

The Voice, of New York, publishes a series of articles on "The Value of Total Abstinence in Relation to Life Insurance."

New York State passes a law providing for scientific temperance instruction in the public schools.

The General Assembly of the Presbyterian Church declares in favor of the utter extermination of the traffic in intoxicating liquors as a beverage.

The United States Senate, by a vote of 25 to 16, passes, for the fifth time, a bill providing for a commission of inquiry on the liquor traffic.

The International Sunday School Convention, held at Louisville, Ky., June 13, recommends the provision of quarterly temperance lessons.

The General Synod of the German Reform Church, at Tiffin, Ohio, denounces "especially the monster evil, intemperance."

In Arkansas 36 counties and several important towns and cities are carried for Prohibition under the local option law.

Rhode Island passes a law providing for the study of scientific temperance in the public schools.

Prohibition is again triumphantly written into the Constitution of the state of Maine by a vote of 70,783 for to 23,811 against.

The General Conference of the Methodist Protestant Church declares for Constitutional Prohibition.

The New York Tribune publishes a scathing editorial against the liquor traffic, on March 2.

Mrs. Mary Clement Leavitt starts from the United

States on a trip around the world in the interest of the creation of a W. C. T. U. organization in all countries and the organization of a World's Woman's Christian Temperance Union.

The national organization of the Woman's Christian Temperance Union, at its national convention, adopts a resolution pledging its influence to the Prohibition party.

The fourteenth national convention of the Catholis Total Abstinence Union is held in Chicago on August 15. Archbishop Feehan of Chicago, Archbishop Elder of Cincinnati, Bishop Ireland of St. Paul, Bishop Spaulding of Peoria, Ill., and Bishop Watterson of Columbus, Ohio, are among those present.

The annual convention of the Law and Order League of the United States is held in Chicago.

A bill is introduced in Congress by Senator Colquitt to submit the question of Prohibition in the District of Columbia to a vote of the people. The measure fails of passage.

The license for bar-rooms in the District of Columbia is raised to $100.

Congress passes an Act approved May 17 for the government of the Territory of Alaska, and prohibits the importation, manufacture and sale of intoxicating liquors except for medicinal, mechanical and scientific purposes.

An army canteen, in which the sale of all forms of intoxicating liquors is forbidden, is established at Ft. Sidney, Neb.

The National Conference of the Unitarian Church in a resolution "affectionately calls on all who may regard their moderate use (of intoxicating liquors) as innocent, to give up such use out of compassion for their weaker brethren."

The General Eldership of the Church of God on May 28, in its meeting at Wooster, Ohio, urges legal Prohibition of the liquor traffic everywhere.

The Reformed Presbyterian Church strongly re-iterates its attitude against the use and sale of intoxicating liquors as beverages.

The Woman's Christian Temperance Union presents hundreds of petitions to the International Committee of Sunday School Lessons at Louisville, Ky., asking for special temperance lessons.

A Grand Council for Kentucky is instituted in Louisville, February 3, by the Royal Templars of Temperance.

Mrs. Mary Clement Leavitt organizes the Woman's Christian Temperance Union of the Hawaiian Islands.

1885

The proposed Constitution for South Dakota is framed by a convention at Sioux Falls, with an article prohibiting the liquor traffic.

The Georgia Legislature passes a general local option law.

A prohibitory liquor law is passed by the Democratic Legislature of Iowa.

A partisan anti-saloon movement is organized in Kansas for the purpose of inducing the Republican party to adopt a platform of hostility to the saloons.

The National W. C. T. U. meets in Philadelphia.

The National Temperance Society petitions the

National Congress to submit a prohibitory constitutional amendment to the Federal Constitution.

Senators Plumb of Kansas and Blair of New Hampshire introduce National Prohibition amendment resolutions in the United States Senate. The Senate committee reports favorably on the resolutions the following year, but the measure does not come to a vote.

Laws providing for scientific temperance teaching in the public schools are enacted in Alabama, Maine, Oregon, Nebraska, Wisconsin, Nevada, Kansas, Pennsylvania, Massachusetts and Missouri.

The National League for the Suppression of the Liquor Traffic is organized in Boston in January.

The International Sunday School Lesson Committee provides for quarterly temperance lessons to begin in 1887.

Washington Territory enacts a local option law.

Father Cleary, a delegate from the Catholic Total Abstinence Union of America to the Centennial Temperance Conference at Philadelphia, declares that "the union has 40,000 pledged total abstainers."

The General Assembly of the United Presbyterian Church declares for absolute and unconditional Prohibition of the liquor traffic.

The Ohio Yearly Meeting of Friends declares for total abstinence and Prohibition.

The General Conference of the United Brethren Church declares for both State and National Prohibition.

The Territory of Dakota adopts Prohibition by a vote of 15,570 to 15,337.

A ruling of Hugh McCulloch, Secretary of the

Treasury, extends the bonding period for distillers seven months.

The sale of beer is introduced into the army canteens.

The third session of the Right Worthy Grand Lodge of the Independent Order of Good Templars is held at Toronto, Canada.

The National Temperance Society calls a centennial temperance convention to meet in Philadelphia.

The fifteenth convention of the Catholic Total Abstinence Union is held at New Haven, Conn., on August 6.

The Citizens' Law and Order League of the State of Pennsylvania is organized.

The Citizens' Law and Order League of the United States holds its convention in New York City.

The East Pennsylvania Eldership of the Church of God, at Shippensburg, Pa., declares it to be the bounden duty of ministers and church members to use every moral and legal influence to destroy the liquor traffic.

The Tennessee Legislature votes to submit a constitutional prohibitory amendment to a vote of the people. It is necessary, however, for the next Legislature to take the same action.

The East Pennsylvania Conference of the Evangelical Association adopts a resolution favoring total abstinence and Constitutional Prohibition. It also condemns the use of wine in the sacrament.

The National Temperance Society reports that up to May 1 the number of copies of the National Temperance Advocate printed since the paper was established is 2,085,695.

The Knights of Temperance are organized under the auspices of the Church Temperance Society of the Episcopal Church.

The Reformed Episcopal Church urges total abstinence.

The no-license election in Fulton County, Ga., including the city of Atlanta, results in a no-license victory by a vote of 3,828 to 3,600.

The Cumberland Presbyterian Church declares for National Prohibition.

The National League for the Suppression of the Liquor Traffic is organized in Boston, Mass., January 1, the first president being Rev. Daniel Dorchester, D. D.

The Oregon Legislature votes to submit a prohibitory amendment to the vote of the people. It is necessary for the next Legislature to take the same action.   1886

The Rhode Island Legislature votes to submit the prohibitory amendment to a popular vote. The prohibitory amendment to the Constitution is approved by the people of Rhode Island by a vote of 15,113 for and 9,230 against (the required three-fifths), and becomes operative on July 1.

The Unitarian Church Temperance Society is organized at Saratoga, N. Y.

The American Convention of the Christian Church declares its hostility to the liquor traffic.

Congress enacts that instruction concerning the effects of alcoholic liquors shall be given in the schools of the District of Columbia, in the military and naval academies, and in all other schools under government control.

Congress passes a local option law for the District of Columbia.

The Dow tax law is passed by the Ohio Legislature.

Judge Brewer of the United States Circuit Court renders a decision in upholding compensation for loss in brewing property occasioned by Prohibition laws.

The national convention of the W. C. T. U. is held in Minneapolis.

Mississippi passes a local option law.

The liquor interests form the National Protective Association.

Twenty-two Republican state conventions declare the liquor question to be one of great political importance.

The Republican state conventions of Massachusetts, Pennsylvania, Michigan, Nebraska, Missouri, West Virginia, Tennessee, Arkansas, Texas and Oregon pass resolutions in favor of submitting prohibitory constitutional amendments to a vote of the people in the several states.

The Republican state conventions of New Jersey, Connecticut, Wisconsin and Indiana resolve in favor of local option.

The Republican state conventions of Maine, Vermont, New Hampshire, Iowa and Kansas resolve in favor of Prohibition and its rigid enforcement.

Rev. George C. Haddock is murdered by pro-liquor ruffians at Sioux City, Iowa, August 3.

Congress passes a law providing for the teaching of scientific temperance in the public schools of the territories and the District of Columbia.

The Commercial Temperance League is formed by traveling men and others in New York City.

Laws providing for scientific temperance instruction in the public schools are passed in Iowa, Maryland and Connecticut.

The state constitutional prohibitory amendment is defeated in Michigan by a vote of 178,479 for and 184,305 against.

On September 16 the convention of anti-saloon Republicans, meeting in Chicago, organize "The National Anti-Saloon Republican Committee."

The New Jersey Legislature defeats the local option bill.

A compact for the suppression of the use of liquor is entered into by representatives of the Cherokees, Choctaws, Chickasaws, Creeks, Seminoles, Comanches, Wichitas and affiliated bands of Indians residing in the southwest part of the Indian Territory.

The Right Worthy Grand Lodge of the Independent Order of Good Templars holds its session in Richmond, Va., and again urges political action to secure the prohibition of the liquor traffic.

The sixteenth national convention of the Catholic Total Abstinence Union is held at Notre Dame, Ind., on August 4.

The Citizens' Law and Order League of the United States holds its annual convention at Cincinnati, Ohio.

1887

A decision handed down by Justice Harlan of the United States Supreme Court in the case of Mulger vs. Kansas and Kansas vs. Ziebold (both men being Kansas brewers whose business had been destroyed by the prohibitory law) on December 5, states: "There is no justification for holding that the state, under the guise of merely police regulations, is here aiming to deprive the citizen of his constitutional rights; for we cannot shut our view to the fact, within the knowledge of all, that the public health, the public morals and the public safety may be endangered by the general use of intoxicating drinks; nor the fact, established by statistics accessible to every one, that the disorder, pauperism and crime prevalent in the country, are in some degree at least traceable to this evil. . . . The power which the states unquestionably have of prohibiting such use by individuals of their property as shall be prejudicial to the health, the morals or the safety of the public is not, and—consistently with the existence and safety of organized society—cannot be burdened with the condition that the state must compensate such individual owners for pecuniary losses they sustain by reason of their not being permitted by a noxious use of their property to inflict injury upon the community."

The two branches of the Independent Order of Good Templars which resulted from a split in the convention at Louisville, Ky., in 1876, are reunited at the convention held at Saratoga, N. Y.

The seventeenth national convention of the Catholic Total Abstinence Union is held in Philadelphia in August.   Ten thousand total abstainers take part in the parade.

The Legislature of Michigan enacts a high license liquor tax law.

The Brooks license law of Pennsylvania is enacted largely as the result of the efforts of the Philadelphia Law and Order Society.

The Citizens' Law and Order League of the United States holds its annual convention in Albany, N. Y.

Miss Jessie Ackerman of California sails from San Francisco on a world lecture tour for the Woman's Christian Temperance Union.

Pope Leo XIII., under date of March 27, writes a letter to Archbishop John Ireland of St. Paul, Minn., expressing his approval of the cause of temperance and the American Catholic Total Abstinence Union. This letter is published in the May number of the Catholic Temperance Magazine.

Laws providing for scientific temperance instruction in the public schools are enacted in the states of California, Delaware, Minnesota, West Virginia and Colorado.

Fulton County, Ga., including the city of Atlanta, votes on the liquor question November 26, with the result that 5,189 votes are cast for license and 4,061 against.

In the Journal of United Labor, under date of July 2, T. V. Powderly writes a strong letter defending his position on temperance and the evil effects of drink on working men.

The provision of a quarterly temperance lesson

goes into operation by act of the International Sunday School Lesson Committee.

The thirty-third annual session of the Independent Order of Good Templars is held at Saratoga, N. Y., in June. The order reports 483,103 members and 139,951 juvenile Templars.

In the "Catholic World" of August, Father Conaty declares that "the battle is really between the saloon and the home," and strongly condemns the saloon.

The Atlanta city council fixes the retail liquor license fee at $1,500 a year.

An attempt to pass a local option bill in the New Jersey Legislature is defeated.

The triennial meeting of the eldership of the Church of God declares against the liquor traffic.

The General Synod of the Reformed Church passes strong resolutions against the liquor traffic.

The Reformed Dutch Church in General Synod passes resolutions favoring temperance.

The General Conference of the Evangelical Church declares for Prohibition.

The constitutional prohibitory amendment is submitted by the Legislature in Tennessee and is defeated by a majority of over 27,000 votes, the vote being 117,504 for and 145,237 against.

Ten counties of Michigan vote dry under the local option law which is enacted early in the year.

The territorial Legislature of Dakota passes a local option law.

Montana passes a county local option law.

The Legislature of Kansas passes a law to suppress the sale of liquor as a beverage at drug stores.

The constitutional prohibitory amendment in Michigan is defeated by a majority of 5,645 votes, the vote being 178,638 for and 184,281 against.

The Citizens' Union of Michigan is organized for Prohibition.

The Minnesota Legislature provides for high license wherever Prohibition is not adopted.

Fifty of the 78 counties of Missouri vote dry under the local option law.

The Legislature of Oregon submits a prohibitory amendment to the vote of the people. The amendment is defeated by a majority of 7,985, the vote being 19,973 for and 27,958 against.

The Pennsylvania Legislature enacts the Brooks high license law.

The Texas Legislature votes to submit a constitutional prohibitory amendment to the people; the amendment is afterward defeated by a vote of 129,-273 for and 221,934 against.

The West Virginia Legislature votes to submit a prohibitory constitutional amendment to the people.

The General Conference of the Wesleyan Methodist Episcopal Church resolves for Prohibition.

Georgia reports 75 counties of the state under Prohibition.

The Connecticut Legislature submits a proposal for a prohibitory amendment to be voted on again at the next session.

The national convention of the W. C. T. U. is held at Nashville, Tenn.

Senator Blair introduces a Federal Prohibition resolution in the United States Senate.

By order of President Cleveland, Alaska is placed under Prohibition.

Local option on the liquor question is incorporated into the Constitution of the State of Florida.

1888

The United States Brewers' convention, held in St. Paul on May 30 and 31, expresses its satisfaction with the internal revenue measure enacted during the Civil War and declares that "the present system, which is perfectly justifiable when viewed from the standpoint of political economy, promotes temperance more effectually than any other measure yet proposed or executed for that purpose."

The War Department issues an order (Oct. 25) for canteens to discontinue the sale of beer at posts where there is a post-trader, as the sale of beer by the canteen is in conflict with the rights of the post-trader.

The eighteenth national convention of the Catholic Total Abstinence Union is held in Boston on August 1.

Supreme authority of the Order of Templars of Temperance is vested in an "International Temple" on June 27.

"The National Anti-Nuisance League" is organized in New York, with W. Jennings Demorest as president and W. McK. Gatchell as treasurer. The object of the league is to assist the fight for Prohibition.

The Citizens' Law and Order League of Pennsylvania and the Philadelphia Law and Order Society are merged.

The Citizens' Law and Order League of the United States holds its annual convention at Philadelphia.

The General Conference of the African Methodist Episcopal Zion Church, with 300,000 members, declares in favor of temperance.

The General Conference of the African Methodist Episcopal Church, with 400,000 members, adopts resolutions favoring temperance.

The Bishop's address to the General Conference of the Methodist Episcopal Church declares against the licensing of the liquor traffic.

The Brooks high license law of Pennsylvania goes into effect.

The National Republican Convention resolves for temperance and morality.

The General Synod of the Moravian Church opposes all traffic in intoxicating liquors.

The General Conference of the Seventh-Day Adventists, in convention at Minneapolis, Minn., resolves for Prohibition.

The Excise Commissioner of New York makes rules and restrictions for the liquor traffic.

The Law and Order League of Sioux City, Iowa, begins proceedings against the transportation companies that have been nullifying the Prohibition laws.

The Legislature of Ohio passes a Sunday saloon-closing law, and adopts township local option.

The Massachusetts Legislature enacts a high license law.

The Prohibition party in national convention at Indianapolis nominates General Clinton B. Fisk of New Jersey for President and John A. Brooks of Missouri for Vice President. In the election the party receives 249,945 votes, all the states except South Carolina returning some votes.

The Constitutional Prohibition amendment submitted in West Virginia is defeated by a majority of 34,887 votes, the vote being 41,668 for and 76,555 against.

The New York General Assembly in April adopts the prohibitory amendment by a vote of 68 to 51 in the Assembly and 18 to 5 in the Senate.

At the request of the National Temperance Society, Hon. J. A. Pickler of South Dakota and Senator Blair, in their respective branches of Congress, present a resolution for the submission of a prohibitory amendment to the states for ratification. On July 9 Senator Blair, of the Committee on Education and Labor, submits a report, concurred in by the majority of the committee, recommending the submission of a prohibitory amendment to the states for action.

1889

Hunterdon County, N. J., votes against license by a majority of 500.

A joint resolution proposing a prohibitory amendment to the Constitution passes the Pennsylvania Legislature.

The Boston Board of Police Commissioners increases the cost of liquor licenses.

The prohibitory amendment to the Constitution in New Hampshire is defeated by a vote of 25,786 for and 30,876 against.

A reform ticket aiming at the closing of liquor shops on Sunday is put into the field at Cincinnati, Ohio.

The Supreme Court of Indiana decides that a license to sell liquor is a special tax, and that no limitations can be placed upon the police power to grant, withhold or annul licenses by any statutory provisions.

The Michigan Legislature fixes the liquor retail tax at $500.

The Rhode Island Legislature enacts a high license law.

The prohibitory clause of the North Dakota Constitution is ratified by the people, the vote being 18,552 for to 17,393 against.

The people of South Dakota approve the prohibitory article of the Constitution by a majority of over 5,000, the vote being 40,239 for to 34,510 against.

A Prohibition amendment to the Constitution of Pennsylvania is defeated by a vote of the people, the vote being 296,617 for and 484,644 against.

The Wisconsin Legislature passes a local option law.

A central Prohibition organization is formed at a convention held in Omaha, Nebraska, 250 delegates representing five nearby states.

The Legislature of North Dakota passes a Prohibition enforcement law which becomes operative on July 1.

The New Jersey Legislature repeals the local option and high license law and enacts another high license law in its place.

The Masonic Grand Lodge of Nebraska expels all saloonkeepers from the Masonic order.

The Nineteenth National Convention of the Catholic Total Abstinence Union is held in Cleveland, Ohio, in August.

The Citizens Law and Order League of the United States holds its annual convention in Toronto, Canada, and changes the name to "The International Law and Order League."

General Order No. 10 dated February 1 issued by Secretary of War William C. Endicott officially recognizes the beer canteen as an institution.

Massachusetts votes on Prohibition, 86,459 for, 133,085 against.

Connecticut votes on Prohibition, 22,379 for, 49,974 against.

Washington votes on Prohibition, 19,546 for, 31,487 against.

Rhode Island votes on Prohibition, rescinding the law by a vote of 9,956 for, and 28,315 against.

1890

The liquor dealers of South Dakota openly refuse to obey the Prohibition law.

Temperance women begin a crusade in Lathrop and other Missouri towns.

President Corbin of the Reading Railroad orders the discharge of all employees who frequent drinking places.

The Prohibition law of Iowa is sustained. The Legislature defeats high license.

The Supreme Court holds that beer sent into the State of Iowa in sealed kegs from Illinois and sold in original packages cannot be seized without violating the Constitution.

The Secretary of War declares that no ardent spirits or wine shall be sold in the canteens.

The Central Labor Union of New York denies admission to the delegates from saloonkeepers' associations.

The United States Brewers' Association, representing $195,000,000 of invested capital, holds its convention at Washington, D. C.

The American Brewing Company opens original package stores at Leachburg, Pennsylvania, and other dry towns.

The Presbyterian General Assembly in session at Saratoga Springs, New York, recommends Prohibition.

The General Conference of the Methodist Protestant Church declares against license.

A whisky war breaks out in Kansas on account of the original package decision by the courts.

The Grand Lodge of the Knights of Pythias takes

a firm stand on the exclusion of liquor dealers from the order.

Judge J. S. West of the United States District Court at Fort Scott, Kansas, declares for the enforcement of the prohibitory law in an original package case.

Irish beer drinkers of Chicago boycott the breweries which have been sold to English syndicates.

The Baltimore & Ohio Railroad issues a circular stating that it will not employ men addicted to intemperance.

A State convention at Topeka, Kansas, composed of 3,000 delegates, resolves against the original package liquor shops.

The Farmers' Alliance and Knights of Labor in South Dakota unite to form an independent party favoring Prohibition.

The non-partisan Woman's Christian Temperance Union is organized at Cleveland, Ohio, on January 22.

The Sons of Temperance call upon Congress to prohibit the exportation of intoxicating beverages from the United States to Africa and the Pacific Islands.

Leland, Iowa, passes an ordinance providing that any person who sells intoxicating liquors shall be tarred and feathered and cow-hided out of the village.

The prohibitory amendment goes into effect in South Dakota. The Legislature enacts a strong enforcement law.

The American Board of Missions petitions Congress to prohibit the exportation of intoxicating liquors to those countries where the missions of the board are located.

The Michigan Supreme Court upholds the local option law.

The Prohibition of the sale of intoxicating liquors in Iowa in original packages becomes effective.

The people of Nebraska reject a Prohibition amendment to the Constitution.

Cambridge, Massachusetts, adopts no-license under the local option law by a majority of 564.

The Maryland Legislature enacts a high license law for Baltimore city.

The Women's Temperance Crusade in Missouri is marked by the forcible destruction of a saloon in Speckardsville.

The Cincinnati Brewing Company, amid much excitement, opens an "original package" store in Leechburg, a dry town.

The Central Labor Union of New York orders a strike against Pool Beer; the Socialists withdraw from the union.

About 800 delegates meet in New York in a temperance convention which declares for Prohibition.

The Reform party meeting in Syracuse, New York, declares for the absolute suppression of the liquor traffic for beverage purposes by National Constitutional enactment.

The New York Citizens' Alliance is organized to work for new excise laws in New York State.

The United States Senate passes an amendment to the Army Bill providing that no liquor shall be sold to soldiers by post-traders, and none by canteens in Prohibition states.

The 46th annual meeting of the Sons of Temperance is held.

The National W. C. T. U. meets in annual convention in Atlanta, Georgia.

The Nonpartisan Woman's Christian Temperance Union holds its convention at Pittsburgh.

The New York Commission of Excise reports that 8,885 places in New York City are licensed to sell intoxicating liquor. This represents 6,742 saloons, 1,098 storekeepers, besides hotels, restaurants and steamboats.

North and South Dakota are admitted to the Union as Prohibition states.

The Twentieth National Convention of the Catholic Total Abstinence Union is held in Pittsburgn, Pennsylvania, on August 6.

The United Christian Commission is revived in the interest of legislation aiding temperance in the United States Army and Navy. Chaplain Orville J. Nave is made corresponding secretary and Rev. Wm. E. Parsons treasurer.

The International Law and Order League holds its annual convention in Boston.

The Universalists of Illinois declare for total abstinence for the individual, and Prohibition for the State and nation.

The first company of the order of "Royal Crusaders" is formed in Brunswick, New Jersey.

As a consequence of the "Original Package" decision handed down by the United States Supreme Court, to the effect that "the State has no power, without Congressional permission, to interfere by seizure, or by any other action, in the Prohibition of importation and sale by a foreign or non-resident imported of liquors in unbroken "original packages," liquor dealers begin opening "original package" shops everywhere defying State and local Prohibition laws.

The "Wilson Law" is passed by Congress (approved August 8) with the intent of making all intoxicating liquors subject to the laws of the State into which they are sent. The Supreme Court, however, weakens this law by a decision that the words of the act "arrival in such State," contemplates their delivery to the consignee before State jurisdiction attaches.

A law enacted by Congress and approved June 13 contains a provision that "no alcoholic liquors, wine or beer shall be sold or supplied to enlisted men in any canteen or post-trader's store . . . in any state or territory in which the sale of alcoholic liquors, wine or beer, is prohibited by law."

Agitation to protect the natives of the Congo Free State from the whisky peddler results in the "Brussels Conference" which establishes a zone around the district in question within which the sale of distilled spirits is to be prohibited. This agreement is ratified by seventeen nations within two years.

Redfield Proctor, Secretary of War under President Harrison, urges an appropriation of $100,000 for fitting up and equipping the military beer canteens. The appropriation is defeated.

General O. O. Howard in an official report recommends the abolition of the sale of beer in the army canteen and the substitution therefor of other beverages.

The building of the Woman's Christian Temperance Union Temple in Chicago is begun.

The New York Legislature passes a Prohibition amendment by a vote of 19 to 13 in the Senate, and by a vote of 66 to 45 in the Assembly. The Attorney General decides that a *bill* on the subject is required and the matter goes over until the next Legislature.

The census reports, and the official reports of liquor organizations, show that the city of Chicago sells more liquor in an average week than is sold during the entire year in the State of Kansas, and that the consumption of liquors in this city for one month is greater than the aggregate sales of the whole twelve months in all of the seven Prohibition States.

1891

The South Dakota House of Representatives passes a resolution to re-submit the prohibitory amendment.

The New York Assembly defends the Stadler special license bill by a vote of 63 to 60.

Twenty-six illicit stills are destroyed in Florida.

The Delaware, Lackawanna & Western Railroad discharges employees who sign petitions of saloonkeepers for license.

Men and women together in a temperance crusade at Bloomville, Ohio, wreck a saloon and destroy the liquors, cigars and billiard tables.

The Maine Legislature passes some very rigid Prohibition enforcement legislation.

The Sunday law in New York is enforced.

The lower House of the Delaware Legislature passes a local option bill by a vote of 14 to 4.

The National Brewers' Association, in session at

Cleveland, rejoices in the defeat of a bill to create a government commission of inquiry on the alcoholic liquor traffic.

Father McNulty, of Paterson, New Jersey, is beaten by a law-breaking saloonkeeper.

The United States Supreme Court upholds the constitutionality of the original package law.

The Mayor of Atlanta, Georgia, vetoes all beer licenses.

The liquor forces hold an anti-Prohibition convention at Janesville, Wisconsin.

The National Prohibition Park on Staten Island, near Port Richmond, is formally dedicated.

Georgia prohibits the sale of liquor within three miles of any church or school except in incorporated towns.

Anti-Prohibitionists of Kiowa, Kansas, petition the woman mayor to resign because she makes continual war on the dives.

The Sunday closing law is strictly enforced in Baltimore.

All liquor dealers at Bar Harbor, Maine, are indicted for violating the liquor law.

Congress passes a law prohibiting the sale of liquor within one mile of the Soldiers' Home in the city of Washington.

A high license law is enacted by the New Mexico Legislature.

The New Jersey Legislature passes a bill requested by the liquor dealers giving absolute power to grant or revoke licenses at their pleasure to boards to be appointed by the Governor.

The lower House of the New Hampshire Legislature rejects a local option bill by a vote of 166 to 148.

The woman mayor of Kiowa, Kansas, succeeds in closing gambling houses and liquor joints in the town.

The general Prohibition enforcement law of Maine goes into effect in May. It provides a fine of $100 and 60 days in jail for the first offense of the anti-liquor selling provision.

The East Maine Methodist Conference protests against the acts of the national administration in endeavoring to enlarge the malt liquor trade with Central American states.

The twenty-sixth annual meeting of the National Temperance Society is held in New York.

The Grand Lodge of the Ancient Order of United Workmen of Milwaukee, Wisconsin, decides by a vote of 114 to 81 that liquor makers and saloonkeepers are eligible to become members.

The Excise Reform Association is incorporated in New York for the purpose of promoting the passage of more stringent excise laws, and the establishment of an excise system that shall impose adequate regulations upon the sale of liquor in that State.

In the District Court at Topeka, Kansas, an original package agent representing a liquor house at Kansas City, Missouri, is fined $500 and sentenced to 90 days in the county jail.

The National Temperance Society holds its annual meeting at Saratoga Springs, New York.

The police of New York are forbidden to receive bribes or to spy into illegal liquor selling during forbidden hours, while the judges refuse to hold the liquor dealers unless the police can testify that they bought the liquor at their saloons.

A monster petition in favor of outlawing the liquor traffic and the opium trade is presented at the great temperance convention in the city of Boston.

The Non-Partisan W. C. T. U. representing seven states holds its annual convention.

The first World's Convention of the W. C. T. U. is held in Boston, Massachusetts, Lady Henry Somerset of England being the honor guest.

The Twenty-First National Convention of the Catholic Total Abstinence Union is held in Baltimore, Maryland. Cardinal Gibbons welcomes the delegates.

The American Medical Temperance Society is organized at the meeting of the American Medical Association at Washington, D. C.

An Encyclopedia of Temperance and Prohibition is published by Funk & Wagnalls.

The International Law and Order League holds its annual convention at Chautauqua, N. Y.

Queen Liliuokalani ascends the throne of Hawaii and discontinues the open use of liquors at her public entertainments and refuses them herself; however, the traffic is not wiped out.

The National Temperance Advocate prints an editorial in February entitled "Appeal to Conscience."

The New York Legislature, after joint resolutions for a vote on a Prohibition amendment had been adopted in the sessions of 1888 and 1890, defeats the bill providing for the submission of the Prohibition Amendment to a vote of the people.

The Annual of Universal Medical Sciences, Vol. 9, letter 1, page 4, gives results of experiments by Blumenau on young men between the ages of 22 and 24 years as to the effects of alcohol on the human system. Deut. Medicin. Wochensch, Leipzig, October 22, gives the results of experiments of Glazer regarding the effects of alcohol on the urine and kidneys. The Journal of Medical Science, September, gives conclusions of Dr. E. McDowell Cocgrove as to "a narcotic rather than a stimulating effect" of alcohol.

Nebraska fails to adopt Prohibition by a vote of 82,292 for, and 111,728 against.

1892

Temperance societies of New York hold mass meetings to protest against the passing of the liquor dealers' excise bill.

Investigations show that there is one saloon in New York for every sixty-two male adults.

The formation of an Anti-Saloon League composing clergymen of all denominations is announced in Massachusetts, but the movement does not materialize.

The police of New York City make a show of enforcing the excise law by making ninety-one arrests.

The general conference of the Methodist Episcopal Church condemns the liquor traffic and the high license system.

Judge Lacombe, of New York, renders an opinion favoring the legality of the whisky trust.

An excise enforcement league is organized in New York City.

Sioux Falls, S. D., decides to experiment with six saloons, one for every ward.

An illicit still in New York, with 6,000 gallons of wine and brandy, is seized by the government.

At a temperance meeting called by Edward Murphy at New Haven, Connecticut, 2,000 persons sign the total abstinence pledge.

The revenue authorities seize ten illicit stills in Wilkes County, North Carolina, and three in Catalba County, destroying the liquors.

Four "moonshiners" are captured near Mount Pleasant, Pennsylvania.

The local option elections in Connecticut result in eighty-eight towns voting for no-license as against eighty which vote for license.

O. B. Williamson, a Prohibitionist, is shot and killed at the municipal election at Warrior, Alabama, by George Kaley who is charged by a coroners' jury with wilful murder.

Doctor Parkhurst seeks to enforce the prohibitory features of the license law in New York City.

Jonathan Hochstetter is killed by moonshiners on Laurel Hill Mountain, Pennsylvania, for testifying against them in court.

The National Temperance Society holds its Twenty-seventh Annual Convention in Broadway Tabernacle, New York.

The Thirty-second Annual Convention of the United States Brewers' Association is held in Boston.

For selling whisky in Lancaster, Kentucky, dry under local option, a negro is fined nearly $1,000,000 after confessing to 1,585 cases, and a white man is fined $157,700 in 1,577 cases.

The National W. C. T. U. meets in Denver, Colorado, having 500 delegates in attendance.

George Cunningham, a Prohibitionist, is killed by

Frank Duffy, a saloonkeeper at Fort Hamilton, New York.

The Sixth National Convention of the Prohibition Party at Cincinnati, Ohio, nominates General John Bidwell of California for President and J. B. Cranfill of Texas for Vice-President. In the election the party receives 270,710 votes.

The existing laws against selling liquor to the Indians are strengthened by the Act passed July 23rd, which prohibits the sale, gift, exchange, or barter of any ardent spirits, ale, beer, wine or intoxicating liquors of any kind.

The War Department makes a distinction between the post-exchange and the beer canteen, the room being set apart for the sale of beer being known as the canteen, while the whole establishment is called the post-exchange.

The Third National Convention of the Non-Partisan W. C. T. U. is held in Cleveland, Ohio.

The Twenty-second National Convention of the Catholic Total Abstinence Union is held at Indianapolis, Indiana, in August. Seven hundred and thirty-eight societies are represented.

The second annual meeting of the American Medical Temperance Association is held in the Y. M. C. A. Hall in Detroit, Michigan on June 9.

The Beer Brewers' Association in its annual convention at Boston in May, reports for educational work a balance of $52,188.91.

CHAPTER VII

Non-Partisan Co-Operation for Local Prohibition—1893-1906

THE year 1893 found the Prohibition movement in the United States at a low ebb. During the fifty years prior to that date eighteen states had adopted state Prohibition, but in eleven of these states the law had been repealed or declared unconstitutional before it had been given a fair chance through any kind of real enforcement, while one other state had practically nullified its Prohibition law by the enactment of legislation giving to the people in certain political subdivisions the right to suspend Prohibition by a majority vote. Thus only six states remained under nominal Prohibition, but even in these states the law was not well enforced. Joints, camouflaged drug stores, speakeasies and numerous other institutions devised for the purpose of evading the prohibitory law, flourished in most of the Prohibition states.

There were thirty-one states in which the people had no legal voice on the liquor question. Only eleven states, in fact, had any form of local veto, and of these not more than six had what might be termed effective local option laws. Post traderships in connection with military forts and army posts had been abolished, thus opening the way for army canteens with the sale of intoxicating liquors at the army posts under the direction of the government.

The Prohibition party, which had aroused strong hopes in earlier years, had not proved equal to the task. After 24 years of organized effort it had been unable to poll in any election as many as 275,000 votes out of a total of more than 12,000,000, or one out of forty-four. Such a showing, after almost a quarter of a century of organized partisan effort, indicated that there was not strong probability that the Prohibition party as such would ever reach the point of being reckoned with as either a political or partisan factor.

In the meantime the liquor interests had perfected one of the strongest political machines that the country had ever known and had injected its dominating influence into the politics of almost every state and city of the nation, controlling conventions and elections and dictating the acts of legislatures.

In short, the partisan plan for Prohibition had failed. The Prohibition wave had receded. The moral forces were fast becoming discouraged. The situation was frequently referred to as hopeless. Reaction had indeed set in and even the religious and temperance forces of the nation had come to the point of realizing that the success of the Prohibition movement depended upon the devising of some new plan which would promise more in the way of the uniting of the temperance forces and the solving of the liquor problem.

It was under such circumstances that the Americanized form of the Gothenburg system presented itself in South Carolina under the name of the dispensary. This proposal, which promised to eliminate the element of private gain from the liquor business and to clothe the traffic with a garment of respectability, vouched for by the state itself, presented the most insidious and dangerous aspect of the liquor problem in America at that date.

The dispensary as a complete solution for the liquor problem had been fathered by the Honorable Benjamin Tillman, Governor of the state of South Carolina. It had the backing of the dominant political party in that state. It quickly made its appeal to the political and moral forces of other states with the result that within a comparatively short time strong temperance advocates and political leaders in many sections of the country were urging the dispensary system as presenting the most helpful suggestion for the solution of the liquor problem.

In many respects the dispensary proposal precipitated the greatest crisis of the entire Prohibition movement in America. It is easy to believe that this system would in all probability have fastened itself upon the southern states and eventually upon the nation as a whole but for two things: the political scandals which promptly developed in connection with the state dispensary in South Carolina, and the nonpartisan movement for temperance reform which presented itself to the temperance and moral forces of the nation in the very midst of this crucial dispensary period.

The non-partisan political plan for coöperation in local Prohibition efforts presented a strong appeal to the religious and moral forces of the nation. This plan proposed to bring all temperance forces into a coöperative effort, regardless of other alliances, affiliations and adhesions. It was indeed interdenominational and omni-partisan. It appealed to the temperance adherents of all parties. Democrats, Republicans, Populists, Socialists, Baptists, Jews, Catholics, Methodists, Presbyterians, Mormons, Hindus, Mohammedans, capitalists, laboring men, professional men, farmers, public servants and the humblest citizens, could stand together on the non-partisan, interdenominational temperance platform presented, without doing violence to either their political, religious or professional relations. This plan, moreover, appealed to the common sense of the public in that it proposed to attack the liquor traffic first at the points of least resistance, namely, the country cross-roads, the townships, the villages and the rural counties. This plan proposed to use sentiment already in existence, crystallizing it for immediate use while at the same time by that very process creating more sentiment for the larger conflicts ahead. The sponsors of the plan recognized the fact that nothing succeeds like success and that nothing makes more sentiment than the proper, active utilization of the sentiment which already exists.

This proposed plan for non-partisan action in local Prohibition contests, moreover, had a strong appeal in that it operated on the fundamental American policy of popular sovereignty on the liquor question. Its demand was that the people of every community have the right to exclude the liquor traffic when the majority of the people of that community so desire. This proposed plan, moreover, was a conservation scheme, dealing with one question only, running counter to no deep prejudices except that engendered by the liquor traffic itself, tying up its fortunes with those of no other problem on which churches, parties, organizations, men and women strongly differ. Thus entangling alliances with other issues were avoided. This plan was political but not partisan. It proposed to work through men instead of parties. It made it possible for the temperance forces to fight on the offensive, choosing the ground and the weapons for each conflict, compelling the liquor traffic to defend itself on that ground and with those weapons. Its object was three-fold, consisting in, first, marshalling and organizing temperance sentiment into active public opinion; second, the crystallizing of public opinion into law; third, the following up of the enactment of law with enforcement and educational work of such a character as to make for permanency. Such was the plan, which at this crucial period in the history of the temperance reform made its appeal to the temperance public in 1893.

The Anti-Saloon League was the embodiment of the above plan. Founded by Doctor Howard H. Russell, a Congregational minister and Christian statesman, directed after the first few years of organization work by Doctor Purley A. Baker, a born reformer, executive and Christian crusader, born in the remarkable Christian moral reform atmosphere of the college town of Oberlin, Ohio, this League, inaugurated in 1893, within an incredibly short space of time spread over the nation, uniting the forces of the church, the adherents and constituents of practically all the temperance and reform organizations and the best men of all political parties, into one united effort for the prompt suppression and the ultimate extermination of the beverage liquor traffic.

The national organization of the Anti-Saloon League came into existence at Washington, D. C., in

1895. Within a few years thereafter state departments had been organized in practically every state and territory. Hundreds of men and women were rapidly employed in the various phases of its work. Its leadership in the early years included men like Howard H. Russell, Purley A. Baker, Edwin C. Dinwiddie, John C. Jackson, and Wayne B. Wheeler, who shaped the early course of this new movement which was destined not only to lead the fight for local Prohibition in the smaller communities, but later to organize the movements for state Prohibition and finally to marshall the moral forces of the nation for permanent National Constitutional Prohibition.

The strongest temperance organizations of the seventies and eighties made an effort at both political and partisan action. The Anti-Saloon League, which came upon the stage in the nineties, was intensely political but insistently non-partisan.

The period of non-partisan local Prohibition effort, inaugurated by the formation of the Anti-Saloon League in 1893, was short but eventful. It covered thirteen years of agitation, legislative campaigning and law enforcement activity, a detailed record of which would fill a library of volumes.

Within a few years after the organization of the League, the temperance revival showed itself in the new life and activity of the reform forces in the towns and counties of practically every state. The few old local option laws of some of the southern states were remodeled and strengthened, while new local option laws were rapidly written on the statute books of most of the states, north, south, east and west.

Before the end of the period, a survey of conditions

showed a remarkable advance in tangible results along Prohibition lines. Three states, with an aggregate population of almost 3,000,000, were under state-wide Prohibition, while three other states were almost entirely under Prohibition by special legislative enactments. Thirty states had adopted local option laws applying either to townships, municipalities or counties, and in some cases applying to all three units. More than half of all the counties, more than 60 per cent of all the incorporated towns and villages, and almost 70 per cent of all the townships in the United States, had gone under Prohibition by the local option route. By 1906, approximately 35,000,000 people in the United States were living in Prohibition territory and the saloon had been banished by law from territory in the United States aggregating more than 2,000,000 square miles.

From 1895 to 1906 the record of practically every year showed an increase in the dry territory and dry population of the United States along with a corresponding decrease in the license territory and license population of the nation. Rural townships and villages which adopted local Prohibition during this period were numbered by the thousands. Before the close of the period, 76 of the 92 towns of Connecticut had adopted no-license; 200 towns and villages in Illinois were under Prohibition, as were also 661 out of the 1,016 townships of Indiana, 250 cities and towns of Massachusetts, more than 400 townships and villages of Nebraska, more than 300 townships of New York, a thousand townships, 450 municipalities and 66 city residence districts in Ohio, more than a hundred towns and villages in Oklahoma, almost half the towns in Rhode Island, 212 out of the 246 towns of Vermont, 50 villages in Washington state, and more than 600 villages and townships in Wisconsin.

County local option had gone into effect in most of the states which were not under either Prohibition or strict license. By 1906, as a result of the operation of county option laws, more than 1,500 counties in all parts of the nation were under prohibitory legislation. At the close of this period, Alabama had 22 Prohibition counties; Arkansas, 50; Florida, 27; Georgia, 110; Iowa, 67; Kentucky, 81; Louisiana, 60; Texas, 125; Virginia, 70; West Virginia, 30; Maryland, 14; Mississippi, 60; Oregon, 12; while most of the remaining license states boasted of a few no-license counties.

During the period South Dakota, Vermont and New Hampshire repealed state-wide Prohibition, but most of the territory in these three states remained under Prohibition by local option provisions.

A number of important events occurred during this period which were of special interest in connection with the Prohibition movement. The World's Temperance Congress was held in June, 1893, in connection with the World's Fair at Chicago. This, perhaps, was the nearest to a great world temperance congress that had ever been held. Representatives from many foreign countries and from practically all temperance and reform organizations in the United States gathered at Chicago and participated in this remarkable gathering. The program of the conference included discussion of practically every phase of the liquor problem and the temperance reform. The minutes of the Congress which were published in two large volumes made an invaluable contribution to the literature of the temperance reform.

It is of interest to note that in 1894 when the liquor interests were making a special effort to corral the vote and influence of organized labor, Typographical Union No. 6 of New York city by a vote of 1,049 to 484 adopted a resolution calling for the complete destruction of the liquor traffic in both state and nation. This was the beginning of the efforts in behalf of Prohibition on the part of organized labor which in many of the state contests have greatly assisted the Prohibition forces.

It was during this period also that the first agreement upon the part of the great nations was reached to protect from distilled liquors the natives of a very large portion of the African continent. This agreement, which was known as the agreement of the Brussels conference, was entered into by the principal nations of Europe and was ratified by the United States in 1899.

At the very beginning of the twentieth century the famous Carrie Nation raids started in the state of Kansas. That state, nominally under Prohibition, had allowed the prohibitory law in certain sections to drift into a state of very lax enforcement. In fact, speakeasies known as "joints" operated in some sections openly and flagrantly. Carrie Nation, who had vainly used various means to secure the enforcement of the law in the town in which she lived, finally in despair proceeded herself to do what the law provided the officials should do.

Perhaps the most important campaign of the period

was that of 1905 in the state of Ohio in which the Anti-Saloon League organized the fight against the re-election of Governor Myron T. Herrick who, under threat of executive veto, had secured the emasculation of a residence district local option measure passed by the Ohio legislature in 1904. Governor Herrick, a Republican, had been elected for his first term in 1903 by a majority of approximately 113,000. The Republican party, under Theodore Roosevelt, had carried the state of Ohio in 1904 by a majority of more than 255,000. As a result of this pronounced wet and dry gubernatorial fight, although the rest of the state Republican ticket was elected by normal majorities, Governor Herrick was defeated by a majority of more than 44,000.

This sweeping victory secured by the anti-saloon forces in a straight Prohibition contest in a great populous state like Ohio was an encouragement to the Prohibition forces for the numerous state-wide Prohibition contests which followed during the next decade.

Among the leaders of this period were such as Howard H. Russell, Purley A. Baker, Anna A. Gordon, John C. Jackson, Ella A. Boole, George R. Stuart, Sam. W. Small, Ervin S. Chapman, George W. Young, Wayne B. Wheeler, Edwin S. Dinwiddie, John G. Woolley, David Stuart Dodge, Doctor A. J. Kynett, Archbishop John Ireland, Mary H. Hunt, Bishop Luther B. Wilson, Senator Jonathan P. Dolliver, Carrie Nation, Wilbur F. Crafts, Dr. T. D. Crothers, William E. Johnson, Margaret Dye Ellis, S. E. Nicholson, Bishop James Cannon, Jr., Mrs. Lillian M. N. Stevens, and many others.

The following chronology gives in considerable detail the facts as to the progress of the movement during the period as evidenced by the Prohibition victories in thousands of local option contests throughout the length and breadth of the nation.

Chronology of the Temperance Reform for the Period 1893–1906

1893

The Ohio Anti-Saloon League is founded by Howard H. Russell at Oberlin, Ohio.

The District of Columbia Anti-Saloon League is organized at Washington, D. C.

The biennial convention of the World's W. C. T. U. is held on the World's Fair grounds at Chicago.

The Evans dispensary law becomes operative in the State of South Carolina.

Governor Tillman, of South Carolina, meets with decided resistance in enforcing the dispensary law in the city of Charleston.

The State Liquor Dealers' Association of Ohio decides to enter politics more actively than before and demands the repeal of the law making it an offense to sell liquor to habitual drunkards, as well as a modification of the Sunday closing law and other restrictive measures.

Members of the W. C. T. U., making a circuit of the joints in Rola, North Dakota, are brutally beaten by liquor advocates.

One thousand women of Owensboro, Kentucky, band themselves together for a crusade against the liquor dealers of that city.

The first convention of the Intercollegiate Prohibition Association is held.

An illicit distillery valued at $75,000 is seized by the Federal authorities at Baltimore, Maryland.

The Long Island Railroad Company's general manager issues an order that heads of departments will be held responsible if they continue to employ men who frequent drinking places during their leisure hours.

"The Anti-Saloon," a monthly temperance paper, is established by Dr. Howard H. Russell as the official organ of the Anti-Saloon League of Ohio.

By the Act of Congress of January 28 the posttraderships in connection with the military service are completely abolished. This opens the way for the complete establishment of the army canteen.

Surgeon General George M. Sternberg protests against the beer canteen as being "an authorized beer saloon kept open under the auspices and with the approval of the government."

The license for bar-rooms in the District of Columbia is raised to $400.

1894

Orders are issued by the St. Louis police department to arrest all saloonkeepers and others having slot machines.

A committee of fifty, with Seth Low as president, is organized in New York to study the liquor question with a view to public and private action.

The Haskell local option bill is defeated in the lower House of the Ohio Legislature, receiving only thirty-six votes.

Archbishop Ireland, of the Catholic church, and Dr. Kynett, of the Methodist church, on a railway train between Chicago and Philadelphia, discuss the temperance question and agree upon the advisability of a plan for the uniting of all the forces opposed to the saloon, similar to the plan later decided upon in the organization of the Anti-Saloon League of America.

The 26th annual convention of the W. C. T. U. meets in Washington, D. C.

The lower House of the Iowa Legislature by a vote of 53 to 45 passes a bill providing for restricted local option for the cities and towns of the State, and allows the assessment of a tax of $600 on any real estate upon which liquor is sold.

Three counties in South Carolina break out in open rebellion against the State Liquor Dispensary law; two citizens and two detectives are killed.

Governor Tillman of South Carolina suppresses opposition to the State Liquor Dispensary law by assuming control of the police and the marshals of all incorporated towns.

An expose of lax law enforcement in New York City is made in an article in "The City Vigilant," which reveals the fact that on Sunday, March 18, there were 2,960 open saloons in nineteen Assembly districts, and that in from ten minutes to half an hour 3,312 persons entered them, not counting eight policemen, while thirty-nine policemen were seen in the immediate vicinity.

Major General O. O. Howard is made president of the National Temperance Society at its annual convention held in New York.

The South Carolina Supreme Court upholds the validity of the Evans Dispensary law.

A Temperance Congress is held at Prohibition Park, Staten Island, N. Y.

Several hundred illicit brandy distilleries are discovered in the mountain districts of California; they are worked mostly by Italians.

A great reception is tendered Miss Frances E. Willard in New York City on her return from Europe.

The Second Annual Convention of the Intercollegiate Prohibition Association of the United States is held in New York City.

The state dispensaries in South Carolina are reopened on August 1.

The New York State Constitutional Convention by a vote of 50 to 86 rejects an amendment offered by Mr. Titus of New York, providing for the free sale of liquor in cities on Sundays.

Judge Gibbons of Chicago directs a judgment of ouster against the whisky trust, which is declared illegal by the court.

More than 100 moonshiners are brought to trial in Kentucky and many illicit stills are destroyed.

The Twenty-first National Convention of the W. C. T. U. is held in Cleveland, Ohio.

The lower House of the South Carolina Legislature passes a bill declaring that intoxication and the use of obscene and profane language are misdemeanors.

Typographical Union No. 6 of New York City by a vote of 1,049 to 484 adopts a resolution calling for the destruction of the liquor traffic in both State and Nation.

The "Mulct Law" is passed in Iowa which has the practical effect of repealing the State Prohibition law.

Kentucky passes a law providing for local option for precincts and magisterial districts.

Missouri enacts a local option law which provides for a vote on the liquor question by counties, exempting cities of 2,500 or more from the operation of the law.

The Act of Congress of August 27 extends the bonding period for distilled liquors to eight years.

1895

At the suggestion of Bishop Luther B. Wilson, the District of Columbia Anti-Saloon League issues a call to initiate a general Anti-Saloon League movement throughout the nation.

The American Anti-Saloon League is organized at Washington, D. C., December 18, by the coalition of the Anti-Saloon League of the District of Columbia, the Anti-Saloon League of Ohio and five other state, national and local temperance organizations.

Dr. Howard H. Russell is chosen the first national superintendent of the Anti-Saloon League of America.

The American Issue, the official organ of the Anti-Saloon League, makes its first appearance, taking the place of the Anti-Saloon, the paper started by Dr. Russell in 1893.

The Indian Territory is placed under Prohibition by Federal enactment.

Congress directs the Bureau of Labor to investigate the economic aspects of the liquor problem.

General Orders No. 46 of the United States army set forth rules for the conduct of the canteen which may be permitted to sell beer and light wines, by the permission of the commanding officer.

1896

State Anti-Saloon Leagues are organized in Pennsylvania, South Dakota, Michigan, West Virginia and Iowa.

The records in Ohio show a decrease of 1,442 in the number of saloons since 1893.

The Harris local option bill is defeated in the lower House of the Ohio Legislature, receiving only fifty votes.

Massachusetts reports seven cities of over 30,000 population free from the saloon.

The Ohio Anti-Saloon League holds at Columbus the largest temperance convention ever held in the State.

The Supreme Court of Indiana holds a saloon to be a nuisance under certain circumstances, and declares that the license fee is no defense.

South Dakota votes to repeal the Prohibition law by a majority of 4,000 votes.

The National Convention of the Prohibition Party at Pittsburg nominates Joshua Levering of Baltimore, Maryland, for President and Hale Johnson of Illinois for Vice-President. The party splits on the currency question. In the election the party receives 130,617 votes.

Kentucky enacts a county local option law exempting from its operation cities of 30,000 or more.

New York enacts a township local option law.

The Second National Convention of the Anti-Saloon League of America is held at Washington, D. C., December 8-10.

1897

The States of Nebraska and Tennessee organize State Anti-Saloon Leagues.

The records of the District of Columbia show a reduction in the number of licenses from 1,100 in 1892 to 689 in 1897.

Van Buren County, Michigan, votes dry under the county option law.

Tennessee extends the Adams law excluding saloons from within four miles of schoolhouses outside of incorporated towns of 2,000 or more.

The number of saloons in New York City is reduced by 1,200 as a result of restrictive laws passed by the Legislature.

Local Anti-Saloon Leagues are organized in Colorado.

A large number of townships in Ohio vote dry under the township option law.

General Superintendent Howard H. Russell, in his annual address to the Anti-Saloon League convention, reports active work along anti-saloon lines in eighteen different states.

The existing laws against the sale of liquors to Indians are supplemented by the Act of Congress approved January 30, which is especially designed to protect Indians to whom allotments of land had been made.

Congress passes a measure (Act of March 3, 1897) giving various privileges to distillers, including the right to "bottle in bond."

1898

The local option law introduced in the Ohio Legislature is defeated in committee.

The Anti-Saloon League movement is started in Northern California, Illinois, Indiana, Minnesota, Vermont, Wisconsin, Maryland and Oklahoma.

The first superintendents' conference of the Anti-Saloon League is held at Delaware, Ohio, and is attended by representatives from twenty states.

The Third National Convention of the Anti-Saloon League of America is held January 11-13 at Columbus, Ohio.

The Fourth National Convention of the Anti-Saloon League of America is held December 6-8 at Cleveland, Ohio.

The agreement made by the Creek Indians with the Commission to the Five Civilized Tribes contains the provision that strict laws should be maintained in the territory of the Creek nation against the introduction, sale, barter or giving away of liquors and intoxicants of any kind or quantity.

Drunkenness in the army camps of Alger, Chickamauga, Mobile and Tampa causes widespread scandal and arouses temperance sentiment over the country.

The Revenue Act approved June 13, 1898, to meet the expenses of the war with Spain, doubles the tax on beer, making it $2 a barrel, but leaves undisturbed the tax on distilled spirits.

1899

Anti-Saloon League state organizations are started in New Hampshire, New York, Colorado, Arkansas and Rhode Island.

Nine-tenths of the territory of Mississippi and five-sixths of the territory of Georgia are reported dry under local option laws.

As a result of the fight made by the Ohio Anti-Saloon League, Hon. John A. Caldwell, the pro-liquor candidate for Lietuenant-Governor of Ohio, runs behind his ticket over 34,000 votes.

The Anti-Saloon League of America opens legislative offices in Washington, D. C., with Edwin C. Dinwiddie as legislative superintendent.

John D. Long, Secretary of the Navy, issues General Order No. 508 abolishing the traffic in beer and other alcoholic liquors both on shipboard and at naval stations.

The American Railway Association, comprising every important railway in the United States, Canada and Mexico, recommends the adoption of a rule forbidding the use of intoxicants by employees while on duty, and providing that the habitual use of intoxicants, or the frequenting places where they are sold, shall be sufficient cause for dismissal.

A decision of the United States Court of Claims, rendered in June, recognizes the official status of the beer canteen features of the post exchange, and declares that post exchanges, being under complete control of the Secretary of War as governmental agencies, are not subject to special taxes as "retail liquor dealers."

An attempt is made, in Kentucky, to compel distillers to pay taxes on the full value of the liquors held by them in bonded warehouses; the distillers having been in the habit of making merely nominal returns which the assessors are compelled to accept as the value of the liquor so held.

Congress enacts a measure providing that no officer or private soldier shall be detailed to sell intoxicating drinks in any post exchange or canteen. The War Department, however, continues the practice of allowing civilians to sell liquors in these canteens.

The Territory of Alaska is given a high license law, to replace the prohibitory legislation, by Act of Congress approved March 3, 1899. Barroom licenses are fixed at $500 to $1,500 per annum according to the population.

The United States ratifies the agreement of the "Brussels Conference" making a zone in which the sale of distilled liquors to native races, in Africa, is prohibited.

1900

The Clarke Municipal Local Option Bill passes the lower House of the Ohio Legislature, but is lost in the Senate by a vote of 15 to 16.

Minnesota passes a Search and Seizure law.

The League's fight on the Governor of Arkansas, who had favored the liquor interests, reduces his majority 20,000 votes. A similar fight on the Governor of Nebraska reduces his majority to 800, while the rest of the ticket wins by 8,000.

Twelve Iowa counties abolish the saloons.

Seventy-five Nebraska towns vote dry.

Queen Anne County, Maryland, adopts no-license.

The Anti-Saloon League is organized in the state of Washington.

The National Convention of the Prohibition Party meeting in Chicago, Illinois, nominates John G. Woolley of Illinois for President and Henry B. Metcalf of Rhode Island for Vice-President. In the election the party received 209,260 votes.

The Fifth National Convention of the Anti-Saloon League of America is held May 24-25 at Chicago.

The Hawaiian Islands are organized as a Territory of the United States, following their annexation, and by the terms of the Act approved April 30, 1900, provision is made for the prohibition of the liquor traffic "except under such regulations and restrictions as the Territorial Legislature shall prescribe." A license law is enacted by the Territorial Legislature with license fees ranging from $250 to $1,000.

1901

Iowa prohibits the soliciting of liquor orders in dry territory.

A strong temperance candidate is elected to the Supreme Bench of Nebraska by 12,000 majority, in spite of all the efforts of the liquor interests to defeat him.

The brewers and liquor dealers organize in every Prohibition State of the Union to break down the prohibitory laws.

Reports indicate that the Anti-Saloon League movement has been inaugurated in thirty-six different States and Territories.

The Anti-Saloon Leagues of Oregon, Virginia and New Jersey are organized.

The Hon. Hiram Price, first President of the Anti-Saloon League of America, dies, and Rev. Luther B. Wilson, D. D., later Bishop Wilson, is elected to succeed him.

Colorado reports five counties dry by action of the County Supervisors.

Private boxes are excluded from the saloons of Los Angeles, and the effort of the liquor forces to open the saloons on Sunday in that city is defeated as a result of a petition containing the names of 13,000 citizens.

The Supreme Court of Indiana hands down three decisions favorable to the temperance forces.

Kansas enacts a Search and Seizure law.

Over 400 liquor cases are started in the courts of Ohio, and convictions are secured in about 85 per cent of that number.

Tennessee reports that out of 500 cities, towns and postoffices, only sixty have saloons.

The Sixth National Convention of the Anti-Saloon League of America is held December 3-5 at Washington, D. C.

The following resolution is introduced into the United States Senate by Senator Henry Cabot Lodge, and adopted: "Resolved, That in the opinion of this body the time has come when the principle, twice affirmed in international treaties for Central Africa, that native races should be protected against the destructive traffic in intoxicants, should be extended to all uncivilized people by the enactment of such laws and the making of such treaties as will effectually prohibit the sale, by the signatory powers, to aboriginal tribes and uncivilized races, of opium and intoxicating beverages."

The Act of Congress approved February 2 prohibits "the sale or dealing in beer, wine or any intoxicating liquors by any person in any post exchange or canteen or army transport or upon any premises used for military purposes by the United States." This is known as the Anti-Canteen Law.

1902

The Ohio Legislature passes the Beal Municipal Local Option law.

Kentucky adopts a stringent law enforcement measure.

Maryland passes twenty-eight different local temperance laws.

Congress appropriates $1,000,000 for canteen substitutes at army posts.

Ninety-three municipalities in Ohio vote dry.

Forty-four Maryland saloons are outlawed.

Forty-four of the seventy-five counties in Arkansas abolish the saloons.

Two-thirds of Los Angeles County, one-half of San Diego County and one-half of San Bernardino County, Cal., adopt no-license.

Missouri closes forty-four dramshops.

Of forty-eight county option elections in Texas, forty-one result in Prohibition victories.

Twenty-eight liquor license remonstrances are successful in Indiana.

New York State outlaws sixty concert hall saloons

in Buffalo, and adds one hundred dry townships to the no-license column.

Oliver W. Stewart, a Prohibition Party candidate, is elected to the Illinois State Legislature.

Local Option elections in Connecticut result in 93 towns voting for no-license as against 75 for license.

The Seventh National Convention of the Anti-Saloon League of America is held December 9-11 at Washington, D. C.

The so-called "New Hebrides" Bill is passed (approved February 14) prohibiting Americans from selling intoxicants, opium and firearms to the natives of the Pacific islands.

A meeting of Indians of the Five Civilized Tribes is called at Eufaula, Oklahoma, November 28, to protest against the admission of Oklahoma into the Union without any provisions for keeping the agreement prohibiting intoxicating liquors.

The Act of Congress approved April 12 removes most of the special taxes levied to meet the expenses of the war with Spain, and reduces the tax on beer from $2 to $1 a barrel.

1903

The Prohibition laws of Vermont and New Hampshire are repealed by the adoption of local option measures in these States.

Virginia passes the Mann law, practically banishing all saloons from rural districts.

North Carolina adopts the Watts law, limiting saloons to incorporated towns and giving the right of local option to all municipalities.

One-fourth of all saloons in the State of Virginia are put out of business by local option.

Eighteen of the twenty-four towns and cities voting in Virginia adopt Prohibition.

Tennessee extends the four-mile law to include all cities of 5,000 or under.

Washington enacts an anti-liquor Search and Seizure law.

Congress appropriates an additional $500,000 for army canteen substitutes.

Five no-license towns are added to the dry column in Connecticut.

One county in Montana votes dry.

Fifty-seven additional towns and cities in Ohio adopt no-license under the Beal law, and 450 convictions of saloon violators are secured in the same State.

Cases against saloon and dive keepers in Maryland result in 430 convictions.

Dr. P. A. Baker is elected General Superintendent of the Anti-Saloon League of America, at the Eighth National Convention of the Anti-Saloon League of America held December 9-11 in Washington, D. C.

Twenty of the twenty-seven municipal local option elections in North Carolina result in Prohibition victories.

Congress passes an Act to Regulate the Immigration of Aliens into the United States, which provides that no intoxicating liquors shall be sold in any immigrant station (Act approved March 3, 1903).

Congress inserts a clause in the Immigration Act, providing that "no intoxicating liquors of any character shall be sold within the limits of the Capitol building of the United States."

A convention is called by the Five Civilized Tribes which takes action for opposing any scheme of statehood for Oklahoma that would endanger the Prohibition laws of the Territory.

1904

Anti-Saloon Leagues are organized in Kentucky, Idaho, Oklahoma and Indian Territory.

Oregon adopts a local option law.

The Brannock residence district option law for cities passes the Ohio Legislature, after being mutilated by action of Governor Myron T. Herrick.

Virginia reduces the number of saloons in that State by 230.

California reports fifty cities and towns under no-license.

The number of licensed bar-rooms in the District of Columbia is reduced to 639.

The anti-saloon forces secure the election of a Prohibitionist member of the Illinois Legislature from the city of Peoria, the world's whisky center.

A movement is inaugurated in Indian Territory for Prohibition statehood.

The Iowa Legislature enacts an anti-bootleggers' bill and inebriates' bill and passes a resolution urging Congress to amend the interstate shipment law in such a way as to prevent the shipment of liquors from one State to the dry territory of another.

The Legislature of Kentucky passes an act to prevent the selling of intoxicating liquors by wholesale in any territory where the retail trade is prohibited.

Seven counties in Missouri vote dry and 200 saloons are closed in the State.

The National Convention of the Prohibition Party at Indianapolis, Indiana, nominates Silas C. Swallow of Pennsylvania for President and George W. Carroll of Texas for Vice-President. In the election the party receives 258,787 votes.

The aggregate vote in the Iowa County elections shows a license majority in the State of 52,358.

The Ninth National Convention of the Anti-Saloon League of America is held November 16-18 at Columbus, Ohio.

1905

Six anti-liquor laws are passed by the Legislature of New York.

Forty-two cities and towns in Wisconsin begin the work of enforcing various laws against saloons and three temperance measures are passed by the Wisconsin Legislature.

The Moore amendment to the Nicholson law of Indiana is enacted, making remonstrances applicable to all requests for licenses in a township. Under this law seventy-four Indiana townships go dry.

North Carolina passes an amendment to the Watts law prohibiting saloons outside of towns of 500 or more.

Five Oregon counties abolish the saloons.

Virginia abolishes one hundred dramshops.

One hundred and fifty-three injunctions against liquor venders are secured in Iowa.

Ninety-one Iowa druggists are deprived of their liquor-selling permits because of law violations.

One hundred and sixty-three convictions against saloonkeepers are secured in Minnesota, and the saloons are closed on Sunday in Minneapolis.

Nebraska witnesses a decrease of 114 in the number of saloons.

Governor Herrick, of Ohio, is defeated for re-election by a majority of over 44,000 by the anti-saloon forces who thus resent his mutilation of the residence district option bill for cities.

The Tenth National Convention of the Anti-Saloon League of America is held November 21-24 at Indianapolis.

CHAPTER VIII

Non-Partisan State Prohibition Movement
1906–1913

BY 1906 the non-partisan movement for Prohibition had come to be generally considered as representing the most effective method of fighting the liquor traffic. The Anti-Saloon League had been organized in practically every state and territory. Many other temperance organizations had been and were doing effective service in connection with the many phases of the temperance reform, but the Anti-Saloon League had come to occupy a place of leadership in the political and legislative phases of the whole Prohibition movement.

Prior to 1906 the Anti-Saloon League did not feel justified in making a general campaign for state-wide Prohibition. There were many reasons for this attitude, the chief of which was to be found in the historic policy of the League, which was to go only so far and so fast in legislative efforts as the public sentiment of the state would justify.

The leaders of the Anti-Saloon League fully recognized the fact that the temperance reform could not be successfully acomplished by any short-cut route; that the mere passage of a law or the adoption of a state constitutional amendment would not secure Prohibition; that any law without the people behind it could never be permanently effective, and that in

the last analysis the success of Prohibition in the
United States was dependent upon the slow but only
sure process of the creation of temperance sentiment,
the crystallization of that sentiment into public opinion,
and the final expression of that public opinion in the
drafting, enacting, and enforcing of prohibitory law.
From the very beginning the leaders of the Anti-
Saloon League had insisted upon such a program and
had consistently refused to be persuaded or driven
from strict adherence to such a program. The radical
element of the Prohibition forces had repeatedly de-
nounced the League and its policy as compromising
and even unmoral. In numerous instances where the
League had refused to be coerced into a premature
fight for state Prohibition it had been charged with
having been afraid to fight or with having been cor-
rupted by the liquor interests, yet the League still insistently held to its course, which in the long run was
bound to demonstrate the wisdom of those who were
responsible for its methods and plans.

The political policy of the Anti-Saloon League had
always been broad-guage, in that the League had constantly refused to lend itself to any political move for
Prohibition which appeared to be too far advanced for
the temperance public to support. Consequently its
efforts in state legislative bodies were always based
upon the degree of advancement to which the sentiment of the state had attained. The League recognized the fact that members of a state Legislature
were peculiarly sensitive, on most public questions, to
the sentiment of a majority of their voting constituency, and that this was especially true where such
issues had been raised and had become prominent in

local contests in the districts which they represented. It had observed that as a rule members of a state Legislature from no-license districts were to be found supporting measures proposed for the suppression of the liquor traffic, while those representing license districts usually opposed restrictive temperance legislation. There were, of course, exceptions to the rule both ways, but in the aggregate the vote for and against vital temperance legislation very closely indicated the number of legislators from Prohibition and license communities.

This being true, the leaders of the Anti-Saloon League took the ground that until a majority of the people in a majority of state legislative districts had reached the point of open hostility to the liquor traffic, efforts of the temperance forces could better be directed toward building sentiment and suppressing the liquor traffic in the local communities than in making a fight for state-wide Prohibition without some probability of success. The experience of the temperance forces in the state Prohibition contests of the fifties and the eighties had been helpful in suggesting the necessity of having a strongly organized public sentiment for enforcement back of any state prohibitory law or state constitutional amendment. The Anti-Saloon League was determined to profit by the unhappy experiences of the past. The League, moreover, very well understood that when the fight began in earnest for state prohibitory legislation in a few states, the psychological effect would inevitably be the projection of state-wide Prohibition campaigns in many states where the temperance sentiment was not sufficiently strong to justify such campaigns.

By 1906, however, the progress of the anti-saloon movement in local option contests throughout the United States had reached the point where in almost half the states of the Union a majority of the members of the state Legislatures represented districts in which the majority of the voting population had been favorable to Prohibition. More than one-third of the population of the United States was living in territory which was under Prohibition by vote of the people. Moreover, it had been found that local Prohibition in municipalities, villages and counties, could not be fully enforced when such local units were bordered by license districts, and that the maintenance and enforcement of Prohibition in local areas required state action which would permit the Prohibition majorities in no-license districts to join with the Prohibition minorities in license districts to secure a majority expression for Prohibition in the state as a unit.

This all indicated that the time had come for the anti-liquor forces in many states to strike for state-wide prohibitory legislation, while in other states it was apparent that the part of wisdom was to continue efforts for local option legislation or the securing of local Prohibition under local option laws already on the statute books.

The signal for the new crusade in the interest of state prohibitory legislation was the appeal for statehood by the people of the Territory of Oklahoma and the Indian Territory. The first legislative contest for Prohibition in connection with the appeal for statehood of this proposed new state came in the halls of the United States Congress. Indian Territory had been under Prohibition by Federal law. Congress recognized the fact that the solemn obligation between the Federal Government and the Indians demanded that protection against the liquor traffic for the Indian Territory should be included in any statehood enabling act which Congress might pass. Prohibition for the Indian Territory portion of the proposed new state therefore was insured by act of Congress for a period of 21 years after Oklahoma should come into the Union as a state. Another battle came in the constitutional convention in Oklahoma in which the anti-liquor forces of the Territory were finally successful, securing the submission of a Prohibition clause in the proposed Constitution.

Under the enabling act of Congress the vote for the adoption of a state Constitution and the vote on a prohibitory clause in that Constitution were taken in 1907, with the result that the people of the proposed new state adopted constitutional Prohibition by a majority of over 18,000. The effect of this successful effort for Prohibition in Oklahoma electrified the moral forces of other states, and the struggle for state prohibitory legislation was promptly inaugurated in many commonwealths, especially in the southern part of the nation.

Alabama passed a prohibitory statute in 1907, which became effective on January 1, 1909. A prohibitory amendment was rejected by vote of the people in 1909 and as a result the complexion of the state Legislature was changed and the state-wide prohibitory statute was repealed in 1911.

Georgia adopted Prohibition in 1907, the law becoming effective on January 1, 1908. For several years the law was not well enforced so far as the sale of beer was concerned. An attempt in 1911, however, to repeal the prohibitory law by the adoption of a beer amendment failed. The enforcement provisions were later amended and improved and the prohibitory law remained upon the statute books until National Constitutional Prohibition went into effect in 1920.

By action of the Tennessee Legislature in 1907 saloons were banished from all but four counties of the state. Two years later state-wide Prohibition went into effect. Mississippi adopted a prohibitory law in 1908, thus bringing under prohibitory legislation the seven remaining license counties of that state. The people of North Carolina during the same year also adopted Prohibition by a majority of 44,000.

Both houses of the Arkansas Legislature in 1909 passed Prohibition measures. The resolutions, however, were not alike and each house refused to pass the prohibitory measure adopted by the other. State Prohibition for Arkansas, therefore, was delayed. In 1911 the Legislature submitted Prohibition to a vote of the people, but it was rejected by a majority of 16,000. Kansas in 1909 greatly strengthened the state Prohibition law, prohibiting the sale of intoxicating liquors with the single exception of that for sacramental use. The state of Wyoming during the same year prohibited the sale of all intoxicating liquors in territory outside of incorporated towns and villages.

The lower house of the West Virginia Legislature passed a Prohibition bill in the session of 1909, but the measure failed of passage in the Senate. Three years later, when the people had an opportunity to vote on the question of a state prohibitory amendment to the Constitution, Prohibition was adopted by a majority of more than 92,000. A proposal to submit Prohibition to the people of Texas carried in the Texas state primaries in 1910 by a majority of 30,000 votes. When the question was submitted, however, in 1911, Prohibition was defeated by a majority of approximately 7,000 out of a total of 466,000 votes.

State-wide constitutional amendments providing for Prohibition were defeated in 1910 in the states of Missouri, Florida and Oregon, the adverse majority in Missouri being more than 200,000, while the majorities in Florida and Oregon were about 4,600 and 20,000 respectively.

The state of Ohio suffered a Prohibition reaction in 1912 by the incorporation of a license clause in the Constitution of the state and the repeal of county local option.

During this period of state-wide Prohibition effort, a number of states where sentiment did not justify an immediate state-wide fight, nevertheless made rapid progress in adding to no-license territory under local option provisions. A general local option law was enacted by the Legislature of Illinois in 1907 under the operations of which in the first general election in the spring of 1908, 1,053 townships in the state voted against license and more than 1,500 saloons were abolished by vote of the people in a single day. Two of the three counties of Delaware also went under local Prohibition by the local option route the same year.

In 1908 the local option laws in the state of Michigan, South Carolina, Oregon and Colorado were strengthened, with the result that before the close of the period, 33 counties in Michigan, 31 counties in

South Carolina and 100 municipalities in Colorado had abolished the saloon. Under the local option law of Oregon, 23 counties had voted for Prohibition prior to 1910, but on account of a constitutional amendment adopted that year, excluding cities from the operation of the county option law, a number of the larger towns and cities in no-license counties went back to the license system. The municipal local option law of the state of Washington and the county local option laws in the states of Idaho, Arizona and Utah, were enacted by their respective Legislatures in 1909. In the case of Utah, however, the measure was vetoed by the Governor.

At the beginning of the period, three states were under state-wide Prohibition. Before the end of the period seven additional states had been added to the Prohibition column. One, however, repealed the law in 1911, thus leaving nine states under state-wide prohibitory laws at the end of the period. Campaigns for state-wide Prohibition, moreover, had already been inaugurated in approximately half of the remaining states, and 15 state capitals were under no-license.

Considerable progress was also made during this period toward advanced temperance legislation in the United States Congress. Several additional appropriations for recreation buildings at army posts were granted by Congress. The National C. O. D. Liquor Shipment bill was passed in 1909 and the Jones-Works law providing for numerous restrictions on the sale of intoxicating liquors in the District of Columbia was enacted in 1912.

As state after state was added to the Prohibition column the problem of enforcement within the borders of each state became serious. Under the Federal Constitution and the numerous interpretations of the provisions of that document by the Supreme Court of the United States, the liquor traffic within a state was subject to state police regulations. The Constitution, however, also gave to Congress exclusive power over interstate commerce, consequently while any Prohibition state had the right to deal directly with shipments of intoxicating liquor from one point in that state to another point in the same state, the state Legislature lacked power to deal adequately with shipments of intoxicating liquors coming into the state from outside points. Numerous efforts had been made to remedy this condition. Two different laws had previously been enacted by Congress which were intended to remedy the difficulty, but under the rulings of the courts these measures had proved entirely inadequate.

While the C. O. D. law passed by Congress in 1909 helped to relieve the situation to some extent, the flagrant violations of state laws and state constitutional amendments continued until after a long, hard fight on the part of the Prohibition forces before Congress, the interstate liquor shipment bill known as the Webb-Kenyon law was enacted by Congress in 1913. This law, which was later upheld by the Supreme Court of the United States, eliminated from the protection of interstate commerce regulations all shipments of intoxicating liquors intended for use in the violation of state laws. This was the crowning victory of the period, not only because of the direct results of the operations of this Federal law, but also because of the fact that the passage of the law under all the circumstances had committed the Congress of the United States to a policy which in reality recognized the liquor traffic as an outlaw trade and which indicated a special desire on the part of Congress to assist the states in the complete enforcement of all prohibitory legislation against the traffic.

The period from 1906 to 1913 was one in which the accomplishments of the Prohibition forces had a most important bearing on the entire Prohibition movement throughout the nation. In the first place, it was demonstrated that the same methods which had worked so successfully in local communities were without doubt the best methods to be used in connection with the fight against the liquor traffic in the state as a unit. In the second place, it had been repeatedly demonstrated that the organized moral forces, operating through legitimate and proper political methods, could win even in uneven contests against the most strongly organized liquor interests working through unscrupulous and corrupt political methods. In the third place, the backbone of the liquor traffic had been broken by the significant fact that the Congress of the United States had committed the Federal Government to a policy of supporting state legislative efforts for the suppression of the traffic.

The following chronology covers the important events of this period.

CHRONOLOGY OF THE TEMPERANCE REFORM FOR THE
PERIOD 1906–1913

1906

Indiana increases the number of Moore law township remonstrances to 187, and abolishes the liquor traffic in seventeen city wards.

Iowa places a time limit on Mulct law saloons.

Georgia extends the local option privilege to all counties where dispensaries have been installed, and five additional counties in that State go under Prohibition.

The number of no-license counties in Arkansas is increased by ten and the total majority recorded against license in the State of Arkansas is 16,618.

Kentucky passes the county unit local option law, which results immediately in fourteen new counties passing into the no-license column. The Governor orders the closing of Sunday saloons in Louisville.

Two temperance laws are placed on the statute books of Louisiana.

Thirty-two local temperance measures are passed by the Maryland Legislature.

Six of the eleven New Hampshire cities and 193 towns vote against license.

Assistant Attorney-General Trickett enforces the Prohibition law in Kansas City.

Governor Cobb is re-elected in Maine on a platform declaring for the continuance of Prohibition and law enforcement.

The Jones Residence District law for cities and a Search and Seizure law are passed by the Legislature of Ohio.

Oklahoma shows a reduction of 128 in the number of saloons.

One thousand law enforcement cases are prosecuted against liquor law violators in Pennsylvania.

One county, three cities and several towns are won for no-license in California.

Six additional municipalities vote dry in Virginia.

The Sunday laws are enforced in Seattle, Tacoma and other cities in the State of Washington.

Congress appropriates an additional $350,000 for army canteen substitutes.

The Oklahoma Statehood bill as passed by Congress, requires the prohibition of the liquor traffic in Indian Territory, and on Indian reservations for twenty-one years, and thereafter until the people shall change the organic law.

Congress prohibits liquor selling in national soldiers' homes, and appropriates $25,000 for the better enforcement of the laws against selling liquor to Indians.

Three Party Prohibitionists are elected to the Illinois Legislature and three are elected to the Minnesota Legislature.

The Eleventh National Convention of the Anti-Saloon League of America is held November 19-22 at St. Louis, Missouri.

Congress appropriates the sum of $25,000 to suppress the traffic in intoxicating liquors among the Indians, of which $15,000 is to be used exclusively in the Indian Territory and Oklahoma.

The Act of Congress of June 21, 1906, amends and strengthens the Act of December 24, 1872, requiring collectors of Internal Revenue to keep for public inspection a list of those who pay special liquor taxes within their district.

An Act of Congress is passed "for preventing the manufacture, sale or transportation of adulterated or misbranded or poisonous or deleterious foods, drugs, medicines and liquors, and for regulating the traffic therein."

1907

Alabama passes a county option law. Jefferson County, Alabama, including the city of Birmingham, votes dry by a majority of 1,800.

Arkansas abolishes all saloons outside of incorporated towns.

Colorado enacts a local option law.

Connecticut passes three new temperance laws.

The Legislature of Georgia passes a state-wide Prohibition measure.

A Sunday closing law is enacted by the Legislature of Idaho.

Local option for townships, cities and villages is adopted by the Legislature of Illinois. One hundred and forty-one precincts voting in Illinois vote no-license.

The Delaware Legislature submits the liquor question to the vote of the people, with the result that every place outside of Newcastle County and the city of Wilmington abolishes the saloons.

Of the thirty-seven county option elections held in Kentucky, thirty-five go dry.

The Massachusetts Legislature enacts the "pony express law," aimed at the illicit selling of liquor in dry territory.

An anti-wine room law is passed by the Legislature of Montana.

Eight additional dry counties are secured in North Carolina.

Ohio destroys 350 speakeasies and fifty additional towns and cities in the State go under local Prohibition.

Several provisions are added to the anti-liquor laws of Nebraska.

A bill calling for resubmission of the Prohibition question is defeated in the lower House of the Legislature of Maine.

Numerous Prohibition victories are recorded in Missouri, Minnesota and Vermont.

South Dakota passes a Search and Seizure law.

An amendment to the Adams law of Tennessee results in the exclusion of the saloons from all but four counties in the State.

Eleven of the thirteen municipalities voting in Virginia go for Prohibition.

A residence district local option law is passed in Wisconsin.

Sixty-three additional townships and four counties are added to the no-license column of Indiana.

Governor Comer of Alabama calls a special session of the Legislature in November, which passes a statewide Prohibition law.

Oklahoma adopts the Prohibition clause of the proposed State Constitution by a majority of 18,103.

The Twelfth National Convention of the Anti-Saloon League of America is held September 16-19 at Norfolk, Virginia.

Congress appropriates $25,000 to suppress the traffic in intoxicating liquors among the Indians.

1908

The Georgia Prohibition law goes into effect January 1.

Illinois in a single day votes 1,053 townships dry, abolishing thereby over 1,500 saloons.

Wisconsin adds one hundred new communities to the no-license column, and abolishes four hundred saloons.

Thirty-two additional towns in Minnesota are gained by the anti-saloon forces.

Thirty additional municipalities in Nebraska vote against license.

Ten additional counties in Michigan abolish the saloons.

Eight additional South Carolina counties go under Prohibition.   Governor Ansell is re-elected on an anti-saloon platform.

Mississippi passes a state-wide Prohibition law.

North Carolina adopts state-wide Prohibition by a majority of 44,000.

Twenty-one of the thirty-three counties of Oregon vote to abolish the saloons under the county option law.

Forty-two municipalities in Colorado adopt no-license.

Arkansas registers a total majority against license in the county option elections of 23,262, and elects an anti-saloon Governor by 80,000 majority.

Leavenworth, Kansas, the last liquor stronghold of the State, falls into line by abolishing the "joints."

Governor Stubbs is elected in Kansas on a Prohibition and law enforcement issue.

South Dakota drives the saloons from Mitchell, and several other important towns, and elects temperance men as Governor and United States Senator.

Texas adds twelve dry counties to the no-license

list, and re-elects Governor Campbell on a straight anti-saloon issue.

Four hundred drinking places in Virginia are closed.

Rhode Island abolishes 429 saloons, and passes a law limiting the number of licenses to one for every 500 of the population, and prohibiting the saloon within 200 feet of a public or parochial school.

Tennessee elects a Legislature pledged to enact State Prohibition.

United States Senator Carmack is shot down in the streets of Nashville, and dies a martyr to the Prohibition cause.

Maine and North Dakota both elect Governors pledged to the strict enforcement of Prohibition.

Two additional counties in California vote dry.

The State of Washington elects a Governor, Lieutenant-Governor and the majority of the members of the Legislature favorable to local option.

Baltimore, Maryland, closes 393 saloons.

An additional county in Maryland abolishes the saloon.

Worcester, Massachusetts, with a population of 150,000, for the second time votes for no-license.

Two hundred and fifteen saloons are outlawed in the State of Massachusetts by elections under the local option law.

Four hundred and sixty-one saloons are abolished in Iowa.

Seven hundred and twenty saloons go out of business in Indiana by the remonstrance route.

The Indiana Legislature called in special session

by Governor Hanly, passes a county local option law.

The Ohio Legislature enacts a county local option law and provides for resident district Prohibition upon petition.

In four months fifty-seven counties in Ohio vote dry, abolishing thereby 1,910 saloons.

More than 11,000 saloons are abolished in the United States by the operation of Prohibition and local option laws, during the year.

The Georgia Legislature passes a law licensing near-beer and locker clubs, which opens the way for wholesale violations of the State Prohibition law.

Congress appropriates an additional $25,000 to suppress the traffic in intoxicating liquors among the Indians. An appropriation of $3,500 is also made for this purpose.

The National Convention of the Prohibition Party meets in Columbus, Ohio. Eugene W. Chafin of Arizona and Aaron S. Watkins of Ohio are nominated for President and Vice-President respectively.

1909

The effort of the liquor forces to repeal anti-saloon legislation in Indiana and Ohio fails.

On the first day of January Prohibition laws go into effect in Alabama, Mississippi and North Carolina.

Tennessee extends the four-mile law to all towns and cities of the State, which means practically state-wide Prohibition, and adopts another measure prohibiting the manufacture of liquor in the State.

South Carolina adopts Prohibition with a referendum by counties, and as a result of the referendum vote, thirty-six of the forty-two counties prohibit the sale, while the other six retain the county dispensaries.

The lower House of the Missouri Legislature passes a resolution calling for a vote on the Prohibition amendment.

Iowa passes five anti-liquor laws limiting the liquor traffic in various ways.

Maine and New Hampshire both write new restrictive law enforcement measures in the statute books.

Washington State passes a municipal and rural county unit option law, and more than forty places in the State promptly abolish the saloons.

Idaho enacts a straight county option measure, and in the first round of elections fourteen of the twenty-three counties abolish saloons.

Arizona enacts a county option law.

Wyoming abolishes all saloons outside of incorporated towns.

Kansas passes a stringent measure prohibiting the sale of liquors for all purposes except for sacramental use.

Nebraska limits the open saloon to the hours between 7 a. m. and 8 p. m. Lincoln, Nebraska, and two counties in the state adopt Prohibition.

Utah passes a county option law which is vetoed by the Governor after the Legislature adjourns, but the people of more than half of the counties of the State are so incensed at the Governor's action that they abolish the saloons by local decree.

Congress passes a C. O. D. liquor shipment measure for the protection of dry territory.

Colorado adds a number of towns to the no-license column, thereby making eleven no-license counties.

Four additional counties are carried for no-license in Illinois.

In the fall election, twenty-eight of the thirty-six places voting in Illinois abolish the saloon.

Nineteen additional counties in Michigan abolish the saloons.

Twelve counties in Texas adopt no-license.

Three new counties are added to the no-license list in Kentucky.

Two counties in Pennsylvania adopt Prohibition.

The lower House of the West Virginia Legislature passes a Prohibition bill. Eight additional counties in West Virginia vote no-license.

The elections in New York result in a net gain for the anti-saloon forces of eighty-eight towns.

Sixty counties in Indiana vote no-license.

A number of anti-liquor measures are passed by the Legislature of Connecticut, one limiting the number of saloons to one for 500 inhabitants.

Six additional counties in California adopt no-license.

Six temperance measures are passed by the Legislature of South Dakota.

A local option bill in the Pennsylvania Legislature is brought to a vote in the House, but is defeated.

The Florida Legislature passes a bill submitting a prohibitory amendment to the vote of the people.

The Alabama Legislature submits a prohibitory amendment to the vote of the people, but the amendment is rejected.

Strong law enforcement measures are passed by

the Legislatures in Georgia and Alabama to assist in enforcing the statutory Prohibition laws.

The Alabama state-wide Prohibition law goes into effect on January 1, closing saloons in the four remaining wet counties, and thirteen dispensary saloons in other counties.

Local option elections in California result in the closing of 439 saloons; in addition by various methods 500 more are closed in the city of San Francisco, thus making a total of 939 saloons closed in the State during the year.

Local option elections in Connecticut result in ninety-seven towns voting against license and seventy-one for license.

Delaware has 76,200 people living in no-license territory.

Florida has thirty-five dry counties out of a total of thirty-seven. Only 330 saloons are left in the State.

Indiana has seventy dry counties out of a total of ninety-two.

The Governor of Kansas declares that no employee addicted to drink will be retained in the employ of the State.

In Kentucky a Legislature strongly favoring prohibitory legislation is elected.

In Louisiana the Gay-Shattuck law goes into effect January 1. It prohibits the sale of liquor to whites and negroes in the same building; prohibits saloons within three hundred feet of any church or school, and makes it unlawful to throw dice or to gamble in any form in saloons. Of the about 2,400 saloons in the State, a majority are in New Orleans.

Missouri gains one Prohibition county.

Through the efforts of Chief Special Officer Johnson of the Federal Indian Affairs Department, two additional counties in Minnesota are placed under Prohibition.

Nevada reports the largest number of saloons per capita in the United States. The city of Reno has one saloon for every twenty male adults, one gambler for every ten male adults and yet there are 2,000 empty rooms in this mining town.

One county and several towns in New Mexico are added to the Prohibition column. The city council of Santa Fe adopts a resolution not to grant liquor licenses after January 1, 1910.

North Dakota Legislature adopts several stringent law enforcement measures.

Ohio reports the tax rate in Prohibition counties decreasing while the tax rate of license counties, for the most part, is increasing. Prohibition cities show an increased number of savings bank depositors.

The Oklahoma Legislature passes a more efficient law enforcement measure.

No-license makes a net gain of three towns in Rhode Island; twenty-seven places in the state grant licenses, eleven are under no-license.

In Vermont, twenty-seven towns vote for license, 219 vote for no-license.

Only about 600 saloons remain in Virginia, nearly all in cities; Charlotteville, the seat of the University of Virginia, on December 7, for the second time, votes for Prohibition by an overwhelming majority.

The Legislature of Delaware passes a law providing for re-submission of the Prohibition question in New Castle County; the vote taken in November results in a majority for license of 748.

The Michigan Legislature enacts a Search and Seizure law and provides for the limiting of the number of saloons to one for every 500 of the population.

Only eight counties in Mississippi are added to the dry column when State Prohibition goes into effect on January 1, the other sixty-nine counties having been under Prohibition through the operation of their county local option law.

The Thirteenth National Convention of the Anti-Saloon League of America is held December 6-9 at Chicago, Illinois.

There are 1,622 breweries in the United States, producing in this fiscal year 56,364,360 barrels of beer.

Congress appropriates $40,000 for suppressing the liquor traffic among the Indians.

1910

The Legislature of Texas passes a measure making the sale of liquors in no-license territory a felony punishable by from three to five years in the penitentiary.

Jasper County, Missouri, including three cities each having a population of 10,000 or more, votes for local Prohibition.

The campaign for state-wide Prohibition in Idaho is launched.

As a result of decision of the United States Supreme Court, saloons are prohibited on the Milwaukee Railroad in South Dakota, and other roads in the confines of reservations.

By decision of the Supreme Court of the State of Arkansas, Texarkana is made no-license under the provisions of the three-mile law.

A monster petition for local option election in the city of Chicago is turned down by the city board of election commissioners.

Seven counties in Texas vote for local Prohibition.

Nez Perce county, Idaho, including the city of Lewiston, with a population of 8,000, abolishes the saloons.

The no-license elections in Vermont result in a net loss of two towns for the temperance forces, thereby increasing the number of wet towns and cities in the state to twenty-nine, and decreasing the number of dry towns and cities to 217.

As a result of local option elections in Minnesota, the temperance forces make a net gain of twenty-nine villages, and for the first time in the history of the State, more than half the towns voting go for Prohibition.

A general local option bill in the Legislature of Maryland is defeated by a majority of two votes.

Of thirty-six counties voting on the local option question in Michigan, twenty adopt no-license, making a net increase of ten counties for the temperance forces, and voting out of business 319 saloons.

The liquor forces win in several city local option elections in Illinois, including those held in Rockford, Decatur, De Kalb, Dixon and Belvidere, while the city of Monmouth changes from license to no-license, the city of Galesburg remains no-license, and the smaller towns and villages for the most part record temperance victories.

A large number of towns and cities in California vote for Prohibition, while several other cities under Prohibition, re-submit the question, but remain in the no-license column.

The largest number of no-license elections ever held in the State take place in Wisconsin, resulting in a net gain of about twenty-five counties for the Prohibition forces.

Fifty-four saloons are voted out of twenty-one towns and cities in South Dakota.

Saloons are closed in the New Mexico cities of Roswell, Endee, Tres Piedras and Shoemaker.

The Minnesota cities of Fergus Falls, Wasseka, Blue Earth and Kasson, vote no-license.

Bonner County, Idaho, banishes the liquor traffic.

Lansing, the State capital of Michigan, together with many other cities and towns in that State, close saloons as a result of the county option elections.

United States Senator Crawford, of South Dakota, introduces a bill in the Senate to prohibit the sale of Federal revenue stamps to persons in Prohibition territory.

The Supreme Court of Washington upholds the local option law in that State.

Lincoln, Nebraska, votes to remain under Prohibition.

Forty saloons are abolished in Idaho between January 1 and June 15, 1910.

Hancock County, Kentucky, votes to remain under Prohibition, Warren County adopts Prohibition, and Bowling Green goes for license by a small majority.

Seventeen precincts in Mendocino County, California, are made Prohibition territory by a local option ordinance.

The Supreme Court of Kansas decides that a club can not maintain lockers in which its members keep liquors for private use.

Three Wisconsin towns go under Prohibition by the use of the remonstrance law.

Territory in Arizona, containing 320 square miles, votes for Prohibition under the precinct provision of the local option law.

Carl Etherington, a special officer, who is compelled, in self-defense, to shoot a speakeasy keeper as a result of a raid in Newark, Ohio, is lynched by a drunken mob on the public square of Newark.

The number of saloons in Baltimore, Maryland, is reduced from 1,600 to 1,406 in one year.

Hon. William Jennings Bryan makes a fight in the Democratic Convention of Nebraska for a county option plank.

Elections held in the counties of Arkansas show a majority against license in the State of 23,262.

Hamilton and Harrison Counties in Texas adopt Prohibition.

Winchester and Fredericksburg, Virginia, vote to remain under Prohibition.

Potter County, Texas, goes for license, being the first of 166 Prohibition counties to reject Prohibition in three years time.

All the saloons in six counties of Minnesota are closed, and large sections of two other counties are made Prohibition territory by order of the Interior Department.

Of the forty-nine cities and towns voting under the local option law of Washington, twenty-eight go for Prohibition, including the two seaport cities of Bellingham and Everett.

Governor R. S. Vassey, of South Dakota, is re-elected in spite of liquor opposition.

Eight cities and twenty-three towns in New Hampshire vote for license, while three cities and 201 towns vote against license.

The anti-liquor forces of Tennessee score a great victory in the election of Governor Hooper and a majority of the Legislature favorable to Prohibition.

A prohibitory amendment to the Constitution of Florida is defeated by a majority of 4,372.

California elects a Governor and a majority of the Legislature favorable to local option.

Two state-wide Prohibition measures are defeated in Oregon by 20,000 majority, and the liquor amendment giving home rule on the liquor question to cities is carried by 3,000 majority.

The county option elections in Arkansas result in seven license counties adopting Prohibition.

The Democratic Legislature of Maine repeals the Sturgis Prohibition law enforcement measure and re-submits the state prohibitory amendment to a vote of the people of the State.

An effort on the part of the liquor forces to repeal the State Prohibition Amendment in Oklahoma results in a Prohibition majority at the polls of 21,077 out of a total vote of 231,159.

Congress appropriates $50,000 to suppress the liquor traffic among the Indians.

The city of Denver, Colorado, remains under license by a large majority.

The number of saloons is reduced in Connecticut, leaving about 1,900 in operation.

Rural Newcastle County, Delaware, remains wet by a majority of 748 on November 8.

Chief of Police Gilman goes into office in Bangor, Maine, on March 1 and begins a vigorous enforcement of the prohibitory law.

Eight out of twelve county elections in Missouri result in Prohibition victories. A prohibitory constitutional amendment is defeated in Missouri by a majority of over 200,000.

Oklahoma elects a large number of State and county officers pledged to strict enforcement of the prohibitory law.

The Supreme Court of Tennessee, in October, upholds the law, making the possession of Federal licenses prima facie evidence of the violation of the Prohibition law.

1911

Only about 2,000 saloons remain in Delaware, the most of them in the city of Wilmington.

In the District of Columbia there are 635 liquor licenses of all kinds, one for every 521 of population.

The Moon law, limiting the number of saloons in Iowa, is upheld by the Supreme Court December 18, and 247 saloons closed at once.

Of 119 counties in Kentucky 95 are dry.

The "Bar and Bottle law" in Massachusetts, prohibiting the sale of bottled goods or liquor sold to be taken out, goes into effect May 1.

The state-wide Prohibition law of Alabama is repealed by the enactment of a county local option law.

Of the thirteen counties in Alabama holding elections under the new local option law, six vote against Prohibition (one voting for dispensary and five for saloons), while seven vote for Prohibition.

The Colorado Legislature refuses to pass two measures introduced by the liquor advocates to mutilate temperance laws already on the statute books.

The result of the local option elections in Connecticut shows ninety-five towns voting for no-license and seventy-three towns voting for license.

The Legislature of California enacts a local option measure which provides for a vote on the liquor question in each incorporated city and town, making supervisorial districts outside of municipalities voting units for the purposes of the act.

As a result of the operation of the new local option law in California, many victories are won by the temperance forces, bringing the amount of Prohibition territory up to 42 per cent of the State's area and closing the saloons in thirty towns and ten supervisorial districts.

Laws are passed in California prohibiting saloons within one and one-half miles of Stanford University or within three miles of the State Agricultural College.

The General Assembly of Delaware passes a druggists' prescription bill which proves to be a splendid temperance measure.

Florida adds one more county to the Prohibition list, thereby bringing the number of no-license counties in that State up to thirty-six out of a total of forty-eight and leaving only sixteen license towns and cities in the entire State.

The Tippins near-beer bill develops a strength of three to one in the Georgia House of Delegates on roll call, but is defeated by a filibuster.

The Georgia Legislature passes a law making the possession of a United States tax receipt prima facie evidence of the violation of the State liquor laws.

Reports from Idaho show that the temperance forces have carried seventeen out of twenty-two county option elections and that only 165 saloons are left in the State.

The General Assembly of Illinois enacts three new temperance laws, thereby prohibiting drinking and drunkenness on railroad trains and interurban cars, establishing a Prohibition zone within a radius of two-thirds of a mile around the Soldiers' and Sailors' Home at Quincy, and prohibiting the sale, gift or use of liquor in any State park.

The Illinois liquor interests are overwhelmingly defeated in their attempt to repeal the township local option law of that State.

The liquor interests of Indiana, led by a brewer Senator, succeed in persuading the Legislature to repeal the county option law and to enact a law providing for city and township units substituted therefor. Another measure protecting the liquor interests is passed by the Legislature.

Forty-six dry counties in Indiana go back to saloons on account of the repeal of the county option law, leaving only twenty-four Prohibition counties out of ninety-two in the State and reducing the number of Prohibition townships to 825 out of a total of 1,015.

A stringent law is passed by the Legislature of Kansas prohibiting the sale of any liquid containing a trace of alcohol to any person in Kansas for any purpose whatsoever, except for sacramental use.

Every candidate on the State ticket in Kentucky who is supported by the liquor interests where the temperance question is involved, is defeated for nomination.

After a vigorous campaign in the State of Maine, a vote is taken on September 11 on the question of the repeal of the Prohibition law of that State, with the result that Prohibition is retained by a majority of approximately 750 votes.

Out of twelve candidates for the House of Delegates in the Second and Third legislative districts of Maryland, five declare for local option and four of the five are elected, while not one of the seven who kept quiet on the local option question is elected.

Reports from Massachusetts show that there have been steady gains in no-license campaigns and that there are four more dry cities and six more dry towns in that State than in 1906.

As a result of the county option elections in Michigan, there are thirty-nine wholly dry counties in the State, which show a gain of thirty-eight dry counties in four years, during which time 1,200 saloons and eighteen breweries have been closed.

Efforts of the liquor forces in the Michigan Legislature to defeat county option and to permit the operation of breweries in dry counties, as well as the operation of saloons on most holidays, are defeated; while on the other hand, several helpful temperance laws are passed, among which are laws governing the writing of prescriptions for liquor.

The State Fair of Michigan is dry for the first time in its history.

Great gains are made in the popular vote for a county option Legislature in Minnesota.

The local option bill in the Minnesota Legislature is voted on for the first time in both Houses of the Legislature, but meets defeat.

A county option bill passes the Missouri House of Delegates by a large majority, but is defeated by being sent to an unfriendly committee in the Senate.

Every local option election in the State of Missouri during the year is won by the temperance forces, the majorities in all cases being larger than ever before.

County option is defeated in the Nebraska Legislature by one vote in each House, but a helpful law is enacted providing for an election on the saloon question upon the petition of thirty freeholders or a majority if there are less than sixty in the corporation, the vote to be mandatory on the license authorities, which law applies to all towns having a population under 10,000.

An amendment submitted by Congress to make the Constitution of New Mexico more easily amendable, is voted upon and carried by 10,000 majority in the new State, thus making easier the way to Constitutional Prohibition.

Five out of sixty-eight legislative bills favorable to the liquor traffic are passed by the General Assembly of New York State.

New York reports a large gain in the number of dry townships.

An effective near-beer law passed by the North Carolina Legislature in March, becomes operative in July.

Several dry counties in Ohio vote for the return of saloons.

Ninety bootleggers are convicted in Oklahoma City during the year, and, in the aggregate, are fined $31,-000 and given 9,000 days in jail. Thirty-seven Oklahoma counties report fines that aggregate $78,000 and jail sentences aggregating 27,154 days.

Lawrence County, Pennsylvania, is made dry by remonstrance, including the city of Newcastle, with a population of 30,000, the largest dry municipality in the State.

In Rhode Island eight towns, with a population of 15,906, vote for no-license, while thirty towns and cities with a population of 526,704 vote for license.

The Legislature of South Dakota passes a law requiring saloons to close each night at 9 o'clock, which affects 500 saloons operating in the State.

Texas votes on a Prohibition Amendment to the Constitution on July 22. The pro-liquor majority is less than 7,000 out of a total of nearly 500,000 votes. Reports show that 168 counties of Texas are entirely under Prohibition.

Reports from the counties of Texas show that 168 counties of that State are entirely under Prohibition.

At the elections held on March 7, only twenty-eight

of the 246 towns and cities of Vermont vote for license, and in twelve of those which vote for license the majorities are so small that a change of forty votes, approximately distributed, would have put them in the no-license column.

The amendment to the charter of Point Pleasant, West Virginia, making that city dry territory, is sustained by the State Supreme Court.

The Legislature of Wisconsin enacts laws regarding the sale of liquors at public auctions, the appearance of intoxicated persons in public places or on railroad trains.

Reports from Wisconsin show that the number of no-license communities in that State has grown from 300 in 1904 to more than 800 in 1911, which 800 communities cover 55 per cent of the State's area.

The Legislature of Idaho enacts a strong Search and Seizure law.

The Thirty-Eighth National Convention of the Woman's Christian Temperance Union is held October 28-November 2 at Milwaukee, Wisconsin.

Congress appropriates $12,000 to suppress the liquor traffic among the natives of Alaska.

Congress appropriates $80,000 to suppress liquor selling among Indians.

The Fourteenth National Convention of the Anti-Saloon League of America is held December 11-14, at Washington, D. C.

New Jersey reports 50 per cent more saloons than in fourteen Southern states.

The Pueblo Indians in New Mexico have formed a total abstinence society of about 500 members and temperance missionary work is planned among all of the tribes.

Sixty-six of the eighty-eight counties of Ohio are reported under Prohibition on January 1.

A special session of the Texas Legislature appoints a committee in both Houses to investigate the use of liquor funds in recent election.

Governor Hooper of Tennessee calls a special conference for November 30 to devise plans for the better organization of temperance forces for the enforcement of the prohibitory law.

Utah on June 27, holds local option election in 110 cities and towns. Salt Lake City and Ogden, and twenty-one other towns, vote for license while eighty-seven towns and cities vote for Prohibition. One hundred and one saloons are closed; 235 are left, of which 141 are in Salt Lake City, and thirty-two in Ogden.

Eight of the nineteen cities of Virginia are under Prohibition, as are also 145 of the 161 incorporated towns.

More people in Washington State are living in Prohibition territory than constituted the entire population of the State in 1900.

The West Virginia Legislature submits a Prohibitory Constitutional Amendment to be voted on in November, 1912.

1912

A vote taken in Arkansas on September 9 on the question of state-wide Prohibition results in a license majority of 15,968, there being 69,390 votes for Prohibition and 85,358 votes against Prohibition.

Reports from Arkansas show that there are about 279 saloons in the State, and that these are confined to twenty-eight towns and cities in twelve counties.

Sixty-seven towns in California vote for Prohibition.

Several Prohibition victories are recorded in local option contests in Colorado.

In the Connecticut local option elections ninety-four towns vote for no-license and seventy-three towns vote for license.

The largest towns in Kent and Sussex Counties, Delaware, prohibit the sale of alcoholic beverages.

Lafayette County, Florida, votes for Prohibition.

The Prohibition forces of Georgia elect a Legislature favorable to Prohibition.

Latah County, Idaho, is put under Prohibition by order of the County Commissioners.

Rockford, Illinois, with a population of 50,000, votes for Prohibition.

Reports from Indiana indicate that twenty-seven out of the ninety-four cities of the State are under Prohibition, and that about 300 of the 360 incorporated towns are without saloons.

Reports from Idaho indicate that out of 830 incorporated cities and towns, 703 are for Prohibition and that there are seventeen Prohibition counties in the State, nine of which have only one wet city each.

The Kentucky Legislature removes the exemption clause from the county unit law, making it apply to all counties alike. The same Legislature also enacts several wholesome law enforcement measures.

Muhlenberg, Montgomery and Pulaski Counties,

Kentucky, vote for Prohibition by more than two to one majority.

A special session of the Maine Legislature rejects a proposed resolution adopted by the lower House to re-submit Prohibition to a vote of the people.

The Maryland House of Delegates passes a local option law, but the measure is defeated by one vote in the Senate.

Of the 320 towns voting in Massachusetts, seventy-three vote for license, and 247 vote against license.

As a result of the spring elections in Michigan, thirty-five counties in that State are dry.

Under a special law enacted by the Michigan Legislature, providing that there shall not be more than one saloon to every 500 of the population, about 200 upper peninsula saloons are closed on May 1.

Congress appropriates $12,000 for the suppression of the liquor traffic among the natives of Alaska.

Congress appropriates $75,000 for the suppression of liquor selling among the Indians.

The National Convention of the Prohibition Party is held at Atlantic City, N. J. on July 10.   Eugene W. Chafin of Arizona and Aaron S. Watkins of Ohio are respectively nominated for President and Vice-President.

Connecticut has 2,120 saloons.

The Legislature of Mississippi enacts three new anti-liquor laws, increasing the penalty for the violation of the State Prohibition law.

Of twenty-four local option elections in Mississippi, twenty-two result in Prohibition victories.

In the local option elections in New Hampshire.

held on November 5, ninety-one towns vote for license and 203 towns vote against license, the total no-license votes being 27,875, while the total license votes are 14,518.

The illegal sale of liquor on railroads in the State of New Jersey is stopped.

The House of Representatives in New Mexico votes to submit a Constitutional Prohibition Amendment to the people by a majority of twenty-seven to fifteen, but the measure fails to pass the Senate.

By a vote of the people in Ohio, an amendment to the Constitution is adopted, licensing the traffic in intoxicating liquors. Out of a total of 1,250,000 electors, only 462,000 vote on this question. Eighteen counties in Ohio vote against Prohibition and twelve counties vote for Prohibition.

The Supreme Court of the United States hands down a decision upholding Federal Prohibition in Indian territory and certain portions of Indian countries in Oklahoma.

The United States Supreme Court hands down a decision upholding the constitutionality of the twenty-one year Prohibition clause for that portion of the new state of Oklahoma which was originally Indian Territory.

The local option elections in Oregon show in the aggregate a majority of approximately three to one favorable to Prohibition.

Decided gains are shown for the temperance forces in the election of members of the Pennsylvania General Assembly.

The Rhode Island local option elections result in

seven towns with a population of 16,850 voting for Prohibition, and seventy-one towns with a population of 525,760 voting against Prohibition.

The Supreme Court of Tennessee upholds the law of that State prohibiting the manufacture of intoxicating liquors.

In the annual elections in Vermont, 225 towns vote for no-license, and twenty-one towns vote for license, showing a gain of 35 per cent in favor of the no-license forces over the preceding year.

A resolution permitting the people to vote on state-wide Prohibition is passed by the lower House of the Virginia Legislature, but is defeated in the Senate by a vote of twenty-four to sixteen.

The people of West Virginia on November 5 adopt a constitutional amendment prohibiting the liquor traffic by a majority of 92,342 out of a total vote of 235,843; the law becomes effective July 1, 1914.

The Thirty-Ninth National Convention of the Woman's Christian Temperance Union is held October 21-25 at Portland, Maine.

The mayor of Jacksonville, Florida, orders the saloons closed during street car strike.

Twenty-five railroads in Illinois agree not to sell liquor on their dining cars or any other part of their equipment.

Cook County, Illinois, has over 7,400 saloons, 7,152 in Chicago. The Chicago Vice Commission presents alarming statistics on the relation of the liquor traffic to vice.

At Quincy, Illinois, the saloon zone near the Soldiers' Home is removed from one-third to two-thirds of a mile from the home; consequently the convictions for drunkenness are reduced from 831 to 319 in six months.

A special session of the Maine Legislature, convening March 20, refuses to submit an amendment to the Constitution providing for the substitution of local option for Prohibition.

Twenty-two of the twenty-four local option elections in Missouri are carried for no-license and 60,000 people added to the population living in Prohibition territory.

Union County, South Carolina, votes for a dispensary making eight dispensary counties and thirty-six Prohibition counties in the State.

Governor B. W. Hooper, Republican, is re-elected in Tennessee by united action of the Prohibition voters of the State.

CHAPTER IX

THE first official declaration by any general temperance organization for National Constitutional Prohibition was made by the order of the Sons of Temperance in 1856. The first resolution introduced in Congress providing for a prohibitory amendment to the Federal Constitution was presented in the House of Representatives by Congressman Henry William Blair of New Hampshire on December 27, 1876. In 1885, a prohibitory amendment resolution was presented in the United States Senate by Honorable Henry W. Blair, United States Senator from New Hampshire, and Honorable Preston B. Plumb, United States Senator from Kansas. This measure was referred to the Senate Committee on Education. It was reported favorably by the Senate committee and placed on the Senate calendar in 1886, but no further action was taken.

The Woman's Christian Temperance Union had repeatedly declared for National Constitutional Prohibition both during the leadership of Frances E. Willard and during the presidency of Mrs. Lillian M. N. Stevens. The Prohibition party, moreover, had repeatedly declared for Prohibition in the national Constitution, while similar action had been taken by the Independent Order of Good Templars, the National Temperance Society and numerous church bodies during the last half of the nineteenth century.

Prior to 1913 the Anti-Saloon League of America had not seen fit to inaugurate a specific campaign in the interest of National Constitutional Prohibition, the leaders of the movement believing that the cause of Prohibition, under the conditions which existed, could be better served by efforts in the interest of state and local Prohibition under state legislative enactments.

The leaders of the League, moreover, naturally applied the same rule regarding legislation in Congress that had been used in determining the proper time for the inauguration of state-wide Prohibition campaigns, feeling as they did that it was very natural to expect that members of Congress would as a rule represent the sentiment of their respective districts on Prohibition legislation in Congress as that sentiment had been expressed in local option or state-wide Prohibition campaigns.

The Anti-Saloon League officials considered that this point was of greater importance in connection with the fight for Prohibition in Congress than it had been in connection with the fight for Prohibition in any of the states. Under the Federal Constitution the passage of a resolution submitting to the states an amendment to the Constitution required a two-thirds vote. Under the rules of the National House and Senate, however, amendments to any such resolutions or changes in any such resolutions as introduced, could be made by a majority vote. It was entirely possible, therefore, that a resolution calling for the submission of a prohibitory constitutional amendment in a Congress where a majority of the members were not favorable might easily have been so emasculated or changed by a majority vote in Congress as to be finally submitted in such form as to protect or legally recognize the liquor traffic as having rights under the Constitution of the United States. There was, of course, not much danger of such a thing happening through the sole efforts of Congressmen favorable to the liquor traffic, but it was entirely possible for such a situation to be created in the fight for a constitutional prohibitory amendment as to unite friends and foes of Prohibition in Congress in such a way as to give recognition to the liquor traffic which the Constitution had never before given and which the high courts of the United States had repeatedly refused to recognize, as inherent rights.

From the Anti-Saloon League viewpoint, therefore, it was exceedingly important to be reasonably sure of a majority for Constitutional Prohibition in Congress before any such measure was introduced or a great nation-wide campaign inaugurated for securing such a resolution at the hands of Congress.

In 1913 not only were nine states under state-wide prohibitory legislation, but the fight for prohibitory laws had already been inaugurated in more than a score of other states in most of which a majority of the population was living in territory made dry by vote of the people under local option laws. The nine Prohibition states in 1913 had an aggregate population of 14,685,961. In the 31 other states operating under local option laws the population living in dry territory at that time was 26,446,810. There were three other states having an aggregate population of 3,693,201 in which the Legislatures had provided for state-wide Prohibition in all sections except those localities where a majority of the voters agreed to waive the prohibitory provisions. Two other states were under state-wide Prohibition for all territory outside of incorporated villages and cities. Congress, moreover, had prohibited the liquor traffic in military forts and reservations, in the United States Navy, in the National Capitol building at Washington, in national and state Soldiers' Homes, and in other specified areas under Federal Government control.

By reason of the operation of all these prohibitory provisions more than 46,000,000 people (more than half the population of the United States) in all the states were living under prohibitory legislation. One-half of all the people living in license territory were living in four states. One-fourth of all the people living in license territory were the residents of six cities, and more than half of all the saloons in the United States were located in fourteen cities. More than 50 per cent of the population and more than 71 per cent of the area of the United States were under prohibitory laws.

A survey of the national Congressional situation in 1913 showed that more than a majority of the members of the national House of Representatives represented Congressional districts in which the majority of their constituents were favorable to Prohibition, as shown by the state, county, municipal and township Prohibition and local option polls. Hence the Anti-Saloon League felt that the time had come for a decisive step to be taken in the interest of National Constitutional Prohibition.

Another factor which strongly influenced the movement for National Prohibition in 1913 was the attitude of the Prohibition and near-Prohibition states on the question of enforcement. Just as it had been impossible fully to enforce township, county and municipal Prohibition without state Prohibition, so it had become apparent that the enforcement of state Prohibition would never be permanently successful until National Prohibition had been secured. Consequently it was natural that the Prohibition majorities in the Prohibition states and the near-Prohibition states should unite with the Prohibition minorities in the license states to secure mutual protection for Prohibition legislation, in harmony with the desire of the majority in the larger unit.

The Fifteenth National Convention of the Anti-Saloon League of America was held in the city of Columbus, Ohio, in November, 1913. This convention unanimously and enthusiastically went on record in favor of the immediate prosecution of a general campaign throughout the length and breadth of the nation for National Constitutional Prohibition. Moreover, the Council of One Hundred, the name of which was afterwards changed to the National Temperance Council, representing the leading men and women in all the national temperance reform organizations of the United States, was organized in the city of Columbus simultaneously with the holding of this epoch-marking convention of the

Anti-Saloon League. From this time forward, all the leading temperance organizations of the nation centered their efforts on the movement for National Prohibition. The National Temperance Council, organized for the purpose of bringing together for consultation the leaders of all temperance organizations, began to play a very important part in the National Prohibition fight by bringing the reform leaders into frequent conferences, by eliminating in some degree the old prejudices which had existed between the organizations, and by emphasizing the important matters upon which all the organizations represented in the body were practically agreed.

The national convention of the Anti-Saloon League at Columbus in November, 1913, had authorized the selection of a Committee of One Thousand Men to meet in the city of Washington, march to the Capitol of the United States, and present to the members of both Houses of Congress the League's proposed resolution providing for the submission of National Constitutional Prohibition. The national Woman's Christian Temperance Union also organized a Committee of One Thousand Women for a similar purpose. When these committees met and formed on Pennsylvania Avenue in the nation's capital city, the Committee of One Thousand Men had been increased to a committee of more than two thousand, while the Committee of Women had also increased beyond the thousand mark, so that as the two committees joined forces they represented a human petition of more than three thousand American citizens, representing practically every state in the Union, appealing to Congress to submit National Prohibition to the Legislatures of the several states. The spokesmen for the Anti-Saloon League Committee on that occasion were Honorable Malcolm R. Patterson, former Governor of Tennessee, and Ernest H. Cherrington, editor of the American Issue and General Manager of the Anti-Saloon League's Publishing Interests. Those who spoke for the women were Mrs. Lillian M. N. Stevens, president of the national Woman's Christian Temperance Union, and Mrs. Ella A. Boole, president of the Woman's Christian Temperance Union of New York state.

The Committee of One Thousand appealed to Congress in harmony with the spirit of Article One of the amendments to the Federal Constitution, guaranteeing "the right of the people peaceably to assemble and petition the government for a redress of grievances." The committee reminded the Congress that a majority of the population of the United States lived under Prohibition; that local and state Prohibition had been thoroughly tried and had fully demonstrated the benefits of such a policy in the diminution of crime, pauperism and insanity and in the increase of wealth, happiness and the general prosperity of the people. The committee called the attention of Congress to the fact that Prohibition had made such progress in the states that there were fewer saloons left south of Mason and Dixon's line than were to be found in the single city of Chicago, and that there were 36 states in the Union in which the aggregate number of saloons was not so large as the number operating in the single city of New York.

The committee moreover called attention to the fact that the United States Supreme Court had repeatedly declared that there is no inherent right in a citizen to sell intoxicating liquors at retail; that under the Constitution of the United States such an employment is not a right of a citizen of any state or of a citizen of the United States, and that under the American form of government the rights of the people of the nation as a whole are paramount, just as the rights of the people of a single state are superior to the rights of the people of any city within the borders of a state; and that, since such a large proportion of the people of the United States had declared themselves in favor of Prohibition as a governmental policy the time had come when it was incumbent upon the Congress of the United States to submit the question of National Prohibition to the several state Legislatures.

The committee declared that its action in presenting this petition to Congress and the efforts of the Prohibition forces throughout the United States, were in full harmony with the objects of the American government, set forth in the preamble to the Constitution of the United States, namely, "To form a more perfect union, establish justice, insure domestic tranquility, provide for the common defense, promote the general welfare, and secure the blessings of liberty to ourselves and our posterity."

The proposed resolution providing for the submission of National Constitutional Prohibition was presented by the committee to Honorable Richmond Pearson Hobson as a member of the National House of Representatives, and to Honorable Morris Sheppard of Texas, as a member of the United States Senate. The measure was promptly introduced by these gentlemen in both Houses of the Sixty-Third Congress and referred to the Judiciary Committee in each House.

The Hobson Joint Resolution was taken up by the House of Representatives by the adoption of a special rule, on December 22, 1914, and on final vote received 197 votes in its favor with 189 votes against it, thus failing for lack of a two-thirds majority necessary for the passage of a resolution providing for the submission of a constitutional amendment. Fifteen absent members were paired, ten for the resolution and five against it, while twenty-seven other members of the House did not vote.

An analysis of the vote in the House of Representatives on the Hobson Joint Resolution showed that the representatives from fifteen states voted solidly for the resolution, that more than three-fourths of the members from each of twenty-one states and a majority of the representatives from each of twenty-seven states voted for submission, only seven states giving a solid vote and only eighteen a majority vote against the resolution.

A joint resolution calling for the submission of a prohibitory amendment to the Federal Constitution was introduced in both Houses of the Sixty-Fourth Congress which convened in December, 1915. The resolutions were presented in the Senate by Senator Morris Sheppard of Texas and Senator J. H. Gallinger of New Hampshire. In the House the resolutions were introduced by Representative Edwin Y. Webb of North Carolina and Representative Addison T. Smith of Idaho. On December 14, 1916, the House Judiciary Committee by a vote of twelve to seven favorably reported the National Prohibition resolution which was placed on the House calendar as House Joint Resolution No. 84. On December 21, 1916, the Judiciary Committee of the Senate by a vote of thirteen to three favorably reported the National Prohibition Resolution which went on the calendar of the Senate as Senate Joint Resolution No. 55. Neither resolution, however, came to a vote, and both died with the adjournment of the Sixty-Fourth Congress.

Similar resolutions were presented in both Houses early in the first session of the Sixty-Fifth Congress and were passed, in the Senate on August 1, 1917 and in the House on December 17, 1917. The final vote in the Senate was sixty-five to twenty while the vote in the House was 282 to 128. Slight amendments were made to the measure when it was adopted by the House on December 17. The Senate, however, on the following day voted to concur in the House amendments and the resolution was thus finally adopted on December 18, 1917.

An analysis of the final vote on the National Prohibition resolution in the House of Representatives shows that the representatives of twenty-four states voted solidly for the measure; that the votes of more than three-fourths of each Congressional delegation in thirty states were cast for the measure, and that the votes of a majority of each of the Congressional delegations in thirty-six states were recorded in its favor, while one-half or more of the delegation in each of forty-two states were thus recorded for submission. The delegations of only two states voted solidly against the measure and the delegations of only six states recorded a majority against it.

An analysis of the vote on the Prohibition Joint Resolution in the Senate shows that both Senators from each of twenty-eight states voted in favor of the resolution, while both Senators from only four states voted against the resolution. In the case of sixteen states, one Senator voted for and the other Senator voted against the resolution.

Something of the progress in the creation of sentiment favorable to the submission of a National Prohibition Amendment is indicated by a comparison of the attitude of the state delegations in the National House of Representatives, when the Hobson Joint Resolution was voted upon in 1914 and when the Sheppard-Gallinger-Webb-Smith resolution was finally passed by the House in 1917. While the delegations from only fifteen states voted solidly for the resolution in 1914, the delegations from twenty-four states voted solidly for the resolution in 1917, and while a majority of the representatives from each of twenty-seven states voted for the resolution in 1914, a majority of the representatives from each of thirty-six states voted for the resolution in 1917.

The representatives from seven states voted solidly against the resolution in 1914, while in 1917
solid delegations from only two states were recorded against it.   In 1914 a majority of the representatives from each of eighteen states was recorded
against the measure, while in 1917 a majority of
the representatives from each of only six states cast
their votes against it.

In the meantime, Congress, which had so thoroughly committed itself to the cause of Prohibition,
enacted numerous measures intended to suppress
the traffic in the territories and in other sections
under Federal control.   Prohibition for the District
of Columbia was adopted in the closing hours of
the last session of the Sixty-Fourth Congress, the
measure having passed the Senate on January 9,
1917, and having passed the House on February 28,
1917.   Prohibition for Alaska was enacted by Congress in February, 1917, becoming effective on January 1, 1918.

Through an enabling act passed by Congress,
Porto Rico was given the right to vote on the Prohibition question, with the result that in July, 1917,
the people of Porto Rico adopted Prohibition by a
large majority, the vote being 99,775 in favor of
and 61,295 against Prohibition, the law going into
effect on March 2, 1918.   Prohibition for the Hawaiian Islands was enacted by Congress on May 24,
1918.   The so-called "Bone-Dry Advertising" Prohibition measure was passed in February, 1917, and
numerous other measures of a restrictive and pro-
hibitive character passed the Congress during the

years when National Prohibition was being considered and before the Eighteenth Amendment to the Constitution was finally ratified.

Aside from the National Prohibition resolution the most important measure passed by Congress was that providing for War-Time Prohibition. Such a bill was presented by Representative Barkley in the House of Representatives on April 26, 1918, and was referred to committee. In May, 1918, however, Representative Randall presented a bill for War-Time Prohibition and the same was passed by a vote of 179 to 137. This measure encountered opposition in the Senate, however, and the Senate Committee finally reported a substitute measure which was passed by the Senate on September 6, 1918. The Randall provision and the provision substituted by the Senate Committee were both amendments to the General Agricultural Bill and while the House of Representatives by a vote of 171 to 34 promptly agreed to the substitute amendment by the Senate, the House disagreed to the other provisions of the agricultural bill. The whole measure, therefore, was thrown into conference and was not finally passed by both Houses until November 21, 1918. This law became effective on July 1, 1919.

Ratification of the proposed prohibitory amendment to the Federal Constitution began almost immediately after the passage of the Joint Resolution by Congress. Mississippi was the first state to ratify, action being taken by the Legislature of that state on January 8, 1918. From that time forward, regular and special sessions of state Legislatures

continued to act favorably on the question of ratification until on January 16, 1919, thirty-six states
had been reported to the United States Secretary
of State as having ratified the amendment. Other
states promptly followed until on the 25th day of
February forty-five states had ratified this amendment, which had been incorporated in the Constitution as the Eighteenth Amendment. New Jersey,
Connecticut and Rhode Island were the three states
which failed to take favorable action on ratification.

It is of interest to note that of the first thirty-six
states to ratify the Eighteenth Amendment to the
Constitution, eighty-six per cent of the population
in all these states was living under Prohibition prior
to the adoption of the National Amendment and
ninety-five per cent of the area of these states was
under Prohibition by state laws.

Something of the reflection of the temperance sentiment of the several states and Congressional districts is shown in the comparative records of the
vote of representatives in Congress and the vote of
state Legislatures on the matter of ratification, in
the first thirty-six states to ratify. Eighty per cent
of the representatives in Congress of these thirty-
six states voted for submission, while eighty-three
per cent of the aggregate members of the Legislatures in these same states voted for ratification.

In the lower Houses of the forty-five states which
finally ratified the amendment, 3,742 votes were
cast for ratification as against 931 votes which were
cast against it, while in the Senates of these forty-
five states, 1,287 votes were cast for and 213 votes

against ratification. In other words, eighty per cent of all the members of all the lower Houses of the forty-five states voted for the ratification of the Eighteenth Amendment, while eighty-six per cent of all the members of all the Senates of the forty-five states voted for ratification.

In addition to those, who as officers of the various temperance organizations stood out as leaders during this period there were a large number of men and women who shared heavily in the leadership of the fight for National Constitutional Prohibition. Among those deserving special mention in this connection are: William Jennings Bryan, Richmond Pearson Hobson, Rev. William A. ("Billy") Sunday, J. Frank Hanly, Louis Albert Banks, Ira Landrith, Clinton N. Howard, Senator Wesley L. Jones, Senator J. H. Gallinger, Senator Morris Sheppard, Mrs. Mary Harris Armour, Daniel A. Poling, Doctor Irving Fisher, Lieut.-Colonel Dan Morgan Smith, Malcolm R. Patterson, and Edwin Y. Webb.

The following Chronology covers the principal events of the period.

CHRONOLOGY OF THE TEMPERANCE REFORM FOR THE PERIOD 1913–1919

1913

The Connecticut Legislature passes a bill providing for a State Farm for drunkards but the measure is vetoed by the Governor.

A number of vicious measures are introduced in the Illinois Legislature by the liquor interests but every one is defeated. An attempt to repeal the local option bill fails. A vigorous and determined effort of the liquor interests to repeal the "Bar and Bottle Law" of Massachusetts fails.

The "Allison" liquor law enforcement act goes into effect in Texas on November 19.

The United States Congress passes the Webb-Kenyon law over the veto of President William H. Taft, thus prohibiting shipment in interstate commerce of intoxicating liquors when such liquors are to be used in violation of law.

As a result of the elections in Arizona, Maricopa County is made Prohibition territory in all portions outside of the city of Phoenix. All of Graham County and parts of Yuma and Apache Counties vote for Prohibition.

The Going law is adopted in Arkansas February 17, 1913. This measure makes it unlawful for any court, town or city council to issue a license to sell intoxicating liquors except in cases where such licenses are asked for by a petition signed by the majority of the white adult population within the incorporated towns or cities where the license is to be issued. Before one can secure such a license the county must have voted for license at the last general election in which the liquor question was an issue.

One hundred and seventeen roadhouses in Sonoma County, California, are closed on January 1.

The California Legislature passes a law compelling saloons to close from 2 to 6 o'clock a. m., thus putting an end to the all-night saloons in San Francisco.

The Hazel anti-shipping law, passed by the Legislature of Delaware, is sustained by the courts.

The Jones-Works bill restricting the liquor traffic in the District of Columbia is passed by Congress in the face of terrific opposition, thus providing for the reduction of the number of saloons to not more than 300 by November 1, 1914.

Under decision of the Supreme Court of Georgia a campaign against near-beer saloons and locker clubs results in the closing of forty-three near-beer saloons and a number of clubs and hotel cafes in large towns and cities of the State.

The Idaho Legislature passes strong law enforcement measures.

The Illinois Legislature passes a four-mile dry zone measure, protecting the University at Champaign and Urbana.

A residence district local option bill is passed by the House and Senate of the Illinois Legislature, but is killed by action of the Speaker.

Of the 28 local option elections held in Illinois on November 4, 22 result in Prohibition victories, the women's vote strongly aiding the victors.

Reports from Indiana show that, within fifteen years, the number of Prohibition towns has been increased from ninety-five to 274, the number of Prohibition cities from none to thirty-two, the number of Prohibition townships from 350 to 825, the number of Prohibition counties from two to thirty-two, and the population in Prohibition territory from 500,000 to 1,600,000.

An important decision of the Supreme Court of Iowa on the Mulct law affects many large cities of the State, and makes it more difficult for saloons to secure licenses.

The Kansas Legislature passes an anti-shipping law to co-ordinate with the Federal anti-shipping law.

The Fifteenth National Convention of the Anti-Saloon League of America is held November 10-13 at Columbus, Ohio.

The enfranchisement of women in Kansas is estimated to have added 300,000 voters to the Prohibition army.

In six local option elections in Kentucky, each involving a license county seat, the Prohibition forces win by good majorities, thus making a total of ninety-nine Prohibition counties in the State as against twenty-one license counties.

Twelve counties out of sixteen in Maine elect officials pledged to the strict enforcement of the Prohibition law.

By raising the license in the city of Baltimore from $250 to $1,000 the number of saloons in that city is decreased from 2,400 in 1907 to less than 1,500 in 1913.

The records show that almost 1,200 convictions for the violation of the Prohibition law of Mississippi have been secured in two years.

In sixteen local option elections in Missouri, between January and October, the population in Prohibition territory is increased by 143,282, and the number of Prohibition counties is increased to seventy-four.

The elections in New Hampshire result in seven license cities and seventeen license towns, as against four no-license cities and 203 no-license towns.

The New Mexico Legislature enacts two local option laws, one permitting municipalities to vote on the liquor question, and the other permitting the territory in any county outside of municipalities to vote on the question.

The Legislature of North Carolina passes an effective Search and Seizure law.

Over 5,000 gambling devices are seized and many pool halls closed in North Dakota.

The Ohio Legislature enacts several law enforcement measures and passes a law providing for the removal of officials who do not enforce law.

The license constitutional provision of Ohio goes into effect.

Twelve municipalities in Oregon vote for Prohibition on November 4 including Salem, the state capital, thus adding 35,000 to the population of Prohibition territory in the State.

The Oregon Legislature enacts a number of measures governing the sale of intoxicating liquors outside of municipalities.

A local option bill in the Pennsylvania Legislature receives eighty-three votes in the House as against seventy-four in 1911, and sixty-six in 1909.

The number of retail licenses in the State of Rhode Island is decreased by about 300 during the year.

Five excellent temperance laws are enacted by the Legislature of South Dakota. By the operation of one of these laws, all but 375 saloons in the State are closed.

An extra session of the Tennessee Legislature is called by Governor Hooper to pass the nuisance bill and the anti-shipping bill.

As a result of elections in Vermont, only eighteen towns and cities in the state license the liquor traffic.

The West Virginia Legislature passes the Yost law, which is conceded to be the most stringent Prohibition enforcement statute in the United States.

The State Supreme Court of Wyoming upholds the constitutionality of the Sunday closing law.

The Oklahoma Legislature amends the Prohibition law, making it a felony to keep a place for the purpose of violating that law anywhere in the State.

The Legislature of Michigan enacts the Lee law prohibiting drinking on other than dining cars, and prohibiting drunken men from riding on trains.

The Missouri Legislature enacts a county unit law which is to be operative throughout the state without exempting cities. The liquor interests, however, secure a referendum on the measure, and it is defeated at the polls.

Although Nebraska had voted under the initiative by a majority of 15,000 in favor of county option, the Legislature fails to pass the law.

The Florida Legislature enacts an anti-shipping and "blind tiger" Search and Seizure law.

The Georgia State Senate by a vote of five to one

passes an anti-shipping law, but the measure is defeated in the House.

Minnesota enacts a municipal local option law.

The number of saloons in Ohio is reduced from 7,800 to 5,300 by the various provisions of the new law.

The Fortieth National Convention of the Woman's Christian Temperance Union is held October 31-November 5 at Asbury Park, New Jersey.

Congress appropriates $12,000 to suppress the liquor traffic among the natives of Alaska and $75,000 for the suppression of the liquor traffic among the Indians.

1914

Arizon adopts a prohibitory constitutional amendment which goes into effect January 1, 1915.

At the November election in Colorado the Prohibition Amendment to the State Constitution submitted to a vote of the people is adopted by a majority of 11,752. The amendment goes into effect January 1, 1916.

Oregon adopts state-wide Prohibition by a majority of 36,480, the Prohibition vote being 136,841 and the license vote being 100,362. Thirty-two of the thirty-four counties in the State record Prohibition majorities.

The bill for an election on state-wide Prohibition which failed in several previous Legislatures in Virginia is adopted in the Virginia House of Delegates by an overwhelming vote and in the Senate by the casting of the deciding vote on a tie by the president of that body. The election under this enabling act is held September 22, and Prohibition is adopted by a majority of 30,365 out of a total of 150,000 votes. The law becomes effective November 1, 1916.

A Prohibition amendment to the Constitution of the State of Washington which is voted upon in the November election, is adopted by a majority of 18,632 out of a total of 361,048 votes, which number is larger by 42,000 than the vote cast at any other election ever held in the State.

The vote on the Prohibition amendment in California in November results in a wet victory by a large majority.

The local option elections in Connecticut result in eighty-seven towns voting for no-license and eighty-one voting for license.

Beginning with November 1, 1914, the license fee in the District of Columbia is increased in the case of barrooms to $500 and in the case of wholesale places to $800.

The three political parties in Idaho pledge themselves in their platforms to the submission of a constitutional amendment prohibiting the liquor traffic.

As a result of the spring elections in Illinois twenty-three counties are added to the Prohibition column, making a total of fifty-one counties in the State where the liquor traffic has been outlawed. As a result of these elections, 1,150 saloons are closed in Illinois, 900 of which are shown to be closed as the result of the women's vote.

The election of Senator Lawrence Y. Sherman to the United States Senate from Illinois, in face of the terrific opposition of the liquor forces, records another significant Prohibition victory.

Two of the leading candidates for United States Senate in Pennsylvania advocate county local option.

In the Vermont local option elections twenty towns vote for license, which is the smallest number voting for license in any year since 1903. The total majority throughout the State against license is 10,195, which is the largest majority yet recorded.

The Prohibition law of West Virginia goes into effect July 1, and is rigidly enforced.

In the spring elections in Wisconsin, thirty-three incorporated cities and villages previously under license vote for Prohibition, and only one village previously under Prohibition votes for license.

The fall elections in Connecticut result in adding 13,000 to the population living under no-license in the State.

In the fall election, a candidate running for Governor of Kansas on a resubmission platform receives only about one vote in every ten, indicating that approximately 90 per cent of the people of Kansas, regardless of party affiliations, are favorable to Prohibition.

Up to November 5, there are issued for the State of Kansas, 263 liquor revenue receipts, 136 of which are for three counties. In seventy-three of the 105 counties of the State, not a single Federal liquor tax receipt is issued.

The Kentucky Legislature amends the local option petition law so that 25 per cent of the voters in any county is sufficient to call an election.

A strong Anti-Shipping law and a Search and Seizure law are enacted by the Kentucky Legislature.

In the election of former Governor J. C. W. Beckham to the United States Senate, the temperance forces of Kentucky score a decided victory.

During the year, the population living in no-license territory in Maryland is increased by 60,435, while the no-license area is increased by 1,548 square miles, closing thereby 105 saloons in the State.

The Massachusetts No-License League and the Massachusetts Anti-Saloon League are merged into one body under the name of the Anti-Saloon League.

Reports from Michigan show that there are now thirty-four Prohibition counties in that State, more than 1,200 saloons and twelve breweries having been closed under the provisions of the local option law during four years.

As a result of the November election in Minnesota, a majority of the members-elect of both Houses of the Legislature are favorable to county option.

A strong Anti-Shipping law is passed by the Legislature of Mississippi.

A majority of the members of the Missouri Legislature elected in November are favorable to advance temperance legislation.

Every city and town in New Hampshire votes on the liquor question, with the result that the total license vote is 32,707 as against a total no-license vote of 40,439, showing a majority of 7,663 for no-license, which is the largest no-license majority ever given in the State.

Two constitutional amendments affecting the liquor traffic are submitted to a vote of the people in Ohio; one of these amendments presented by the Prohibition forces providing for state-wide Prohibition is defeated by a majority of 83,000, although the Prohibition forces muster more than 504,000 votes. The other amendment presented by the liquor interests repealing the county option law is adopted by a majority of 12,000 on the face of the returns.

On December 22 the Hobson resolution providing for the submission of a prohibitory amendment to the Federal Constitution is voted upon in the lower House of Congress, 197 votes being recorded in favor of the measure and 189 votes against it. Since however, a two-thirds vote is required for such a resolution it fails of passage.

On June 1, Josephus Daniels, Secretary of the Navy, issues General Order No. 99, strictly prohibiting the use or introduction for drinking purposes of alcoholic liquors on board any naval vessel or within any navy yard or station.

Congress appropriates $100,000 for the suppression of illegal liquor selling to Indians.

Congress appropriates $15,000 for the suppression of the liquor traffic among the natives of Alaska.

The tax on beer is raised to $1.50 per barrel by the Act of Congress of October 22.

The Forty-First National Convention of the Woman's Christian Temperance Union is held November 12-18 at Atlanta, Georgia.

1915

The Legislature of Alabama by an overwhelming majority passes a state-wide prohibitory law which is vetoed by the Governor and then passed by the Legislature over the Governor's veto. The law goes into effect January 1, 1916.

By a majority of seventy-five to twenty-four in the House and thirty-three to two in the Senate, the Arkansas Legislature adopts a state-wide Prohibition law which goes into effect January 1, 1916.

The Legislature of Idaho by a large majority votes to submit to the people of the State a constitutional prohibitory amendment, following this by the adoption of a state-wide prohibitory law which goes into effect January 1, 1916.

The Legislature of Iowa repeals the Mulct law, thereby returning the State to state-wide Prohibition January 1, 1916. The Iowa Legislature also submits the question of a prohibitory constiutional amendment to a vote of the people. Des Moines, Iowa, goes under Prohibition on February 15, 1915, through a decision of the Supreme Court.

The South Carolina Legislature submits the question of state-wide Prohibition to a vote of the people, which vote is taken on September 14, and results in the adoption of Prohibition by a majority of 24,926.

The state-wide prohibitory law goes into effect in Arizona January 1, thus making ten states where state-wide Prohibition is in force.

The United States Senate votes on the question of taking up for consideration a rider on the District of Columbia appropriation bill providing for absolute Prohibition in the District, the resolution being defeated by a narrow margin.

The Legislature of Utah adopts a resolution submitting the question of state-wide Prohibition to the voters of the State.

Governor Brumbaugh of Pennsylvania in his inaugural address declares for county option and calls upon the Legislature to enact a county local option law.

The Texas Anti-Saloon League is re-organized and begins an aggressive fight for a state-wide prohibitory law.

The Supreme Court of Arizona upholds the prohibitory amendment to the State Constitution.

The elections in Connecticut result in 79 towns voting no-license as against 88 for license.

Under the operation of the county option law of Idaho between 1909 and 1915 twenty-one counties vote for Prohibition as against nine for license; as a result fewer than 200 saloons remain in the State.

The efforts of the liquor interests to defeat existing temperance legislation in Illinois by a law providing for so-called Home Rule for cities and villages are defeated in the Legislature.

The saloons of Chicago are closed on Sunday by order of the mayor.

An Anti-Roadhouse law is passed by the Minnesota Legislature, thus closing the saloons in the rural districts surrounding each large city in the State.

New Hampshire enacts a law providing that any person convicted of drunkenness shall not be permitted to have liquor in his possession for twelve months.

Jnjunctions are placed on the railroads of North Dakota restraining them from delivering liquors to be used in violation of law.

By an overwhelming vote in both Houses, South Carolina adopts an Anti-Shipping law.

The Legislature of North Carolina passes an Anti-Jug bill.

The Alabama Legislature passes a measure over the Governor's veto to prohibit newspapers published in the State from printing liquor advertisements, and preventing the circulation in the State of newspapers published outside of Alabama which carry liquor advertising.

The Wyoming Legislature votes down a resolution providing for submission of state-wide Prohibition by a vote of twelve to fourteen, two-thirds majority being necessary.

As a result of the local option elections in Massachusetts, there is a net gain of seven Prohibition towns and cities.

The Oklahoma Legislature passes a resolution memoralizing Congress to adopt the Sheppard-Hobson resolution for National Prohibition.

The Legislature of South Dakota passes a resolution submitting the question of state-wide Prohibition to a vote of the people of the State, the vote to be taken in November, 1916.

Statutory Prohibition goes into effect in Alabama July 1, 1915.   Liquor advertisements in newspapers, on billboards, or in any other form, are prohibited within the State.   The shipping of intoxicating liquors for any purpose except for personal use is also prohibited.

The California Legislature passes a law which makes all places where liquor is sold illegally, public nuisances, and authorizes any citizen to bring action for the abatement of such nuisances; also a law forbidding the sale of liquor to people of Indian blood, or to people of part Indian blood, or to white people who live with or habitually associate with Indians.

The Colorado Legislature passes a stringent law providing for the enforcement of the State Prohibition Amendment, which goes into effect January 1, 1916. The liquor interests of the city of Denver submit a charter amendment providing for "home rule" for the city, which is adopted by a majority of 2,600 but is overruled by the State Supreme Court.

The General Assembly of Connecticut enacts a law governing the sale of liquor in clubs and also passes several other minor amendments to the anti-liquor laws.

The Hazel Anti-Shipping law is repealed by the State Legislature of Delaware.

The Florida Legislature enacts a law which prohibits treating, drinking in saloons, free lunches, screens, blinds, tables and chairs, and also compels the closing of saloons from 6 o'clock p. m. to 7 o'clock a. m. During the year two new counties are formed, namely, Broward and Okaloosa. Both counties are under Prohibition. Two other counties, Marion and Franklin, change from license to Prohibition during 1915.

The Sixteenth National Convention of the Anti-Saloon League of America is held July 6-9 at Atlantic City, New Jersey.

A special session of the Georgia Legislature is called and enacts a law to secure effective enforcement of Prohibition. This law prohibits the sale of all liquors containing any portion whatsoever of alcohol, prohibits liquor advertising, and makes it unlawful to import liquors except for personal use. The law goes into effect May 1, 1916.

A great mass convention of temperance workers is held in Lansing, Michigan, in November, and petitions are circulated calling for a vote on a Constitutional Prohibition Amendment, which vote is to be taken on November 2, 1916. During the year 1915, 342 saloons are closed in the State, through county option elections. The Legislature passes a bill providing that before the consignee of liquor shipments can receive same he must make affidavit that he is of full legal age and not disqualified under the law of Michigan to receive same. An anti-liquor advertisement law is also passed, also a measure giving township boards the right to reject all applications for liquor licenses and a law prohibiting the selling or furnishing of intoxicating liquors at lumber camps or along the right of way of logging railroads to any employee thereof. A statutory Prohibition bill containing a referendum clause is presented to the State Legislature but fails of passage.

The Minnesota Legislature enacts a county option bill which becomes law on March 1. Within seven months thereafter, fifty-seven counties in the State hold county elections, with the result that forty-five counties vote for Prohibition and twelve counties vote to retain the saloons. About 500 saloons are closed in the State during 1915, together with twelve wholesale houses and the same number of small breweries. The

United States Indian Bureau takes aggressive action to enforce Prohibition in the territory covered by old Indian treaties.

Eleven out of seventeen local option elections held in Missouri are won by the Prohibition forces.

Richland County, Montana, votes for Prohibition on October 13, 1915. The General Assembly of Montana submits a Prohibition statute referendum bill, to be voted on in 1916. It also enacts an anti-race track gambling law; a law closing saloons within one mile of cities of the first class from 12 o'clock midnight to 8 a. m.; a law closing saloons from 10 p. m. Saturday until 1 p. m. Sunday; a law prohibiting the sale of liquor within five miles of railroad grade, public works, etc., under construction, except where sold in a town of 50 or more persons, or by dealer in business two years before the beginning of such works; the issuance of new licenses on a basis of one to every 500 persons; after December 31 all saloons are to be closed in places having less than 50 persons within one-fourth mile of the place where the liquors are to be sold; a law providing for the filing of protests against the re-issuance of saloon licenses and the commissioners are given discretionary power in the issuance thereof. The petitioners for, or the remonstrance against the issuance of a license are given the power to appeal to the District Court. A law is passed prohibiting sale of intoxicating liquors to drunkards, minors or Indians, and holding the person breaking this law liable for damages to any person injured thereby in property, money or means of support.

In Ohio, a state-wide Prohibition amendment is voted on at the general election in November, and de-

feated by a majority of 55,408 votes. A so-called
Stability League amendment, introduced by the brewers, which is intended to prevent another vote on the
liquor question for a period of six years, is defeated
by a majority of 64,891.

The Tennessee Legislature passes laws known as
the Soft Drink Stand law, and the Ouster law, materi-
ally strengthening the anti-liquor laws of the state.

The Utah Legislature enacts a strong Prohibition
bill, with only five votes against the measure in the
House of Representatives and two in the Senate.
Governor Spry however, holds the bill until after the
Legislature has adjourned, and then attaches his veto
to the measure.

The Vermont Legislature passes a state-wide prohibitory law, referring the same to a vote of the people, to be taken March 7, 1916.

The West Virginia Legislature passes a number of
additional law enforcement measures, strengthening
the Prohibition laws of the State.

The Wisconsin Legislature changes the limit on the
number of saloons, making the ratio one saloon for
every 500 people.

A joint resolution calling for the submission of a
prohibitory amendment to the Federal Constitution is
introduced in both Houses of the Sixty-Fourth Congress, which convened in December. The resolutions
are presented in the Senate by Senator Morris Sheppard of Texas and by Senator J. H. Gallinger of New
Hampshire; in the House by Edwin Y. Webb of
North Carolina and A. T. Smith of Idaho.

A bill providing for the absolute prohibition of the

sale of intoxicating liquors in the District of Columbia is introduced early in the first session of the Sixty-Fourth Congress by Senator Morris Sheppard of Texas. The bill is submitted to the District of Columbia committee, reported back to the Senate and placed on the calendar.

The Forty-Second National Convention of the Woman's Christian Temperance Union is held October 9-14 at Seattle, Washington.

The second session of the Alaska Legislature on March 3 submits to the people a referendum bill providing for the prohibition of the traffic in intoxicating liquors after January 1, 1918.

1916

The Judiciary Committee of the United States Senate, by a vote of 13 to 3, on December 21 favorably reports to the United States Senate the National Prohibition Resolution known as Senate Joint Resolution No. 55.

A referendum vote on Prohibition is taken by the voters of Alaska, which results in a large majority in favor of Prohibition.

An amendment intended to weaken the Arizona Prohibition law is defeated by a majority of over 12,000.

Prohibition goes into effect in Arkansas, Colorado, Idaho, Iowa and Washington on January 1, 1916.

In Arkansas a bill is submitted to repeal the prohibitory law and allow saloons to return, but is defeated by 50,000 majority.

Two Prohibition amendments to the Constitution of California are voted on at the general election, and both are defeated. One would prohibit the sale or gift of intoxicating liquors in places of public resort, after January 1, 1918, while the other would prohibit the manufacture, sale, importation and transportation within the State of all alcoholic liquors after January 1, 1920.

In Colorado an amendment to exempt beer from the operations of the state-wide Prohibition law is defeated by a majority of 85,792.

A law prohibiting the sale of all liquors containing alcohol, and also prohibiting liquor advertising, goes into effect in Georgia May 1.

Idaho adopts a constitutional amendment for state-wide Prohibition, by a vote of about three to one, at the November election.

The Louisiana Legislature passes the Johnson near-beer bill, prohibiting the sale of all malt liquor in Prohibition territory.

Prohibition goes into effect in St. Mary's County, Maryland, May 1, 1916. The question of state-wide Prohibition for Maryland is presented to the Legislature in the form of a statute with a referendum attached. The bill is changed so that the measure which is finally passed provides for the submission of the question to the city of Baltimore and to the other wet sections of the State as separate units. At the November election, Havre de Grace and the counties of Frederick and Washington vote for Prohibition.

The Massachusetts Legislature passes a bill prohibiting the peddling of liquor in no-license towns.

Michigan adopts a prohibitory amendment to the

State Constitution by a vote of 353,378 to 284,754, on November 7.

A state-wide Prohibition measure is defeated in Missouri, at the November election, by a majority of 122,538.

The city of Duluth, Minnesota, votes for Prohibition at a local option election, by a majority of 364.

Montana adopts state-wide Prohibition by a vote of 102,776 to 73,890, at the general election in November.

Constitutional Prohibition is adopted in Nebraska by a vote of 146,574 to 117,132, at the November election. A prohibitory statute is also passed by the Legislature.

A petition for a state-wide prohibitory statute is filed in Nevada, under the initiative and referendum, but is rejected by the Legislature.

In Oregon an amendment to permit the manufacture and sale of beer is defeated by a majority of 54,-626, at the November election. At the same election an amendment forbidding the importation of intoxicating liquors is adopted, thus strengthening the anti-liquor laws of the State.

South Dakota adopts Constitutional Prohibition by a majority of 11,505 votes, on November 7.

At an election held on July 28, the voters of Texas give a majority in favor of submitting a Constitutional Prohibition Amendment to the electorate, but this amendment is defeated in the Legislature.

An election on the question of state-wide Prohibition in Vermont, held in March, results in the defeat of the Prohibition measure.

State-wide Prohibition goes into effect in Virginia on November 1. A stringent law enforcement measure is passed by the State Legislature.

State-wide Prohibition goes into effect in Oregon on January 1, closing 900 saloons and 18 breweries.

State-wide Prohibition goes into effect in Washington on January 1. The liquor forces of the State initiate two measures to weaken the state-wide Prohibition law, which measures are defeated by majorities of 146,556 and 215,036 respectively.

The prohibitory amendment to the State Constitution of Colorado becomes effective on January 1, closing 1,800 saloons and seventeen breweries in the State.

The last bond representing the indebtedness of Kansas incurred under the open saloon regime prior to 1881 is paid off and the bonds burned at a public celebration at the State Capital.

Hon. Carl Milliken is elected Governor of Maine on a platform calling for strict enforcement of the prohibitory law.

Michigan defeats a proposed amendment to the Constitution aimed at weakening the anti-liquor laws, by a majority of 122,599 votes.

Michigan reports forty-five of the eighty-three counties already under Prohibition through the operation of the county option law.

In New Hampshire 207 towns vote for Prohibition at the regular election.

The National Convention of the Prohibition Party meets in St. Paul, Minnesota July 18-22. J. Frank Hanly of Indiana is nominated for President and Ira

Landrith of Tennessee is nominated for Vice-President.

The Seventeenth National Convention of the Anti-Saloon League of America is held June 26-29 at Indianapolis, Indiana.

The number of breweries in the United States is 1,332, and the amount of beer produced is 58,564,508 barrels per annum.

The sum of $100,000 is appropriated by Congress for the suppression of the liquor traffic among the Indians.

The Forty-Third National Convention of the Woman's Christian Temperance Union is held November 17-22 at Indianapolis, Indiana.

1917

The resolution submitting to the states the National Prohibition Amendment to the Constitution of the United States, is adopted by the United States Senate on August 1, and by the House of Representatives on December 18.

The Federal Anti-Liquor Advertising bill, carrying with it the Reed Bone-Dry Amendment, is adopted by the United States Senate on February 15 and by the House of Representatives on February 21.

The Supreme Court of the United States, on January 8, 1917, hands down a decision upholding the constitutionality of the Webb-Kenyon Interstate Liquor Shipment law.

A bill providing for Prohibition in the territory of Hawaii is presented in both Houses of the Sixty-Fourth Congress, and is reported out by the House committee on January 27, 1917.   The measure fails to come to a vote, however, in either House.

The District of Columbia is made Prohibition territory by a bill passed by the United States Senate on January 9, and by the House of Representatives on February 28.

A bill providing for Prohibition in the territory of Alaska is presented in both Houses of the United States Congress early in January, 1917, and is adopted by the Senate on January 31, and by the House of Representatives on February 2.   The Prohibition measure goes into effect January 1, 1918.

A provision for a vote on the question of Prohibition in the island of Porto Rico is passed by the United States Congress, as an amendment to the Porto Rican Citizenship and Civil Government bill.   At a special election held in July, 1917, the voters of Porto Rico approve the Prohibition measure by a vote of 99,775 to 61,295.

A Food Control bill is passed by the House of Representatives containing a provision forbidding the use of any foods, food materials, or feeds for the production of alcoholic beverages, except for governmental, industrial, scientific, medicinal, or sacramental purposes, and also, authorizing the President of the United States to commandeer alcohol and distilled spirits for government requirements.   Because of a threatened filibuster against this food control bill by the friends of the liquor interests in the United States Senate, a request is made by the President of the United States to the anti-liquor forces, as a result of which the bill is finally changed so as to make the prohibition of the use of food materials in the manufacture of beer and wine, optional with the President of the United States. The bill as finally passed by the Senate on August 8 and signed by the President on August 10, provides for the prohibition of the manufacture of distilled spirits for beverage purposes, prohibition of the importation of distilled spirits, and authorized the President to commandeer whisky in stock as well as in bond, at his discretion, to reduce the alcoholic content of beer and wine, and to limit, regulate or prohibit the use of food materials in the manufacture of beer and wine. According to the terms of this measure, the manufacture of distilled spirits in the United States ceased on September 8, 1917.

On January 22 both Houses of the Arkansas Legislature pass a bone dry law by a large majority.

The Connecticut Legislature passes a bill calling for the submission of a State Prohibition Amendment, which under the Constitution goes over to the Legislature of 1917 for further action.

The Loose Anti-Liquor Shipment bill is passed by the Delaware General Assembly.

North Carolina makes the manufacture of liquor a felony; the State becomes bone dry July 1.

Eleven cities are added to the Prohibition column in California, eight adopting absolute Prohibition while three others—Los Angeles, San Jose and Santa Clara—abolish saloons, prohibit all distilled liquors, but permit wine and beers not having over 14 per cent of alcohol to be sold in original sealed packages or served in hotels.

The Legislature of Delaware submits the question of Prohibition to a vote in the city of Wilmington and rural New Castle County as separate units; as a result of the election the city remains under license by a majority of about 2,000, while rural New Castle County votes for Prohibition by a majority of 1,270, thus closing twenty-six saloons and making the entire State Prohibition territory, with the exception of the city of Wilmington, which retains 161 saloons, five wholesale houses and thirteen merchant license places.

At a special session of the Georgia Legislature called by Governor N. E. Harris, a bone dry prohibitory law is enacted which bars even the possession of liquor for personal use. The law becomes effective immediately upon its passage.

The Idaho Legislature passes a stringent law enforcement measure, also a measure prohibiting the advertising of intoxicating liquors. Constitutional Prohibition becomes effective in Idaho on January 1st, statutory Prohibition having already gone into effect.

A bill providing for a Prohibition referendum in Illinois is passed in the Senate, but defeated in the House. A bill providing for a Prohibition zone of five miles' radius around the U. S. Naval Training Station at Waukegon also passes the Senate but fails of passage in the House.

The General Assembly of Indiana passes a state-wide prohibitory statute, to go into effect April 2, 1918.

In Iowa, a prohibitory amendment to the State Constitution submitted by the Legislatures of 1915 and 1917 is defeated at a special election by less than

1,000 majority. A bone dry law is enacted by the State Legislature, which strengthens the prohibitory statute and prohibits liquor advertising.

A constitutional amendment is adopted in Maine, giving the Governor power to remove delinquent county sheriffs and to appoint others in their places.

The Massachusetts Legislature passes the Express Permit bill, strengthening the anti-liquor legislation of the State.

The Minnesota Legislature submits the question of Constitutional Prohibition to a vote of the people, which vote is to be taken in November, 1918.

The Missouri Legislature passes two laws providing for clean elections, and also refers a constitutional state-wide Prohibition Amendment to a vote of the people, to be taken at the general election in November, 1918.

Constitutional Prohibition goes into effect in Nebraska May 1.

New Hampshire adopts state-wide Prohibition, by act of the State Legislature, in April, 1917.

New Mexico adopts constitutional state-wide Prohibition by vote of the people on November 6.

The New York Legislature passes a city local option bill, which enfranchises, on the liquor question, more than 8,000,000 people living in the cities of the State.

The North Dakota Legislature passes a bone dry law which is signed by the Governor on March 9th.

At the third general vote on state-wide Prohibition in Ohio, Prohibition is defeated by a majority of 1,137 votes out of a total of more than 1,000,000 votes.

Oklahoma adopts a bone dry law as well as other enforcement measures.

The South Carolina Legislature adopts an anti-liquor advertising law.

State-wide Prohibition goes into effect in South Dakota on July 1.

The Tennessee Legislature enacts the following laws: The storage bill, which abolishes the mail order houses July 1, 1917; the bone dry anti-shipping law which goes into effect March 1, 1917; an anti-club law which takes effect immediately after its passage; and a bill making bootlegging a felony, which takes effect immediately after is passage.

Statutory Prohibition is adopted by the Utah Legislature, the bill being signed by the Governor on February 8, and becoming effective August 1. A prohibitory amendment to the State Constitution is also submitted by the same Legislature, the vote on which is to be taken in November, 1918.

The Washington Legislature passes a state bone dry law.

The West Virginia Legislature passes a law prohibiting the carrying of liquor into the State by common carriers. Liquor carried into the State, or from one point to another within the State, is limited to one quart within thirty consecutive days.

The Wyoming Legislature adopts a resolution submitting state-wide Constitutional Prohibition to a vote of the people.

The District of Columbia prohibitory law becomes effective November 1, closing 267 saloons, twenty-two barrooms in hotels, nine in clubs, eighty-nine wholesale places and four breweries.

Florida by additional provisions strengthens the Anti-Shipping and Search and Seizure law enacted in 1913.

Massachusetts records show that from 1881, when the municipal local option law of the State became effective, to 1917, there have been held in the State under this law 12,520 local option elections, of which number 2,979 resulted in license victories and 9,541 in no-license victories.

New Jersey enacts a local option law under which forty-nine municipalities containing a population of 180,278 vote dry within six months after the passage of the law.

Of thirty-four municipal local option contests in Ohio, twenty-one result in Prohibition victories. Of twenty-two township contests, eighteen give majorities for Prohibition.

The Legislature of Montana passes strong law enforcement measures providing for search and seizure and the abatement as nuisances of places selling liquor contrary to law.

The Eighteenth National Convention of the Anti-Saloon League of America is held December 10-13 at Washington, D. C.

Hawaii has 127 saloons, controlled by a Board of Commissioners appointed by the Governor.

Congress appropriates $150,000 for the suppression of the liquor traffic among the Indians.

The Forty-fourth National Convention of the Women's Christian Temperance Union is held December 2-7 at Washington, D. C.

1918

The National Prohibition Amendment to the Constitution of the United States is ratified by the Legislatures of the following States:—Mississippi, Virginia, Kentucky, South Carolina, North Dakota, Maryland, Montana, Texas, Delaware, South Dakota, Massachusetts, Arizona, Georgia, Louisiana, Florida.

Prohibition goes into effect in Alaska on January 1, 1918.

A bill for war-time prohibition of the manufacture, sale, importation, and transportation of intoxicating liquors for beverage purposes during the period of the war and the period of demobilization, is introduced in the House of Representatives of the United States Congress, by Representative Barkley of Kentucky, on April 26.

An amendment to the Agricultural Appropriation bill is offered in the United States House of Representatives, by Congressman Randall, providing that no part of this appropriation shall be available unless the use of grains in the manufacture of beer be prohibited. An amendment to this bill is offered in the Senate by Senator Jones, to prohibit the use of cereals and fruit in the manufacture of intoxicants. The Agricultural Appropriation bill is passed by the Senate on September 6th, with a Prohibition amendment, and approved by the President on November 21. The law as finally approved prohibits the manufacture of beer and wine, after May 1, 1919, and forbids the sale of distilled, malt and vinous intoxicants after June 30, 1919.

On December 1, 1918, the use of foods and food materials in the manufacture of beer is ordered stopped by the food administration of the Federal government.

A state-wide Prohibition Amendment is defeated by the voters of California.

The bone dry law, adopted by vote of the people, goes into effect in Colorado on December 16.

Florida adopts state-wide Prohibition by a majority of 8,242 at the November election.

A bill providing for Prohibition in the territory of Hawaii during the period of the war and thereafter unless the same shall be repealed by vote of the people within two years after the conclusion of peace, is passed by the United States Congress, and becomes a law May 24.

The dry forces of Chicago, Illinois, circulate a petition for a vote on the wet and dry issue in that city. The petition is filed with 150,000 names attached, but the election commissioners throw it out, declaring over 40,000 names fraudulent or illegal.

Prohibition goes into effect in Indiana on April 2, thereby closing 3,500 saloons.

The Kentucky Legislature submits a state-wide Prohibition amendment to the Constitution, to a vote of the people at the November election in 1919. An anti-liquor shipping law and a law prohibiting the owning or operating of moonshine stills are also passed by this Legislature.

The Louisiana Legislature meets in regular session in May, and fails to ratify the National Prohibition

Amendment by a tie vote in the Senate. At a special session called in August, however, the National Prohibition Amendment is ratified by a vote of 69 to 41 in the House, and 21 to 20 in the Senate.

A prohibitory amendment to the Constitution of Minnesota is voted on at the November election. The amendment receives a majority of 15,932 votes, but fails to pass by 756 votes, according to the provisions of the State election law.

The Mississippi Legislature passes a bone-dry law prohibiting the possession of whisky and also prohibiting liquor advertising.

The Forty-fifth National Convention of the Woman's Christian Temperance Union is held in Chicago, Illinois, on December 3-6.

A constitutional amendment for state-wide Prohibition is defeated at the general election in Missouri, by a vote of 300,354 to 227,501.

State-wide Prohibition goes into effect in Montana on December 31, in New Hampshire May 1, and in New Mexico October 1.

State-wide Prohibition is adopted in Nevada at the November election and goes into effect on December 16.

The New Jersey Legislature passes a municipal local option bill.

Under the city local option law of New York, thirty-nine of the fifty-nine cities of the state vote on the license question on April 16, twenty out of this number voting dry.

The Supreme Court of Oklahoma decides that the

State prohibitory law does not forbid the importation of wine for sacramental purposes, even though no specific exemption of wine for this purpose is made in the State law.

Prohibition goes into effect in Porto Rico on March 2.

The Senate of Rhode Island, by a vote of 20 to 18, indefinitely postpones consideration of the resolution for ratification of National Prohibition.

South Carolina enacts a law allowing the possession of one quart of whisky for medicine.

The Texas Legislature adopts a ten-mile zone law, and a statutory Prohibition measure. The Prohibition statute is declared unconstitutional by the Court of Criminal Appeals in October, 1918, but the Attorney-General's department closes every saloon that attempts to open. The Court of Civic Appeals holds that the law is constitutional.

Utah adopts a prohibitory amendment to the State Constitution at the November election.

A bone dry amendment to the Constitution of Washington is adopted by a majority of 41,778 votes.

The Wisconsin Legislature passes a state-wide Prohibition referendum bill by a vote of 21 to 11 in the Senate and 55 to 38 in the House, but the bill is vetoed by the Governor.

State-wide Prohibition is adopted at the general election in Wyoming, by 15,000 majority.

The Legislature of Maryland passes bone dry laws for Somerset and Caroline counties and closes the saloons at Chesapeake Beach in Calvert County.

The prison farm in Kent County, Michigan, is closed because of lack of prisoners to work it.

The prohibitory amendment to the Constitution of Michigan becomes effective May 1, thereby closing 3,285 saloons and sixty-two breweries.

The records of the State of Missouri show that there are 3,100 saloons in 10 per cent of the territory of the State, 90 per cent of the territory being under Prohibition through the operation of the county option law.

Several law enforcement measures are enacted in New Jersey.

The Legislature of Florida submits a Prohibition amendment to the vote of the State with the result that at the election held in November the amendment is adopted by a majority of 8,242, every county in the State giving a Prohibition majority.

Ohio adopts state-wide constitutional Prohibition by a majority of 25,759, the vote being, for Prohibition 463,654, against 437,895; only nine of the eighty-eight counties give license majorities, the Prohibition majorities in the other seventy-nine counties overcoming the wet majorities in Cleveland, Cincinnati, Toledo and other license centers.

CHAPTER X

WHEN CONGRESS voted to submit to the states a constitutional amendment providing for National Prohibition of the sale, manufacture, importation and transportation of intoxicating liquors in the United States, the liquor traffic as a legalized institution was doomed. No one knew this fact better than those who had closely followed the progress of the Prohibition movement and who as Prohibition workers in the several states understood something of the overwhelming sentiment for Prohibition which existed in most sections of the nation outside the great cities. More than 65 per cent of the population of the United States was under Prohibition either by virtue of the operation of local option or state-wide Prohibition laws.

Adoption of the proposed Federal Prohibition Amendment required ratification by the Legislatures of three-fourths of the 48 states. The liquor interests of the nation still felt secure because they realized that all that was necessary to prevent final ratification was for the friends of the liquor traffic to succeed in preventing favorable action in one branch of each of thirteen state Legislatures, while on the other hand it was necessary for the Prohibition forces to secure favorable action on ratification by both branches of the Legislatures in each of at least thirty-six states. In other words, the liquor interests needed to hold only a bare majority in thirteen legislative branches, while the Prohibition forces needed to secure a majority vote for ratification in at least seventy-two state legislative branches.

Twenty-eight states, however, had already adopted state-wide prohibitory laws, thus committing themselves beforehand to the Prohibition policy. In seven other states, more than a majority of the people were living in territory under Prohibition by vote of the people in the counties, villages and townships, while a majority of the members of the Legislatures in three other states represented legislative districts which were under local Prohibition by a majority vote of the people. The leaders of the Prohibition movement, therefore, realized that if each legislator in both branches of the Legislature of each state voted on ratification in harmony with the expressed will of the majority of his constituents, at least 38 states would ratify the Federal amendment, thus giving the necessary three-fourths of the state Legislatures with two states to spare. This knowledge inspired confidence in the Prohibition forces, especially in view of the fact that under the Federal Constitution the failure of any state to ratify a constitutional amendment did not preclude the taking up of the matter by any succeeding Legislature in that state during the seven-year period provided for in the Federal resolution, while in the case of any state which voted favorably on ratification the chapter was closed so far as that state was concerned, since there was no chance thereafter for a succeeding Legislature to rescind or change such action.

It was not strange, therefore, that the Prohibition forces, confident of the adoption of National Constitutional Prohibition, began to plan for the future with the idea of making Prohibition effective and permanent. Neither was it remarkable that these forces promptly began to look forward to the possible extension of the benefits of Prohibition to other countries of the world, especially in view of the fact that the entire movement for Prohibition in the very nature of the case had been from the very beginning a great missionary project.

International activity along temperance lines was not new. For many years, several temperance organizations had been conducting their work along international as well as national lines. The first general temperance organization in the United States, founded in 1826, sent missionaries abroad in the interest of international temperance reform. The Woman's Christian Temperance Union had been in the international field for a considerable period and had organized to some degree the temperance movement among women of practically every continent. In many countries, in fact, practically all the organized temperance work which had been accomplished prior to 1920 had been accomplished through the agencies of the World's Woman's Christian Temperance Union.

The International Order of Good Templars was perhaps the best organized international movement of record prior to the adoption of Prohibition in the United States of America. While this organization had its birth in America, it had attained to a higher degree of success in its activities in many European countries and in other parts of the world, the strongest and largest National Grand Lodges under its jurisdiction being located in the countries of Northern Europe.

The Rechabites, the Sons of Temperance and numerous other organizations had conducted a part of their work along international lines and had been successful not only in organizing temperance movements in numerous countries but in developing a spirit of international coöperation on the part of temperance organizations in practically all countries of the world.

The Anti-Saloon League of America, in harmony with the idea that the non-partisan method for Prohibition activity should be projected into the international field, called a special conference of officers and workers which convened in Columbus, Ohio, in November, 1918. At this conference practically every phase of the international Prohibition question was considered both from the viewpoint of the American Prohibition forces and from the viewpoint of the numerous representatives of temperance organizations in foreign countries who were in attendance at the conference and took part in its deliberations.

As a result the Anti-Saloon League of America decided upon a course of action which involved the sending of official representatives of the American Commission to meet with representatives of the temperance organizations of foreign countries at the Paris Peace Conference, and which also inovlved an immediate movement for securing coöperation on the part of temperance organizations in other countries, in the effort to organize a world-wide movement for non-partisan activity against the liquor traffic.

The commission appointed by the Anti-Saloon

League of America to represent its views and co-operate with other national temperance organizations at the proposed conference to be held in Paris, France, consisted of Bishop James Cannon, Jr., Edwin C. Dinwiddie, Bishop William F. Anderson, Mr. L. B. Musgrove, Doctor Henry Beach Carrê, Mr. Wayne B. Wheeler and Mr. Ernest H. Cherrington.

On account of the inability of some of the members of the American League Commission to go to France, negotiations in Paris were largely conducted for this commission by Bishop James Cannon, Jr., Doctor Henry Beach Carrê, and Mr. L. B. Musgrove, who, together with the representatives from many other countries, appeared before the subcommittees of the Peace Conference and urged especially that the peace treaty contain some provision for the protection of native races against the ravages of alcohol as that which had been put into effect by the nations of Europe and America in the Brussels Conference of 1898. It is of interest to note in this connection that the provision for excluding distilled liquors from the native race countries of Africa, which was finally agreed upon by the Paris Peace Conference, was far more comprehensive and enforceable, even, than the original agreement of the Brussels Conference.

By joint action of the Anti-Saloon League of America and the Dominion Temperance Alliance of Canada, arrangements were made for a World-wide Prohibition Conference to be held on the American continent during the latter part of May and the first week of June, 1919. This conference was opened in Toronto, Canada, on May 22, 1919, and was adjourned to meet in the city of Washington, D. C., U. S. A., on June 4, 1919. This conference was attended by representatives from more than fifty different countries of the world. Official representatives from leading temperance organizations from fifteen different nations were present and took part in the deliberations, as a result of which there was organized on June 7, 1919, at Washington, D. C., the World League Against Alcoholism, under the following constitution:

CONSTITUTION OF THE WORLD LEAGUE AGAINST ALCOHOLISM

ARTICLE 1. NAME

The name of this League is the World League Against Alcoholism.

ARTICLE 2. OBJECT

The object of this League is to attain, by the means of education and legislation, the total suppression throughout the world of alcoholism, which is the poisoning of body germ-plasm, mind, conduct and society, produced by the consumption of alcoholic beverages. This League pledges itself to avoid affiliation with any political party as such, and to maintain an attitude of strict neutrality on all questions of public policy, not directly and immediately concerned with the traffic in alcoholic beverages.

ARTICLE 3. MEMBERSHIP

The membership of this League is limited to organizations which are in harmony with the objects, and which are national in the scope of their operation. Such organizations whose officers or accredited representatives are signatories to this constitution shall be considered active members of this League when the action of their officers or accredited representatives in signing this document has been officially ratified by the proper authorities of such organizations. Other similar organizations may be added to the membership of the League from time to time by a three-fourths vote of the General Council of the League, or of the Permanent International Committee, present and voting, to extend an invitation to such organizations eligible under the provisions of this constitution, provided that at least six months' notice shall be given before the vote is taken.

The Permanent International Committee shall have the right to admit individuals as associate members of the League, but such associate members shall not be represented in the General Council or Permanent International Committee.

ARTICLE 4. OFFICERS

The officers of this League shall be: Four Joint Presidents, a Vice-President for each country represented in the membership of this League, a Treasurer and a General Secretary, each of whom shall be chosen for a term of three years and shall be elected by the General Council upon the nomination of the Permanent International Committee.

ARTICLE 5. GENERAL COUNCIL

There shall be a General Council composed of three members from each organization holding membership in the League, chosen by such method as may be determined by said organization, and additional members elected by the Council, but the number of additional members thus chosen shall not at any time exceed one-third of the total membership of the Council.

ARTICLE 6. PERMANENT INTERNATIONAL COMMITTEE

There shall be a Permanent International Committee consisting of (1) the officers, (2) one member from each organization holding membership in the League. Each member shall be elected for three years by the organization which he represents on the committee by such method as may be determined by the said organization, and each member shall hold office until his successor shall have been duly elected and his election duly certified to the Permanent International Committee. (3) Additional members elected by the Permanent International Committee, but the number of additional members thus chosen shall not at any time exceed one-third of the total membership of the Council.

ARTICLE 7. EXECUTIVE COMMITTEE

There shall be an Executive Committee consisting of the Presidents, Treasurer, and General Secretary, and not fewer than seven nor more than fifteen members elected annually by the Permanent International Committee.

Article 8.   Finance

The League shall be supported by assessments to be fixed by mutual agreement between the Permanent International Committee and each member of the League. The Permanent International Committee shall devise ways and means for the securing of additional financial support to meet special demands.

Article 9.   Conventions

Conventions of this League shall be held once in every three years, the time and place to be fixed at least twelve months beforehand by the Permanent International Committee. By a two-thirds vote, special conventions may be called at such time and place as may be determined by the Committee.

Article 10.   Amendments

Amendments to this Constitution may be made at any regular meeting of the General Council by a two-thirds vote of the members present and voting, providing the amendment has been recommended by a two-thirds vote of the Permanent International Committee; or in the absence of such recommendation, by a three-fourths vote of the members present and voting. The final vote upon any proposed amendment shall not be taken within six hours after the amendment shall have been presented to the Council.

(Signed)

Australian Alliance Prohibition Council—R. B. S. Hammond, James Marion.

The Council of the Dominion Alliance of Canada—Miles Vokes, Sara R. Wright, Ben Spence.

Denmark Grand Lodge I. O. G. T.—Larsen Ledet.

United Kingdom Alliance—J. H. B. Masterman, G. B. Wilson, William Bingham. *Wesleyan Methodist Church of Great Britain*—Henry Carter. *National Commercial Temperance League, Strength of Britain Movement*—C. W. Saleeby.

Ligue Nationale contre l'Alcoolisme—JEAN LETORT.

Temperance Committee of the Irish Presbyterian Church, Irish Temperance League—JOHN GAILEY.

National Temperance League of Japan—TAKESHI UKAI, M. YAMAGUCHI.

National Anti-Alcohol Association—EPIGMENIO VELASCO.

New Zealand Alliance for the Abolition of the Liquor Traffic—JOHN DAWSON.

Scottish Permissive Bill and Temperance Association—W. J. ALLISON, THOMAS REA.

Swiss Total Abstinence Federation—R. HERCOD.

Anti-Saloon League of America—WILLIAM H. ANDERSON, P. A. BAKER, JAMES CANNON, JR., ERNEST H. CHERRINGTON, ARTHUR J. DAVIS, F. SCOTT McBRIDE, L. B. MUSGROVE, HOWARD H. RUSSELL, WAYNE B. WHEELER.

This constitution of the World League Against Alcoholism and the action of those who signed the document was later ratified by the several national temperance organizations thus represented, and the World League became operative in the interest of international temperance reform.

During the first year of the World League's operations, considerable advance was made in survey work, in getting points of contact with temperance and reform forces in all countries of the world, in assisting several no-license and Prohibition campaigns in a number of countries outside the United States, and in a very large distribution of literature throughout the world.

The program of the World League Against Alcoholism for the future is a large program. It is hoped in the first place that this World League may prove to be a foundation for coöperation and federation upon the part of all national temperance organizations in every country of the world for international temperance activity. If this can be done, the world liquor problem will undoubtedly soon be in the way of permanent solution.

The following chronology gives the most important events of the temprance reform for the period:

CHRONOLOGY OF THE TEMPERANCE REFORM FOR THE PERIOD 1919–1920

1919

The amendment to the Constitution of the United States, providing for National Prohibition, is ratified by the Legislatures of three-fourths of the states, on January 16, 1919, and becomes the Eighteenth Amendment to the Constitution of the United States. The Acting Secretary of States issues a proclamation on January 29, declaring this amendment a valid part of the Constitution of the United States. During the early part of the year 1919 the amendment is ratified by the following State Legislatures: Michigan, Ohio, Oklahoma, Maine, Idaho, West Virginia, Washington, Tennessee, California, Indiana, Illinois, Arkansas, North Carolina, Alabama, Kansas, Oregon, Iowa, Utah, Colorado, New Hampshire, Nebraska, Missouri, Wyoming, Wisconsin, Minnesota, New Mexico, Nevada, Vermont, New York and Pennsylvania, thus making forty-five states which have ratified.

War-Time Prohibition for the United States of America goes into effect on July 1. The advent of National Prohibition puts out of business 236 distilleries, 1,090 breweries and 177,790 saloons and other places where intoxicating liquors were sold.

The Delaware Legislature passes a Prohibition enforcement measure, to go into effect January 16, 1920.

A bone dry law for the District of Columbia is passed by the United States Congress and goes into effect on February 25.

State-wide Prohibition goes into effect in Florida on January 1.

The Supreme Court of Illinois decides that the election commissioners of Chicago acted illegally in throwing out the petition for a vote on license in 1918, and directs that a vote be taken on the question.

An amendment providing for the manufacture and sale of beer and wines in Michigan, is initiated by the wet forces, and defeated by a large majority on April 7.

A bill to legalize the sale of beer and light wines is defeated by the Legislature of New Hampshire.

A resolution providing for ratification of the National Prohibition Amendment is defeated in the New Jersey Senate by a vote of 10 to 8, on March 10.

The Senate of Rhode Island votes to indefinitely postpone consideration of the National Prohibition Amendment to the United States Constitution, by a vote of 25 to 12, on February 6.

The Tennessee Legislature passes a law requiring the destruction of all seized contraband liquors under the direction of the judge of the Circuit and Criminal Courts.

The Texas Legislature submits to a vote of the people a prohibitory amendment to the State Constitution. The vote, taken May 24, results in a Prohibition majority of 25,000.

The Legislature of West Virginia passes a bone

dry law, as well as a number of amendments strengthening the Prohibition laws of the State. These include a law making moonshining a felony.

The Supreme Court of West Virginia decides that the "one quart" law of that State is nullified by the so-called Reed bone dry amendment enacted by Congress.

The Legislature of Wyoming unanimously adopts a bone dry law to go into effect June 30, 1919.

North Dakota enacts an inspection measure for purposes of law enforcement.

Ohio by popular vote refuses to repeal the state-wide prohibitory amendment to the Constitution.

The New Mexico Legislature enacts a law enforcement measure to make Prohibition effective.

The Forty-sixth National Convention of the Woman's Christian Temperance Union is held November 15-20 at St. Louis, Missouri.

The Attorney General of Arkansas holds that a referendum on the ratification of the National Prohibition Amendment would be illegal.

New York brewers seek an injunction to restrain the Federal officers from interfering with the production of 2.75 per cent beer.

Judge Hamilton of Porto Rico decides that it is a violation of the Reed amendment to bring liquor into Porto Rico even for personal use.

A Prohibition enforcement measure is adopted by the Minnesota Legislature.

Attorney General Palmer on May 15 renders an opinion holding it to be the lawful duty of the Internal Revenue Department to collect a tax on malt beverages with alcoholic content "in excess of that permitted by law."

Attorney General Price of Ohio holds (May 9) that the state-wide Prohibition Amendment abrogates all license laws and regulatory local option laws.

President Wilson in his message to Congress on May 20 recommends the repeal of the War-Time Prohibition act in so far as it applies to wine and beer.

Judge Hand of the Federal District Court, New York, hands down a decision on May 17 declaring that only the manufacture and sale of beer that "is in fact intoxicating" is prohibited by the War Prohibition act.

Missouri passes a law enforcement measure.

Federal Judge Mayer of New York City on May 23 grants an injunction restraining government interference with the manufacture of beer containing 2.75 per cent alcohol.

The Secretary of State of Arkansas refuses permission to circulate petitions for a referendum on the ratification of National Prohibition.

State-wide Prohibition becomes effective in Ohio May 27.

The State Supreme Court of Nevada upholds the constitutionality of the state-wide Prohibition law on May 29.

The Nineteenth National Convention of the Anti-Saloon League of America held at Washington, D. C., June 4-6.

The distillers in convention at Chicago on January 7 agree to raise one billion dollars if necessary to beat the Federal Bone Dry act.

"No beer, no work" is the slogan adopted by the Essex county, N. J., Building Trades Council on February 6. In New York "No beer, no bonds" buttons are worn.

The Michigan Supreme Court holds that the search and seizure clause of the bone dry state law which became effective on May 1, 1918, is invalid.

Restrictions on the use of grain in the manufacture of "near-beer" and other non-intoxicating beverages are removed by the government on February 20.

Breweries throughout the country are told by the New York Lager Beer Board of Trade and the United States Brewers' Association, on March 17, to go ahead forthwith with the sale of beer of alcoholic content of 2.75 per cent.

The New Jersey Assembly on March 18, by a viva voce vote, rejects the Eighteenth Amendment to the Constitution of the United States.

The Jacob Hoffman Brewing Co. of New York files in the Federal District Court application for an injunction restraining Federal authorities from possible criminal prosecution of alleged violations of the Internal Revenue Department's ruling that beer containing one-half of 1 per cent alcohol or more is intoxicating. It is aimed to make the government a party to action of the definition of intoxicants. Several brewers resume making 2.75 per cent beer.

The manufacture and sale of near-beer in Nevada is prohibited under a decision by the State Supreme Court.

The Presbyterian Church on March 30 resolves in favor of a world-wide fight for Prohibition.

The World League Against Alcoholism organizes at Washington, D. C., on June 7, adopts a constitution and elects officers.

Governor Lowden of Illinois signs a search and seizure bill to enforce Prohibition.

New Hampshire enacts a strong enforcement law.

Brewers of Philadelphia decide to continue the manufacture of 2.75 per cent beer, and pass resolutions declaring that such beer is non-intoxicating.

New Mexico enacts a bone dry Prohibition enforcement measure.

The governor of Montana vetoes a bill which would permit the manufacture of liquor containing .5 of 1 per cent of alcohol, also another bill intended to weaken state Prohibition.

The Connecticut Brewers Association meets at New Haven and announces that they will begin manufacture of beer of 2.75 per cent alcoholic content immediately.

Seven breweries operated by the Central Pennsylvania Brewing Company begin the brewing of beer on March 19.

The Lager Beer Brewers Board of Trade in New York, representing forty-two brewery concerns, on March 17 announce that on advice of counsel its members will sell beer containing 2.75 per cent alcohol.

A Prohibition enforcement measure is passed by the Delaware Legislature, prohibiting alcoholic beverages containing one-half of 1 per cent alcohol.

The Brewers Association of Massachusetts adopts resolutions recommending that brewers begin the manufacture of 2.75 per cent beer.

On March 13 a resolution is introduced in the Rhode Island Legislature instructing the Attorney General to begin action in the name of the state to protest the constitutionality of the Prohibition Amendment to the Constitution.

A general remonstrance against the granting of any liquor licenses in Pittsburgh and specific remonstrances against 66 licenses are made by representatives of the Ministerial Alliance.

The number of saloons in Panama is reduced from 680 to 100 by the law which goes into effect March 1.

Alabama passes a stringent bone dry enforcement measure.

President Wilson signs the War Revenue bill on February 24, by which measure the tax on whisky is doubled.

Bone dry Prohibition goes into effect in Washington, D. C., on February 24, by the terms of an amendment to the War Revenue bill, providing that the Reed bone dry law shall apply to the District of Columbia.

The House Judiciary Committee on February 24 approves a Prohibition law enforcement measure.

On February 25 a sub-committee of the Senate Judiciary Committee favorably reports the Sheppard War-Time Prohibition Enforcement bill.

A Prohibition enforcement measure, to make effective the National Prohibition Amendment, is adopted by the California Legislature.

Wet forces win an uncontested license election in Chicago on April 1; more than 150,000 voters voting on candidates fail to vote on the license proposal.

The Attorney General of Alabama rules that the Alabama Prohibition law prohibits the sale of all beer substitutes.

Liquor forces in California circulate petitions for a referendum on the ratification of National Prohibition.

The Maine Supreme Court on June 7 rules against

the sale or possession of Jamaica ginger as an intoxicant.

Michigan adopts a law enforcement measure designed to remedy defects in the state Prohibition law.

The Rhode Island Legislature passes an act providing that all beverages containing 4 per cent of alcohol or less shall be deemed non-intoxicating.

A meeting of citizens of the Virgin Islands endorses the Eighteenth Amendment to the United States Constitution.

The Oregon Supreme Court rules on April 29 that a referendum cannot be had on the ratification of the National Prohibition Amendment by the Oregon Legislature.

The Attorney General of Washington rules that a referendum cannot be held on the ratification of the Eighteenth Amendment, in that state.

William E. ("Pussyfoot") Johnson, a representative of the Anti-Saloon League of America, is attacked by a mob in London, England, on November 13, forcibly taken from the platform of Essex Hall and carried through the streets of London by medical students and others protesting against the Prohibition movement. Mr. Johnson sustains the loss of an eye, but discloses rare qualities of sportsmanship and becomes a hero for his remarkable diplomacy in handling a serious situation in the interest of the Prohibition cause.

On December 15, the United States Supreme Court hands down a decision upholding the constitutionality of the War-Time Prohibition law.

The Volstead Prohibition Enforcement Code is passed by the United States House of Representatives

on July 22, 1919, by a vote of 287 to 100, and by the
Senate on September 4, without roll call. The measure
then goes to conference. The Senate concurs in the
conference decision on October 8, and the House concurs by a vote of 321 to 70, on October 10. The
measure is vetoed by President Wilson on October 27,
and passed over the President's veto, by a vote of 176
to 55 in the House of Representatives and by a vote of
65 to 20 in the United States Senate.

1920

The Eighteenth Amendment to the Constitutuion,
providing for national prohibition of the sale, manufacture, transportation, importation and exportation
of intoxicating liquors, goes into effect at midnight,
January 16.

The Supreme Court of the United States on January 5 renders a decision holding that Congress has
power to define intoxicating liquors, and to fix the
standard of alcohol at one-half of 1 per cent by
volume.

The United States Supreme Court on January 7 decides "two-thirds majority of Congress" means two-
thirds of a quorum present and voting.

The records of the United States Internal Revenue
Department show that when the constitutional prohibitory amendment becomes operative in the United
States there are 69,233,000 gallons of distilled liquors
in bonded warehouses of which 38,134,000 gallons are
in Kentucky warehouses.

The General Conference of the Methodist Episcopal
church in session at Des Moines, Iowa, in May,
strongly declares for pressing the movement for Pro-

hibition throughout the world and endorses the World League Against Alcoholism.

The New York State Legislature in defiance of the provisions of the National Prohibition law enacts a statute permitting the sale of beer having 2.75 per cent of alcohol.

The Democratic State Convention of New York declares for the amending of the National Prohibition Enforcement Law so as to permit the sale of beer and light wine.

The Ohio Legislature enacts a prohibitory enforcement law which, under the referendum provision of the state, is referred to the people for final action.

A strong effort to weaken the Prohibition enforcement law in the Legislature of Virginia is defeated.

The National Republican Convention in session at Chicago in June, makes no reference in its platform either to the Prohibition Amendment to the Constitution or the Volstead Prohibitory Enforcement Code.

The National Convention of the Democratic Party in session at San Francisco in June declares against the adoption of a Prohibition plank in the platform by a vote of 929½ to 155½. On the same day the Convention rejects a beer and wine plank by a vote of 726½ to 356.

The National Prohibition Party holds its national convention at Lincoln, Nebraska, in July and nominates William Jennings Bryan for President. Upon Bryan's declination to accept the nomination the convention nominates Rev. A. S. Watkins of Ohio for President and Doctor D. Leigh Colvin of New York for Vice-President.

The Massachusetts State Legislature passes a bill

providing for 2.75 per cent beer but the measure is promptly vetoed by Governor Calvin Coolidge.

The United States Supreme Court on January 13 decides that the Reed Amendment prohibits a person from carrying liquor into a Prohibition state on a street car for his own use, even though the law of the state permitted such transportation of liquor.

On June 1, the United States Supreme Court decides that the referendum by a state on a proposed amendment to the Constitution of the United States was invalid.

The Supreme Court of the United States on June 7 unanimously renders a decision upholding the validity of the Eighteenth Amendment to the Constitution, and the Volstead Enforcement Act.

A large delegation of women representing the Woman's Christian Temperance Union of the United States attends the World's Woman's Christian Temperance Union convention in London, in June.

The records of the first year of Prohibition in the United States under the War-Time Prohibition Measure which went into effect on July 1, 1919, and the National Prohibition Amendment which became operative on January 16, 1920, show a remarkable decrease in crime and overwhelming benefits of every kind.

The Fifteenth International Congress Against Alcoholism is held in Washington, D. C., Sept. 21-27, both inclusive.   The Congress is conducted by the direction of the United States Department of State under the authority and appropriations of the United States Congress.   The United States government officially invites every nation with which it has diplomatic relations to send delegates to this Congress.